ALTERNATIVE TRACKS

D1160249

The Johns Hopkins Series in Constitutional Thought

Sotirios A. Barber and Jeffrey K. Tulis, Series Editors

Alternative Tracks

The Constitution of American Industrial Order, 1865–1917

GERALD BERK

The Johns Hopkins University Press
Baltimore and London

© 1994 The Johns Hopkins University Press
All rights reserved
Printed in the United States of America on acid-free paper

The Johns Hopkins University Press
2715 North Charles Street
Baltimore, Maryland 21218-4319
The Johns Hopkins Press Ltd., London

Library of Congress Cataloging-in-Publication Data will be found at the
end of this book.

A catalog record for this book is available from the British Library.

For my mother and the memory
of my father and his father

CONTENTS

PREFACE

No sooner had pluralists and Marxists agreed that the modern corporation placed structural constraints upon democracy than its defining features were called into question. Scholars now agree that the technological paradigm underlying corporate capitalism—mass production—fell into crisis in the 1970s. Where bigness, hierarchy, and an extreme division of labor had once been assets to efficiency under conditions of stable and growing markets, intense competition, fragmented markets, and rapid technical change made them liabilities. So too was the American corporation's relationship to the state called into question. Where redistributive policies had once served national prosperity by expanding the market for mass-produced goods, they now appeared to be a drag upon investment and economic growth.

For well over a decade now, Americans have experimented with and fought over law and public policy in an effort to reproduce the level and kind of prosperity associated with the "golden age" of mass production after the Second World War. Few would disagree that the outcome of current conflicts over regulatory, industrial, labor, welfare, and fiscal policy will determine the shape of American political economy in the twenty-first century. Yet, when we look back upon the origins of mass production and redistributive government, the idea that politics determined the world of our parents often seems counterintuitive. In our profession and our culture, we have so internalized the defining features and organizing principles of corporate capitalism as inevitable byproducts of industrialization that we look back upon politics in the age of enterprise as epiphenomenal and adaptive. But current uncertainties reopen questions about the past. Did the modern corporation emerge from economic and technological constraints well beyond the will of democracy? Or were there plausible alternatives to the twentieth-century industrial order of corporate capitalism and redistributive government which were suppressed for reasons of politics, not technical inferiority?

The title of this book, *Alternative Tracks*, suggests my answer. In arguing the latter, however, I do not share the view of Progressive Era intellectuals that Gilded Age robber barons corrupted the American regime. Instead, through a critical study of the railroads, I show how industrial technology was initially applied in ways far more diverse than commonly thought. The choices Americans made among them, moreover, were inescapably collective, determined through protracted political conflict, not Darwinian market competition.

This historical journey will take us well into the technical worlds of business management, corporate jurisprudence, and regulatory policy. By probing disputes over the legal and economic principles upon which the modern corporation and redistributive regulation were constructed, we shall see that industrialization and statebuilding in the United States were much more contested and open-ended than twentieth-century learning suggests. At the current juncture, when generalizations about capitalist democracy once thought settled no longer seem to hold, this excursion into the past also promises to enlarge our sense of the institutional possibilities by which we might reconcile our constitutional aspirations both to democratic self-government and material prosperity.

Many people have contributed directly and indirectly to the development of this study. Two, in particular, deserve special mention at the outset: Thomas K. McCraw and Stephen Skowronek. Although this book disagrees with their interpretations of industrialization and statebuilding in the United States, it literally could not have been written without their scholarship and personal generosity. I hope, through debate, I have advanced the project they have done so much to cultivate.

My teachers—Walter Dean Burnham, Joshua Cohen, Morton J. Horwitz, and Charles Sabel—each made unique contributions to this study. Their ideas, individually and collectively, have inspired the questions I have addressed; their criticisms have forced me to focus and sharpen my arguments (even as I hold stubbornly to positions they disagree with); and each, by example, has shown me special qualities to strive for as a teacher and a scholar.

Others have been generous with their time, criticism, and encouragement well beyond the call of collegiality and friendship: Stephen Amberg, Tom Baker, Donald Critchlow, Robert Gordon, Victoria Hattam, Takashi Hikino, Anthony Levitas, James Livingston, Edward Lorenz, Gretchen Ritter, Philip Scranton, Richard Valelly, and Jonathan Zeitlin. If I have neglected to show my appreciation along the way, I do so now. My editors, Henry Tom, Sotirios Barber, and Jeffrey Tulis, have been a pleasure to work with.

The help of archivists and librarians at Baker Library and the Minnesota Historical Society was indispensible to this project. The University of Notre Dame Institute for the Study of the Liberal Arts generously funded research on the Chicago Great Western Railway. Portions of chapters 2, 3, 4, and 6 have been previously published in *Studies in American Political Development* and the *Journal of Policy History.*

Finally, I thank my family, Karen and Adrian. They, more than anyone, have provided me with the humor and perspective to see this project through. It is no exaggeration to say it could not have been done without them.

CHAPTER ONE

Toward a Constitutive Political Economy

Modern American politics is child to the industrial revolution. The private business corporation—internally hierarchical, powerful in the market, privileged in polyarchy—has shaped the institutional boundaries and aspirations of mainstream American politics for nearly a century. Designed to countervail corporate power in the market and politics, the independent regulatory commission, industrial trade unions, and the welfare state were to ensure that the material benefits of industrial capitalism would be widespread. At its best, this industrial order of big business and redistributive institutions generated a virtuous circle of economic growth and a rising standard of living. The larger the mass market generated by collective bargaining, regulated monopoly, and public social provision, the greater the economies of scale achieved by America's leading corporations. Thus buttressed by the universal promise of increasing material prosperity for more and more Americans, the modern corporation became central to the American or "Fordist" model of political economy.[1]

To be sure, there were always limits to this industrial order. Casual observation and social scientific research found that corporations routinely turned state power to private ends; a part of the American population structurally dispossessed seemed permanently locked out of the virtuous circle of Fordism; and the American labor movement never completely secured a commitment to full employment from the federal government.[2] Nonetheless, the best cause for most twentieth-century liberals, if not many conservatives, was to universalize the benefits of corporate enterprise by extending the reach of redistributive institutions.[3]

In the United States, however, perhaps more than in any other advanced industrial society, nagging doubts remained about the modern corporation's compatability with liberty and democracy. From muckraking journalism to social protest and critical scholarship, twentieth-century Americans have always worried that corporate power undermines self-determination and self-government. Indeed, by the late 1970s many mainstream pluralist theorists who had long defended polyarchy against the charge of systematic class bias, came to agree that the corporation held a privileged position in pluralist democracy. Charles Lindblom even argued that so much do ruling governments depend upon private investment for full employment that they inevitably become hostage to corporate demands. And though pluralists noted the empirical correlation between market economies and polyarchical democracies, following a long line of critics from Louis D. Brandeis to Lewis Mumford, Lindblom's collaborator and colleague Robert Dahl argued that the private business corporation had become an "impediment to democracy in the United States." The evidence, they charged, shows that the corporation's vast economic resources are readily converted to political resources; its internal hierarchy meant that a large portion of the demos lived out its lives within systematic structures of subordination; and its private status formed an ideological barrier against control by a government measurably more democratic. Moreover, hierarchical as secondary redistributive institutions are as well, they are a poor substitute for corporate reform. Only by some combination of economic decentralization, internal corporate democracy, and public control over socially consequential decisions would the corporate impediment to pluralist democracy be diminished.[4]

Such criticism has reappeared like clockwork since the industrial revolution to challenge the "trusts," the "interests," and the "establishment." And yet each time reformers seem to fall far short of their egalitarian aspirations: hierarchies in state and society have remained relatively secure; the privileged position of corporate enterprise, though altered at the margins, has remained structurally constant; and redistributive regulation has retained its grip on the political imagination of the left. Thus, the gap between ideals and institutions, as cultural critics from Walter Lippmann and Louis Hartz to Richard Hofstadter and Samuel P. Huntington point out, is a permanent fixture in American politics. For, despite the persistent American "creed" of yeoman individualism, equality, and self-government—our continuing "agrarian myth"—the limits to reform lie in the *administrative* imperatives of modern economy and governance. Americans in the twentieth century are ambivalent about corporate power: they desire its material benefits as they deride its size and hierarchy. At best, they muddle through, periodically placing "moral" restrictions upon the corporation and the administrative state which weaken, but do not fundamentally alter, their hierarchical form. At worst, as the cultural critics point out, an indiscriminate aversion to *all* concentrations of power and authority weakens the capacity of the administrative state to realize American ideals—individual liberty, equality, and democracy.[5] Just when these generalizations about American politics seemed most secure—shared, more often than not, by left and right—those institutions that marked the limits to political realism in state and economy were no longer achieving their universal promises. In the 1970s and 1980s, the corporate bellwethers of American economic prowess, General Motors, DuPont, even IBM, failed to generate the economic growth they once did. In a world of increasingly stiff international competition, rapidly changing technologies, and bewildering diversity in product markets, the defining features of the American model of corporate success—internal hierarchy, formal rules, and huge size—now seemed a liability.[6] Nor did the institutions designed to redistribute corporate wealth achieve their promise. Liberals and conservatives alike came to agree that trade unions required thorough reform; that airlines, telecommunications, banking, trucking, and rails ought to be deregulated; and that the welfare state had not solved poverty.[7] All in all, the institutions intended to balance corporate powers and maintain its positive social role no longer appeared desirable.

New developments and current doubts have reopened questions about the past once thought long settled. Was twentieth-century American democracy destined to succumb to the constraints of corporate capitalism? Did Americans willingly sacrifice their commitments to equality, individual liberty, and self-government to their desires for material prosperity? Was the modern corporation the inevitable byproduct of industrialization? Or were there alternatives, as critics of the corporation have asked, more consistent with the American commitments to liberty, equality, and democracy? Finally, if the "American model" of the twentieth century no longer seems as compelling as it once was, what lasting generalizations remain possible about the relationship between modern capitalism and democracy?

With these questions in mind, this book returns to the perennial American passion with the railroads. Business historians have taught us that the railroads were the first big business in the United States. As such they knit together a vast continent of "island communities" into a single national market. The leading sector of the industrial revolution, they so increased the speed of transportation and the size of domestic urban markets that, without them, the large-scale managerial enterprise would have been literally unimaginable in industries like steel, oil, tobacco, sugar, and chemicals. Railroads also became the organizational prototype for other industries. Although this industry began the long road to decline by the 1920s, the modern firm in automobiles, pharmaceuticals, aeronautics, and telecommunications, among others, mimicked the features pioneered here. Moreover, America's first experiment in federal redistributive regulation came in response to this industry. Established in 1887, the Interstate Commerce Commission (ICC) became the model for modern institutions of countervailing and redistributive power. Thus, if the coming of managerial capitalism placed unassailable constraints upon twentieth-century state structure and democratic politics, one is sure to find them in this industry.

If, on the other hand, there were alternatives to corporate capitalism as we know it—if the aspirations of reformers are to be taken seriously as *possible* and not merely as utopian or reactionary musings—we are also likely to find them here. For every innocent grammar-school student has learned of the Gilded Age revolt against the "trusts." Was this just another example of American "creedal passion," "irrational Lockian liberalism," or "the paranoid style in American politics," or was something else viable in practice?

As we re-evaluate the defining features of the modern corporation and its place in American democracy at the turn of the twentieth century, the stakes in looking back to its origins once again loom large. For, as Bruce Ackerman has written of constitutional interpretation, the narratives we share about the past, as a profession and as a polity, weigh heavily upon our collective identity and sense of agency in the present. Suppose we find that the modern corporation was the inevitable byproduct of industrialization. Intellectual maturity and political realism would suggest that a trade-off between democracy and material prosperity, between equality and efficiency, is just a fact of modern life. However, suppose that corporate capitalism was no more than a "historic commitment," that is, the outcome of an "overt, bitter . . . and prolonged" conflict with "alternatives [which] seemed open to the principal historic actors" involved. If so, then its compatibility with pluralist democracy remains an open question, subject, in principle, to re-evaluation and collective choice. Thus, the stakes in answering these questions remain high; they go to the heart of our profession's capacity to distinguish the economically or politically necessary from the democratically possible in the American experiment.[8]

In *Alternative Tracks* I will argue that there was more than one path to industrialization possible in the United States, and the railroad corporation was at the center of an overt and prolonged conflict over which one was chosen. Corporate capitalism as we know it in the twentieth century vied with a more decentralized, less hierarchical, and more public alternative. Furthermore, redistributive regulation, so typical of twentieth-century politics and administration, also vied with an alternative designed not so much to displace the market with public command as to "regulate competition" by subjecting it to publicly enforced substantive norms. This alternative form of industrial order will be called "regional republicanism."

Regional republicanism has remained largely invisible to students of American political and economic development because they have drawn the empirical line between the economically necessary and the politically contingent, between nature's laws and mere historic commitments, in the wrong place. By so doing, political scientists and historians have not only systematically underestimated the range of institutional forms by which Americans could have reconciled industrialism with democracy in the past, but also perpetuated a narrative in the profession and the culture about what we can become as a nation that cannot withstand a critical encounter with historical fact.

The Existing Narrative

The Modern Corporation and the New Business History

The publication of Alfred Chandler's *The Visible Hand* in 1977 buttressed the idea that there is an eradicable gap between American ideals and institutions. No single work has done more to dispel the myth of the robber barons—buccaneer capitalists whose greed corrupted democracy and the self-regulating market—than this one. The real architects of the modern corporation, Chandler showed in theoretically informed detail, were a new class of professional managers. In a deliberate effort to economize on capital and energy-intensive technologies, they reorganized the capitalist enterprise from the small-scale, competitive, proprietary firm to the large-scale, hierarchical, oligopolistic corporation. If the result was an economic institution that exercised substantial power in the market and indirectly in politics, this was the unintended consequence of efficiency gains.[9]

Railroads figure prominently in this transition from proprietary to managerial capitalism in two ways: first, as paradigm for other industries, and second, as cause to national market integration.[10] On the former, railroads were the first of America's industries in which the fixed cost of plant and equipment had become so high relative to the variable costs of labor and raw materials. Consequently, the railroads faced unprecedented "economies of scale," that is, the cost per unit of output dropped precipitously as the volume of output increased. But these were only the physical traits of technology. In order to reap economies of scale, Chandler argues, the railroads pioneered three sorts of organizational innovations that would be mimicked in other industries. First, they invested in sufficiently large plant and equipment to achieve scale economies. Second, by consolidating end-to-end lines into huge national systems, they achieved economies of "high-volume through-put" or "speed" unthinkable on smaller scale railroads. This innovation turned out to be the model for *vertical integration* in manufacturing and processing industries. In oil, for example, the effort to reap scale economies in refining was facilitated by "backward integration" into crude production and transportation and "forward" integration into marketing. The third investment was in human resources: railroads were the first American enterprise to recruit and train a hierarchy of middle managers to supervise the flow of resources throughout these vast national systems. Although the organizational problems associated with capital-intensive technologies varied from industry to industry, railroad innovations were copied in steel, oil, chemicals, tobacco, meatpacking, and farm machinery.[11]

The railroads were, however, more than the prototype for other industries; they also figured causally in the transition from competitive to corporate capitalism. The coming of the railroads, Chandler writes, was a necessary condition for the extension of America's domestic market. By the 1880s a vast rail network had integrated formerly isolated regional markets into a single national market and furnished mass producers with the reliability and speed necessary for high-volume vertical flows of resources into and out of capital-intensive production. Thus, without the railroads, mass production would have been unthinkable in other industries. In steel, oil, and chemicals, for instance, management would have found it impossible to reach the "minimum efficient scale" necessary to profitably reap the scale economies inherent in technology.

Thus, technology and markets are exogenous in this account of the transition to corporate capitalism. By force of cost structure and demand these variables disciplined management behavior and thereby determined plant size, internal firm organization, and the extent of industrial concentration (the number of firms in an industry and their market share). To be sure, intervening variables, like culture and politics, would alter the particular form or the pace of development of industrial capitalism. In a subsequent work, for example, Chandler demonstrated how they stymied the transition to corporate capitalism altogether in Britain. Nonetheless, capital-intensive technology and large-scale markets remain necessary conditions; and when coupled with investment in sufficient plant size, vertical integration, and managerial hierarchy, regardless of intervening factors, they are sufficient for the transition from proprietary to managerial capitalism.[12]

My objections to this account of railroads, in particular, and corporate capitalism, in general, are two. The first is the now-familiar fallacy of technological determinism. This is the idea, as Chandler puts it, that different technologies have inherent efficiency characteristics, which, in turn, determine the best form of economic organization. But, as Michael J. Piore, Charles F. Sabel, Jonathan Zeitlin, Philip Scranton, and others have shown, technologies can typically be put to more than one use, each having unique and nonordinal efficiency advantages. That is, some uses will be superior on one performance criterion, while others will be superior on another. Absent a metarule of efficiency, there is no noncontroversial, or at least nonpolitical, way to choose among them. These studies show that such choices are determined by the standing distribution of legal entitlements and power. Rights allocating access to credit, for instance, will allow the proponents of one form of organization to impose a solution to technical or efficiency problems, where there were in fact practical alternatives.[13] This was the case for railroads. Economies of scale was only one possibility. The other was "economies of scope," or "networking." Quite roughly, in railroads, the latter involved careful mixing of heterogeneous freight through many switching nodes throughout regional systems. Although Chandler recognizes the importance of economies of scope in manufacturing, he fails to see how scale and scope clashed on the railroads, for economic and political reasons.[14]

Moreover, building upon Piore and Sabel, I contend that the outcome of this conflict would not be determined solely by the distribution of background entitlements. Political struggles in Congress, the courts, and the ICC over rights to credit and ratemaking not only shaped the choice of one form of efficiency over another, they also determined those variables new business historians take to be exogenous: technology and markets. These variables, like the modern railroad corporation itself, were politically constructed as well.

Consider first technology. It is not hardware per se that determines economies of scale, but the ratio of fixed to variable, capital to labor, cost. But cost structure, we know, will be determined as much by the allocation of power and property rights as by physical technology. The ratio of capital to labor costs, for example, is always determined by workers' bargaining power and collective entitlements. Similarly, capital costs will be shaped by the allocation of rights in capital markets and corporation law. During the period of rapid industrialization in the United States, however, capital or credit entitlements themselves became the subject of a prolonged political struggle, in which management figured prominently. In an effort to shield the many national railroad systems that had fallen into bankruptcy from dismemberment, managers enlisted the power of the federal courts in a systematic effort to restructure corporate capital costs and the rights attached to them. Management was compelled by the logic of the model itself to effect the parameter said to determine its behavior. Thus, we cannot hold the cost structure of technology exogenous to the development of the railroads.

This problem is as vexing for markets as for technology. We shall see that in order to choose between forms of efficiency (scale or scope), railroad managers were compelled to organize demand. Their ability to form stable alliances with shippers of choice, however, depended upon the allocation of ratemaking entitlements. Those rights became subject to a long and heated struggle over what sorts of market landscape railroads ought to serve: a national hierarchy of centralized markets or a decentralized pattern of regional markets. Indeed, this conflict was the heart of regulatory politics from 1870 to the turn of the century. The outcome of that contest, not natural selection disciplined by market competition, determined the choice between scale and scope.[15] Because railroad organization and landscape were interdependent, management was compelled to affect the variable—namely, markets—presumed to discipline its behavior.[16]

The regionalist alternative to corporate capitalism, then, remains unintelligible only when we take technology and markets as exogenous. Once one recognizes how plastic these variables were in the midst of rapid industrialization and how self-consciously management acted to reshape them, one can no longer conclude that the modern corporation, as we know it, was the inevitable byproduct of industrialization. The hypotheses that there were equally efficient rivals and that causal choices were determined politically becomes compelling.

Statebuilding and the New Institutionalism

If background entitlements—that is, institutions—matter so much to technology and markets and through them to economic development, then the analytic emphases of state-centered new institutionalism would seem especially appropriate to my project. This school has hypothesized that state actions and politics are not only relatively autonomous from economic structure, but more important, they have independent effects on group formation, collective behavior, the content and definition of the interests of sectors of society, and economic development. Like the approach taken here, state-centered scholarship has pressed back the boundary between economic necessity and political contingency. In so doing, it has opened new scholarly terrain for work on the state and politics in their own right (not merely as epiphenomena to economic or social structure). By questioning the functionalist assumption that the structures of all societies converge as they modernize this school has opened our eyes to institutional diversity, dysfunctional structures, and the politically contingent in history.[17]

Unfortunately, in practice the new institutionalism has not fully realized its promise to test the independent effects of politics upon interest formation and economic development. Its practitioners have taken the defining features of industrialization to be largely exogenous to late nineteenth- and early twentieth-century statebuilding, party development, and class formation in the United States. The result, however, is a shared narrative which systematically underestimates the diversity of institutional paths open to Americans and tends to mistake the contests among them for conflict between an old order and a new one in birth.

In this view, the American administrative state is comparatively weak because of its exceptional past. Unlike its European counterparts, the United States industrialized without a preexisting central state bureaucracy and with relatively high levels of democratic participation for a full generation, that is, with a state of "courts and constituent parties." Absent a federal bureaucracy capable of appropriating public resources and initiating comprehensive policy, parties allocated governmental largesse to loyal patrons and the judge-made law became the final word in public policy. However weak, the nineteenth-century American state was strong enough for a decentralized agrarian society; that is, until industrialization placed demands upon it which could not be met by the state of courts and parties. The coming of the modern corporation, in this view, nationalized distributive conflicts among formerly isolated groups, hardened class conflict, and integrated economic crises across formerly autarkic communities.

Moreover, industrialization produced a new class of vanguard intellectuals, relatively autonomous from the centers of power in industrializing America: the old state and the new corporation. Drawn from professional cadres of elite lawyers, social scientists, and military professionals, these were to become the architects of the new administrative state. In alliance with innovative presidents, they labored to build a regulatory state sufficiently strong to moderate distributive conflicts between the corporation and noncorporate classes and autonomous enough to resist rent-seeking claims that would threaten the prosperity of all.[18]

This program was not advanced without a fight: cosmopolitan statebuilders found themselves in a protracted struggle with old-order judges and politicians. In alliance with particularistic interests in society, the latter defended their place and status within the state. As a result, administrative government was born, but into a constitutional stalemate between old order and new that significantly weakened the modern American state. For example, although regulated monopoly emerged in the pathbreaking railroad sector, it was subject to ongoing conflicts of authority, exceptional mistrust between business and government, and the inability to defend regulation from insatiable redistributive claims.

Once we take seriously the hypothesis that the defining features of industrialization were forged in politics, statebuilding can no longer be conceptualized as an adaptive enterprise, its politics understood as a struggle between old order and new. The line presumed to distinguish the necessary from the contingent becomes problematic, and the criteria by which one differentiates patronage from rational policy, provincial from cosmopolitan ideas, or atavistic from prophetic behavior must be skeptically assessed. Accordingly, two empirical problems with the new institutionalist account of American statebuilding become evident. First, this scholarship systematically overestimates the constraints of the political and economic division of labor (old and aborning) upon the policy preferences of public officials and their allies in society. Second, and corollary, new institutionalists underestimate the range of coherent options for building administrative capacity, in general, and regulating modern industry, in particular.

Consider the implications of our critique of the new business history for the behavior and policy preferences of two key actors: politicians and cosmopolitan intellectuals. In order to defend their prerogatives within the state, politicians follow nineteenth-century convention: distribute discrete patronage to loyal clients. By what criteria, however, were rural politicians to best serve their agrarian constituents? In railroad regulation, for example, did midwestern farmers need low long-haul rates to seaboard markets or low intraregional rates capable of cultivating regional development and trade? As we shall see, these policies were in conflict, and politicians were hard put to choose by referring to the place of their constituents in a territorial or sectoral division of labor. For it was precisely that division of labor that was subject to politics. Whether they intended to or not, in order to choose among policy *means*, politicians were compelled to grapple with the *ends* of industrial society. Patronage or not, they had little choice but to engage in programmatic politics. The new institutionalism is correct that political parties did not become the vehicle for class-based politics in the European sense. Still, because democratization came prior to an industrialization whose defining features were genuinely uncertain, politicians were forced to think in terms vastly more universal than the prevailing account suggests.

This dilemma was not unique to politicians. If the form of industrialization cannot be conceptualized as exogenous to politics, the new theorists of administration were also hard put to devise "rational" regulatory policy prior to the outcome of critical struggles over the cost structure of technology or the organization of markets. Their policy ideas changed fundamentally as some options were closed off and others opened. The role of intellectuals in statebuilding, then, is better seen as a political learning process than as a problem in forging administrative structures equally autonomous from an old order and the particularistic interests of society. Indeed, we shall see that there were divisions among the ranks of virtually all classes enmeshed in the struggle over railroads—judges, statebuilders, merchants, even railroad managers—on foundational questions concerning citizenship, market landscape, economic efficiency, the corporation, and regulation.

In short, the content of policy preferences and the principles of administrative rationality became the subject of statebuilding politics. Since the coming of the railroads threw the old boundaries between state and society into disarray, timeworn routines no longer guided old-order public officials. Coupled with genuine uncertainty about the fate of the railroad corporation, actors in state and economy had little choice but to rethink the relationship between the politically good and the economically possible. Such efforts resulted in a protracted and overt conflict over two fundamentally different tracks to twentieth-century industrial order. This contest not only better explains a project not fully appreciated so far by the new institutionalism—the regional republican alternative to corporate capitalism and redistributive government—but it also takes seriously the hypothesis that interest formation and industrial organization are, in fact, politically determined.

Alternative Tracks

This study draws a distinction between constitutive politics and the politics of power. Like Bruce Ackerman's notion of "constitutional moments," Dahl's of "historic commitments," or Walter Dean Burnham's "realigning sequences," I conceive of constitutive politics as epochal. These are periods when overt and protracted conflicts occur over those standards by which we organize the political and economic institutions that shape our daily lives. In constitutive politics, fighting over what had once seemed routine issues inexorably opens conflict over the very grammar by which actors are made available to one another, identify allies and adversaries, and through which legitimate claims upon the state are recognized.[19]

Such periods, then, are experienced as truly nonroutine, a time when the institutional maps by which actors find their way about no longer retain the practical hold over economic and political behavior they once did. Like Piore's and Sabel's notion of an "industrial divide" or Roberto M. Unger's of "context making," constitutive eras necessitate experimentation in business strategy, constitutional interpretation, and public policy.[20] Moreover, efforts to extend and consolidate local experiments inevitably necessitate allies in state and economy. By definition, however, collaborators cannot be enlisted on the basis of objective affinities of interest in constitutive politics, because the exogenous conditions, which tend to determine interests and behavior during more stable periods, lose their hold at such times.

Recall, for example, midwestern farmers could not identify natural allies on the railroad question from a territorial or sectoral division of labor, which was itself up for grabs in the politics of regulation. But this was a general problem: all key actors in the development of the modern corporation and adminstrative state had little choice but to engage in constitutive politics. As Clifford Geertz writes, it is just at such inchoate moments that social agents engage in "ideological activity," that is, the generation of evaluative models of social reality which "render otherwise incomprehensible social situations meaningful, to so construe them as to make it possible to act purposefully within them."[21]

This process occurs piecemeal: competing models of industrial order did not occur to politicians, managers, farmers, or statebuilders in comprehensive and programmatic detail. Still, at critical moments of crisis and conflict, the architects of political economy did emerge to articulate constitutive norms and programmatic policy in remarkable detail. The empirical problem of this study, then, is not to explain how a conflict of interests (fixed in the background conditions of state and society) shaped the transition from an old institutional order to a new one. Rather, it is to examine a diversity of business and regulatory experiments that emerged during the industrial revolution; the strategies and logic critical actors adopted to institutionalize them in economy, law, and public administration; and the conflicts occasioned by such efforts. Once such turning-point conflicts are resolved, conceptualizing politics as a clash of fixed "interests" among actors fighting over well-recognized signs of status, wealth, and advantage becomes more appropriate. In contrast to the constitutive politics of industrial order, I call this the politics of power.

The late nineteenth century was just such a constitutive period in the development of American political economy. No two events did more to throw old patterns of economic and political practice into disarray than the Civil War and the coming of the railroads. Together they made it possible to imagine conquering the West anew, to surmount isolation over a vast continent, and to launch America onto an economic growth trajectory unprecedented in its history. But they also threw open the organization of work and its rewards to contention and revision; called entitlement patterns in public and private finance into question; and led Americans to pose penetrating questions about the place of the corporation in a market democracy, the organization of economic landscape, and the role of national government in shaping economic practice.

Not only did the railroads figure prominently as the cause of this constitutive era, but they also found themselves at the center of a nearly half-century-long struggle to reimpose order on an inchoate world. As the first industry to make extensive use of the corporate form, railroads became the center of a contest over the form and place of the modern corporation in an industrial democracy. Since they were also infrastructure to economic development, a protracted battle raged over what sort of markets railroads ought to serve. Though these contests were not of a piece and they took place in segmented arenas, they were coherent. Two evaluative models of industrial order emerged to vie for institutional hegemony: corporate liberalism and regional republicanism. In theory and in practice, they traveled separate tracks, colliding at critical turning points in the state legislatures, the courts, Congress, and, after 1887, in the Interstate Commerce Commission.

Drawing from different cultural, political, and economic resources, the architects and practitioners of regional republicanism and corporate liberalism nonetheless attempted to solve many of the same problems: a sectoral overproduction crisis, instability in market alliances, productive efficiency, cutthroat competition, and carrier-shipper conflicts. Any viable alternative had to confront these issues. Not just any political discourse, though, carried weight in late nineteenth-century America. Both models drew from longstanding constitutional debates over the nature of the American regime. Finally, the Civil War had transformed capital markets and the state in ways that placed genuine constraints upon economic and political choice. Nonetheless, much more was possible within these constraints than the new business history or the new institutionalism suggest.

On the first model, corporate liberalism, railroads would become huge national firms, hierarchically organized, and characterized by the separation of property ownership from managerial control. They would attain "economies of scale" (declining per-unit costs with increasing output) by serving primarily high-volume, long-haul freight between relatively large centralized national markets. National market development, or dominant city urbanization, was the geographic counterpart to this model. But corporate liberalism was well more than the economic institutions we have come to associate with modern capitalism. It had an ideological and public counterpart. Drawing from the same cultural well as conservative republicanism in Reconstruction, Gilded Age social Darwinism and Progressive Era new nationalism, corporate liberalism conceived property and economic development prior to the will of collective or democratic choice. "The laws of trade," its adherents were fond of saying, "are stronger than the laws of men." Thus, the modern corporation, like the liberal person, owed its existence first and foremost to private purposes. If the result of economic development rooted in such presocial entitlements was to concentrate market power in huge monopolistic firms, this was deemed inevitable. The only economic role left for the liberal democratic state was to redress the concentration of excessive wealth in the modern corporation through regulated monopoly. The goal of regulation, in other words, was to balance the interests of consumers in redistribution with those of the corporation in accumulation.

On the second and competing model, regional republicanism, railroads would be moderate in size, regionally based, and characterized internally by flatter hierarchies and shared authority between owners and managers. They would achieve "economies of scope" (declining "joint production costs") by carefully mixing and networking long and short, carload and less-than-carload, relatively heterogeneous freight, within and between regional markets. Regional market development, or decentralized urbanization, was the geographic corollary to this model. But regional republicanism was also far more than an alternative economic practice. It, too, had ideological roots and a public counterpart. Drawing from the cultural resources of civic humanism articulated by the founders, and the antimonopolism voiced by radical Jacksonians, Populists, Knights of Labor, and greenbackers, regional republicanism conceived property and the corporation to be public conventions, necessarily embedded in history and politics. As such, its adherents justified regulating the public corporation to collective ends. Railroad ratemaking would be subject to substantive republican norms, namely, decentralized market development. Moreover, once the outer bounds of acceptable corporate behavior were established, the state would agree to set limits upon its own conduct. In between, however, regulators would search for mutual gains from moderate bargaining and cooperation.

At most times, corporate liberalism and regional republicanism traveled autonomous tracks to industrialization and statebuilding. Nonetheless, as actors in economy and the state attempted to perfect and extend their strategies, they clashed over regulation, finance, and corporate structure. At critical turning points, those conflicts were mediated and channeled through the courts, Congress, and the Interstate Commerce Commission. During these fights, the architects of industrial order attempted to control the scope of conflict by enlisting allies to practical solutions to economic and regulatory problems. In so doing, however, they had little choice but to engage in constitutive politics, that is, to make their moral premises so explicit and their programs so comprehensive that a range of groups might evision a place for themselves. Thus, *Alternative Tracks* explores both the autonomous development of regional republicanism and corporate liberalism in railroad, regulatory, and judicial practice, and the critical junctures at which they clashed.

The Narrative in Brief

Alternative Tracks is organized in three parts: "Corporate Entitlements and National System Building," "Regional Republicanism," and "The Corporate Liberal Basis of Group Politics." Parts I and II explore the constitutive politics of twentieth-century industrial order. Together they follow the practitioners of corporate liberalism and regional republicanism along separate tracks in state and economy and analyze moments when they clashed in the courts, Congress, and the ICC. Part III turns from constitutive politics to the politics of power by explaining the consolidation and limits of corporate liberalism. As such, it establishes the institutional form, policy assumptions, and administrative frailties familiar to students of twentieth-century distributive politics.

Part I tests the hypothesis that the victorious railroad strategy—what Chandler calls interterritorial system building—was politically constituted in two ways. First, this strategy was initially driven by the distribution of entitlements in postbellum capital markets, rather than by technology and market geography. Second, when interterritorial systems suffered a life-threatening crisis, the federal courts provided their architects with the coercive power to protect systems from dismemberment and to restructure capital costs.

Chapter 2 describes the transformation of capital markets and the status of railroads in American economic development during the Civil War. The result was to channel unprecedented savings into corporate—that is, railroad—investment. This turned out to be a mixed blessing for the carriers. On the one hand, it made enormous resources available for expansion. On the other, it fueled a competitive rivalry over territory that resulted in investment and building well beyond realizable demand.

Moreover, the boom-and-bust cycle of railroad investment that ensued reopened Civil War capital markets to constitutive politics. Proposals for structural reform issued from both the ranks of corporate elites and greenback radicals on grounds remarkably homologous to the corporate liberal and regional republican principles that shaped the contest over railroads. However, neither side was able to muster sufficient power to impose a solution or the will to compromise; hence capital-market reform locked into a three-decade stalemate after the depression of 1873. As a result, periodic crises of corporate overinvestment were left to *sectoral* resolution. A conflict of weighty social significance was all but privatized for historically contingent, not economically necessary, reasons.

Drawing from the theoretical and historical insights of critical legal studies, Chapter 4 shows how railroad fixed costs (that is, debt) and the rights attached to them were reconstituted to buttress national systems, not, as the new business history has it, the other way around. Having overbuilt and overcapitalized, many huge systems collapsed in the 1880s and 1890s and fell into court-ordered receivership. Here federal judges made choices that had profound effects upon the development of the industry and the internal structure of the modern corporation. Under prevailing norms of corporate doctrine, which granted priority to property (debt) holders, the architects of national railroads would have been divested of authority and their systems threatened by dismemberment into regional parts. Like historians looking back, however, many on the federal bench were convinced that only incumbent managers were capable of reorganizing these systems. The law, they concluded, would have to adapt, even if this meant stripping debt holders of their traditional property rights in insolvent corporations. Yet the "facts" were ambiguous, and receivership courts had choices. The transformation of receivership law did not occur without contentious professional debate. Moreover, the economic effects of breaking huge systems into their regional parts were also ambiguous. As I show in Part II, smaller-scale regional railroads were both viable and valuable. Still, the result of the transformation in receivership practice during the 1880s and 1890s was to institutionalize national systems, the legal doctrine that the corporation was a natural entity, and to reduce the fixed costs of railroad technology on average by one-third.

All dominant institutions, writes Unger, rest on defeated and repressed alternatives. The national railroad system and the corporate person—two defining features of the industrial order I call corporate liberalism—were no exception. The regional railroad and a public or mutualist theory of the corporation—two defining characteristics of regional republicanism—were successfully tried and politically defeated. Part II describes the autonomous development of regional republicanism in state and economy and the critical junctures at which its architects clashed with those of corporate liberalism. At those moments, we shall see, the evaluative models of both sides were made most explicit and their programs most complete.

"History," it has been said, "knows no possibilities." On this view, by definition, if regional republicanism was defeated, it was not in fact a "real" possibility. Yet as Weber points out, it is impossible to establish historical causation without positing an "imaginative construct" in which the course of events is altered through the modification of known facts. A historical alternative, Weber argues, can be said to be "objectively possible" when we are able to construct an ideal type from historical fact which stands up to plausible counterfactual argument. Furthermore, few dominant institutions ever fully displace or subjugate their alternatives. Recent research has found that traditional customs not only survive in the midst of industrial societies, they often become interdependent with modern economic and political practices; in "dual" industrial economies some segments are organized according to "modern" corporate, others according to more "traditional" proprietary principles; and modern social movements have often located the will to challenge dominant institutions in churches, civic organizations, and informal networks well beyond the boundaries of the corporate and redistributive institutions that have shaped so much of twentieth-century American political economy. On both criteria, Part II will provide evidence to show that regional republicanism was "objectively possible": it was a coherent and empirically verifiable ideal type in economic and policy practice, and it survived as a deviant practice, well into the twentieth century.[22]

Part II is organized in two chapters: the first describes regional republicanism in legislative politics and regulatory practice, the second in railroad organization and management. In addition, both chapters explore representative and turning-point clashes with the practitioners of corporate liberalism. Chapter 5 reinterprets the origins and early administration of the Interstate Commerce Act of 1887 as a limited but quite real victory for the forces of regional republicanism. Fighting over regulation was occasioned not by monopoly profits, but by the efforts of national system builders to organize markets through *differential* ratemaking. In their quest to maximize high-volume through traffic over interregional systems, traffic managers generated a rate structure that systematically favored the long haul over the short, carload over less-than-carload freight, and the large-scale centralized national market over the moderately sized decentralized regional market. It was in this sense that national system builders were compelled to act upon the exogenous constraint—market structure—said by the new business history to discipline their behavior.

No single issue so mobilized the forces arrayed in favor of regulation than such "discriminatory" ratemaking; and, unlike the reconstitution of capital structures, this conflict became fully socialized. Those who hoped to alter the status quo and nurture regional market development were compelled to articulate a coherent theory of the corporation, the state, market landscape, and railroad ratemaking. The battle over regulation, then, is better understood as one over worldview and program than economic interest narrowly conceived or a struggle between "parochials" and "cosmopolitans" in the state. For interests were at best ambiguous during this constitutive era in political and economic development. Farmers, railroad managers, politicians, and intellectuals were divided over foundational questions and regulatory policy in ways that cannot be explained by institutional or economic conditions alone. Drawing from the republican school of United States historians, from J. G. A. Pocock to Lawrence Goodwyn, I argue that the regionalist program is better understood as a "moral economy"—an evaluative model or vision of industrial order with republican roots—than a reflection of economic or institutional interest narrowly conceived. Rereading the legislative history of the Interstate Commerce Act of 1887 from this perspective, Chapter 5 shows that it was a limited but quite real victory for the adherents to regional republicanism.

If fundamentally ambiguous *economic* interests were only fixed through shared evaluative models of industrial order, this was equally true for the policy ideas of America's new statebuilders. Some, we shall see, looked with disdain upon the claims of regionalists as parochial and self-serving. Others, however, like the ICC's first chief commissioner, Thomas M. Cooley, drew from a republican idiom, even if he did not recite all of its old axioms. Building upon the regionalist provisions of the Interstate Commerce Act of 1887, Cooley designed a regulatory architecture intended to cultivate self-restraint (a sense of republican citizenship) among shippers and railroads, by locating grounds for mutual gain. Cooley's goal was not so much to supersede the market with the state as it was to "regulate competition" in the name of regionalism *and* railroad rate stability.

Despite his remarkable success, regulated competition ran aground on the shoals of judicial review. The conflict between regional republicanism and corporate liberalism was never more stark than it became in the clash between court and commission in the 1890s. It was here that both would make most explicit their competing notions of regulation. If the corporation was a natural entity, a liberal person with presocial property rights, the Supreme Court said, the problem was to distinguish its *objectively* private activities from those "affected with the public interest," and to protect the former from state intrusion. From this corporate liberal point of view, regulated competition was incoherent, an oxymoron. For if competition in the market reigned, then by definition railroad ratemaking was a private activity, protected from state regulation. Thus, with Cooley's architecture in a shambles after judicial review, the ICC capitulated to corporate liberalism and rethought its mission.

From the political constitution of background conditions—capital structures and market landscape—Part II returns to the railroad corporation itself. Chapter 6 affirms the finding that technologies can be put to more than one use, each having unique and nonordinal efficiency advantages, by comparing a modest-size regional carrier, the Chicago Great Western Railroad, to its larger interregional competitors on four dimensions: morphology, traffic management, ratemaking, and finance. Like the distinction Piore and Sabel draw between mass production and flexible specialization in manufacturing, this chapter shows that a similar contrast existed in transportation at the turn of the century.

Chapter 6 shows that the Great Western achieved comparable levels of productive efficiency through remarkably different principles of efficiency than those prevailing on the interregionals. Where the latter attained scale economies by maximizing long-haul, high-volume, relatively homogeneous freight between large-scale markets, the Great Western achieved "economies of scope" by flexibly mixing diverse traffic: long and short haul, bulk and specialty, and carload and less-than-carload freight. However, in contrast to "batch" manufacturers, who attain flexibility through the use of general purpose machinery, I show how this was done in transportation through a complex pattern of traffic networking and freight mixing at key nodes throughout this regional system. This strategy, moreover, was facilitated by the Great Western's hub-and-spoke form.

Like its flexible counterpart in manufacturing, on the other hand, economies of scope in railroads put a high premium on the exercise of discretion by skilled workers out in the field and rapid communication between central traffic management at the hub and station agents throughout the system. As a result, just when the interregional railroads were thickening their managerial hierarchies, the Great Western abolished a key layer of middle management in its traffic department.

In ratesetting, as well, the Great Western differed dramatically from its larger scale competitors. Its president, A. B. Stickney, shared with the regionalists who drafted the Interstate Commerce Act, a bias for relatively decentralized market development. Hence, Great Western traffic managers set rates to nurture the development of "agricultural market towns"—decentralized markets, which were expected to diversify from agricultural distribution centers into food processing, farm implements and machinery, and construction-related industries. Finally, unlike the national systems that emerged from receivership in the 1890s with a clear legal and practical separation of property ownership from managerial control, the Great Western experimented with a condominium of ownership and management. By establishing a permanent finance committee in London, empowered to oversee all major capital expenditures, Stickney hoped to ensure his unorthodox railroad with a permanent source of credit.

From an account of business practice, this chapter returns to the struggle over the background conditions that ultimately determined the success of one railroad strategy over another. In both capital markets and regulation, the Great Western failed to secure the support necessary to consolidate and extend its regional strategy. By the turn of the century, both institutions had come to internalize the principles of scale economies; national, rather than regional, market landscape; and a corporate liberal theory of the corporation. Nonetheless, the Great Western survived, even if its architects lost control and many of its defining characteristics were modified. Thus, if railroad regionalism was pressed to the margins of twentieth-century practice, this was for political and relatively contingent, not economically necessary, reasons.

Part III explores the consolidation of and limits to corporate liberalism in railroad regulation. It shifts focus from constitutive politics to the politics of power within the institutional and conceptual boundaries familiar to students of modern American politics. Chapter 7, "The Predicament of Regulated Monopoly," reinterprets three defining characteristics of the modern American regulatory state: its redistributive focus, its relative weakness in the face of entrenched group conflict, and the exceptionally adversarial nature of business-government relations.

With the alternative to these features—regulated competition—dashed by the Supreme Court in the 1890s, the ICC rethought its mission. So had the commissioners internalized corporate liberal principles that they fundamentally reconceptualized Cooley's understanding of the corporation, railroad economics, and legitimate regulation. No longer was the corporation conceived as a public entity intended to serve the mutual interests of the corporators and the democratic state, the industry as a complex blend of competition and monopoly, or regulation as a cooperative enterprise. Instead the ICC capitulated to the judiciary's corporate liberalism: the corporation, it said, was a *natural* entity, a person with economic status prior to collective choice; the industry was a *natural* monopoly; and regulation was merely a matter of redistributing monopoly rents without confiscating corporate property. By definition, the proximate interests of state and corporation were adversarial. Therefore the regulatory problem, as the court instructed, was an empirical one: to discover the rate level that best balanced corporate and consumer interests in the distribution of wealth.

Though the ICC took this mandate literally, the promise of a *factual* solution to an inescapably political problem remained elusive: no estimate could avoid value judgements about the future of the industry. However, steeped as it had become in an adversarial model of regulation, the Progressive Era ICC was unable to escape the problem its ancestor had labored so diligently to solve: namely, how to generate consensus and compromise among railroads, shippers, and the state. So convinced had commission and carriers become that there was an *objective* solution to the political problem of wealth distribution, that they locked horns in a bitter stalemate. And so paralyzed did regulation become, that it stalled the transition from extensive to intensive railroad development. Tragically, then, the predicament of regulated monopoly set the seeds for twentieth-century railroad decline. But adversarial regulation was not the inevitable result of the sequence of democratization, industrialization, and statebuilding in the United States. A cooperative alternative had been tried. It was defeated in the realm of politics, not necessity.

Part I   CORPORATE
ENTITLEMENTS
AND NATIONAL
SYSTEM
BUILDING

CHAPTER TWO

Corporate Capital
Markets Transformed

No single fact shaped Gilded Age railroad politics more than overproduction. For three decades after the Civil War railroads were built and capitalized well beyond remunerative demand. Just how investment would be realized and how demand would be constituted became the subject of prolonged, if fragmented, fighting among investors, managers, shippers, and bankers. Like its consequences, the causes of overcapacity were also political: wittingly or not, the Civil War accorded railroads a novel priority in economic development. Nurtured not only by Republican party land grants and subsidies but also, and more important, by a capital market poised to mobilize savings for economic development on a continental scale, the railroad corporation emerged the dominant sector from the war. By the boom of the early 1870s, annual construction doubled its antebellum zenith. When it collapsed in the Panic of 1873, 30 percent of all railroad mileage fell into court-ordered receivership —fully twice the peak before the war.[1]

The conventional explanation of railroad overcapacity is technological, not political. According to the new business history, no project had ever necessitated such huge capital outlays. Railroads were not just big projects, though; they were marked by discrete ("lumpy") and immobile technology: once built, railroad track and roadbed stayed put and were subject to single use. There was little choice, then, but to construct railroads in large and discrete pieces. Therefore, it was only natural that demand lag behind capacity. In addition, since railroad market share is by its very nature territorial, preemptive building and acquisition of existing lines became a strategic necessity: entrepreneurs were compelled to risk investment beyond short-run remuneration. In short, late nineteenth-century railroads suffered from overcapacity and overcapitalization for the inescapable reason that technology was lumpy and capital intensive, and market share was measured territorially.[2]

By the same token, corporate capital markets were no more than a mediating factor—an intervening variable—in railroad development, equally derivative of technology. Chandler, for instance, argues that all of the elements of a modern corporate capital market were set in place well before the Civil War. The railroad boom of the 1850s necessitated such huge investment that dramatic innovations in capital mobilization were inevitable. By the time the antebellum construction mania collapsed in 1857, railroads had spawned an extensive call loan market, a spot market for corporate securities (in the New York Stock Exchange), and a new class of private investment bankers.[3]

There is no denying capital-market innovations before the war or interterritorial competition after. Nonetheless, nineteenth-century capital markets were equally, if not more profoundly, transformed by the triumph of republicanism, the Civil War, and Reconstruction. The result was to channel unprecedented domestic and international savings into railroad expansion. Overcapacity reached new heights after the war, as did the magnitude of routine bankruptcies: between 1870 and the turn of the century virtually half of all railroad mileage in the United States collapsed and fell into court-ordered receivership. Railroads were accorded a new priority during the 1860s—not just by the state, but more important, by private capital markets as well. Politics, not technology, better accounts for railroad overcapacity and overcapitalization in the late nineteenth century.

Even though business historians have all too often missed the independent effects of postbellum capital markets on the boom-and-bust cycle of railroad construction, many contemporaries understood it well. Especially in prostrate times, railroad overcapacity became a public marker for the ills of federal monetary, banking, and fiscal policy. Even so, contemporaries disagreed about the implications. Demands for structural change issued from the remarkably different perspectives of corporate and greenback reformers. This contest, remarkably homologous to the one over railroads, became mired in stalemate until 1896. Hence, the problem of railroad overcapacity was left to sectoral resolution. Nonetheless, postbellum capital markets were not only politically constituted, they were also contested. Like the case of railroads, if the corporate or administrative model of capital-market organization emerged victorious, this was for politically contingent, not technologically necessary, reasons.

The Transformation of Capital Markets

Investment Banking

Looking back from the 1880s, there were no more than a half-dozen investment banking houses prominent in railroad finance that had been in practice before the war. The Clarks, the Drexels, and the Vermilyes, the Boston bankers John Murray Forbes and Henry Lee Higginson, were all important players in the railroad boom of the 1850s. By the early 1870s, however, the field had crowded considerably. Many new entrants became permanent fixtures in railroad promotion, expansion, and reorganization. Moreover, without exception, the established firms were reorganized during the 1860s. The war decade left no part of investment banking untouched, including its relationship with corporate capital markets. As board members, reorganizers, and permanent financial agents, investment bankers pegged their ambitions to the railroad corporation well into the new century.

Still, the 1860s witnessed discontinuity between the growth of railroads and investment banking. During the peak growth years for private banking, 1862 to 1870, railroad construction collapsed. When it recovered in 1869, it did so at double its prewar level. No small part of this quantum leap was attributable to the many new private bankers who had entered the world of corporate finance.[4]

Where did these railroad bankers come from? Why did investment banking prove so attractive? And how do we account for the novel attention given to railroads? No single group provided more personnel to postbellum investment banking than seaboard merchants. Having all but lost their prominent status in antebellum politics and commerce, many seized the opportunities afforded by the war to secure a new place in the postwar division of labor. Tied as they were to Atlantic trade and king cotton, merchants and bankers from the largest of seaboard cities had actively opposed the Republican party's alternative to slavery until 1866. Republicans had long angered seaboard merchants by pledging federal aid to railroads and other "internal improvements," a homestead act based on preemption, and worst of all, the protective tariff. Merchants well understood the implications of this program. It "would reduce the volume and value of raw materials exports and of manufactured goods imports," the staples of their trade. As such, it would "tend to reduce the incomes and demean the functions of established merchants and bankers."[5]

In 1860 New York merchants announced their intention to ally with New England textile merchants against the protective tariff. The following year they signaled opposition to the party program by virtually boycotting the treasury's $150 million war-bond issue. In 1863 they opposed congressional decisions to issue fiat currency and legislate a national banking system, both of which threatened to undermine the functions and status of state commercial banks.[6] Admittedly, seaboard merchants were not unanimous in their opposition to republicanism. Moderates from east and west tended to accept the party's program piecemeal, often in the guise of the necessities of war.

Nevertheless, with their southern allies absent from Congress for the duration of the war, seaboard merchants and bankers had little choice but to capitulate, as Republicans enacted their "blueprint for modern America." Merchants and bankers were hardly relegated to obscurity, however. Republicanism, though obnoxious to Atlantic trade premised on the export of raw materials and on the import of manufactured goods, was not bereft of profitable opportunities. For one thing, the fiscal aspects of war provided merchants with incentives to enter investment banking. Some $2.8 billion in war debt, refunded regularly over the next decade, gave merchants, especially those with overseas correspondents, a powerful reason to abandon commerce. But western subsidies, greenback inflation, and a revolution in commercial banking also gave investment bankers aborning a special incentive to turn from Atlantic trade to western investment. Together, the realignment of American politics in 1860 and the Civil War sparked the emergence of a new class of private bankers, who, as the century wore on, pegged their ambitions to the settlement of the trans-Allegheny West.

Three groups seized the opportunities afforded by Republican legislation and the war: domestic sales agents for the House of Cooke, the German-Jewish merchants, and the Yankee houses.[7] The first emerged in 1861, after the treasury failed to place $150 million in war bonds in the open market. Reluctant as they were to support the early war effort, metropolitan bankers and large eastern investors refused to subscribe.[8] Still worse, the British market for American debt of all sorts had collapsed as a result of the uncertainties of secession. With a large stock of unsold war bonds, Treasury Secretary Salmon Chase provided huge blocks directly to the House of Cooke for commission sales. Over the next five years Jay Cooke effectively revolutionized American investment banking by establishing a vast network of domestic agents to mass market war bonds to small investors. Not only had Cooke opened the door to a new market for securities, he also had provided ample opportunity for his agents to amass sufficient capital and experience to enter the field themselves. Many investment houses prominent in postbellum railway finance got their start as participants in Cooke's Civil War operations.[9]

The firm of Fiske and Hatch, made immortal by Charles Francis and Henry Adams's muckraking account of railroad finance in *The Chapters of*

Erie, was organized in 1862 as a Cooke correspondent. Similarly, Vermilye and Company, though founded in 1830, remained obscure until it joined the Cooke organization during the war. In two short years, Vermilye accumulated a reserve of well over a million dollars and attained a trusted name in the New York money market. In 1860 another key player in postbellum railroad finance, Henry Clews, abandoned the woolen trade to open a private investment house. But, it was not until two years later, when he formed the partnership Livermore and Clews, in order to market Cooke's 5-20s, that the firm blossomed. Finally, John J. Cisco, undersecretary of the treasury for Lincoln, left public service in 1864 to start his own private bank to market war debt as part of a Cooke syndicate.[10]

Every one of these firms was to become a prominent railroad banker, promoter, and underwriter during the decades following the war. Moreover, Cooke introduced innovations that would become stock-in-trade in late-century corporate finance. His complex of correspondent and agent sales was a precursor to the postbellum financial syndicate, in which several houses agreed to market a railroad issue. Cooke also set the groundwork for securities underwriting, a practice that took off with the railroad reorganizations of the 1880s.

Although they also responded to the positive opportunities afforded by war finance, a second group of new entrants, the German-Jewish bankers, better illustrates the impact of the collapse of king cotton and Atlantic-based trade. Antebellum immigrants by and large, they had become successful merchant wholesalers before the war. Positioned at the axis of Atlantic, as well as northern and southern trade, they would search for new opportunities as the war shook those channels to their foundation.[11]

Likely the most prominent of this group was the Seligman family. Until 1862 they had been import-export merchants in New York. With the collapse of the cotton trade, however, they abandoned mercantile activity and opened private banking houses in New York and Frankfurt. With this overseas connection in place, the Seligmans succeeded in placing $200 million in unsalable war bonds in European markets during their first months in business. J & W Seligman and Company grew swiftly, opening branches in London, Paris, Amsterdam, and Berlin over the next decade.

Others followed in the Seligmans' footsteps. Lehman Brothers, a New York-based cotton brokerage house with a network of branches throughout the South, also abandoned the cotton trade during the war. In 1863 the Lehman Brothers opened a successful private bank in New York. Two years later Kuhn, Loeb and Company also gave up its merchant wholesaling business, moved to New York, and opened an investment house to market refunded war debt. As it turned more and more to railroad finance in the years following the war, Kuhn, Loeb would be joined by one of the two most prominent of Gilded Age railroad financiers, Jacob Schiff. Schiff, too, had left mercantile pursuits just after Appomattox for private banking, as did the founders of the prominent German-Jewish house, Goldman, Sachs. Like Cooke's correspondents, these firms became permanent railroad financiers and the innovators of modern investment banking, pioneering such functions as underwriting, merchant sales, placing new issues, and in the eighties and nineties, corporate reorganizations.

A third group, the "Yankee houses," were also established in New York during the 1860s. Similarly affected by the war and Reconstruction, they too drew from the mercantile community engaged in foreign and domestic trade. "It was this group," historian Vincent Carosso has written, "that produced the greatest American investment banker of all time, John Pierpont Morgan."[12]

In 1860 Morgan left his position in Duncan, Sherman and Company to organize J. Pierpont Morgan and Company. Four years later, he was joined by Charles H. Dabney, to form the partnership Dabney and Morgan. Over the next six years, this firm became a mainstay of government refunding operations. Often joined by a second Yankee firm, Morton, Bliss and Company, these two houses provided powerful competition to Cooke's refunding syndicates.[13] Morton, like many of the German-Jews, had been driven from his mercantile business by the war. In 1861, unable to collect debts from his southern customers, he was forced into bankruptcy. Slower to recover than the Seligmans, he waited two years before opening a private bank on Wall Street, L. P. Morton and Company. Joined by another former merchant, George Bliss, in 1869, the partnership changed its name to Morton, Bliss and Company.[14]

Fritz Redlich adds to this group of Yankee firms established in the sixties the First National Bank of New York. A premier example of a firm mixing commercial and investment services, the First National incorporated in 1863. Over the next decade its business originated primarily in war debt, buying and selling public reissues, and participating in refunding syndicates. Eventually led by George Baker, the First National would become a permanent ally to Morgan during the high years of railroad building, struggles for control, and reorganization.

Private investment banking had thus been transformed by the war. The union's fiscal revolution and the collapse of the cotton trade saw many a prominent merchant move into private banking. Even those firms established before the war were substantially reorganized. For instance, thanks to his success in government refunding sales in the late sixties, J. P. Morgan was offered a partnership in Drexel and Company in 1871. In this way, Drexel, Morgan and Company secured an overseas alliance with Morgan's father, Junius Spencer, in London. Similarly, Levi Morton, Henry Clews, and virtually all the German-Jews opened international offices or secured partnerships with correspondents in London, Amsterdam, and Frankfurt in order to market war bonds. The war also introduced the private bankers to syndicate sales, rudimentary underwriting services, and the practice Cooke's biographer, Henrietta Larson, calls "rigging the market" in order to maintain the price of a large issue of securities. Each of these innovations became standard practice in postbellum railway finance.

Indeed, by 1867 investment bankers, old and new, began to diversify from public to corporate debt. In 1869 alone, new railroad mileage doubled its peak year in the fifties; as many new miles were built between 1870 and 1872 as were built during the entire antebellum decade. Of course, investment banking alone did not drive the postwar railroad boom. Republican subsidies and land grants helped. So, too, did the reorganization of commercial banking. Still, during the sixties the New York banking and mercantile community had shifted its focus from Atlantic trade to the West and from king cotton to railroads. The city's National Board of Trade indicated as much by changing its position on the money question in 1870.

The Board, Irwin Unger has written, was the closest thing to a barometer of opinion among New York merchants and bankers. Throughout the sixties it had been the citadel of hard money orthodoxy. Dominated by creditors, many of whom traded internationally in gold, its members had denounced greenback inflation and excessive war debt and demanded a return to the gold standard. Moreover, since international commerce was transacted in gold, which traded at a premium to greenbacks, excess paper currency had the effect of driving down the price of domestic goods relative to imported goods. This de facto tariff angered international merchants and served to harden their opposition to fiat currency.[15] The National Board of Trade was unified in its position until 1870, when prominent members began to soften their position on greenback contraction. As the economy fell into recession in 1869, Jay Cooke, John Cisco, and Henry Clews, all three deeply invested in railroads by then, denounced Treasury Secretary McCulloch's contractionary policies. By 1870 neither the National Board of Trade nor the New York Chamber of Commerce could muster a majority in favor of rapid contraction or species resumption.[16]

Prominent board member Simeon B. Chittenden expressed the shifting sands of opinion among New York investors: "Had we resumed we should

not have had the great development of railroads which has come as an inci-
dent to our paper money, and which may yet prove, contrary to all history,
that a great war and paper money may be a great blessing . . . [The future
might yet show] that the magnificent development of our country was an in-
cident of the great rebellion and of the prodigious amount of paper which
consequently was circulated through the country."[17] Cooke, Cisco, the Seligmans, Lehmans and Drexels, Morton, Bliss, Fiske, and Hatch, among others,
all took advantage of the flush times afforded by war and abundant currency.
In so doing, they placed railroad promotion on a new plane after the war.
Nonetheless, the railroad boom of 1870 and those following it were not produced by private bankers alone. Changes in commercial banking wrought by
the war tipped the balance of domestic capital markets toward corporate investment as well.

Commercial Banking and Fiscal Policy

The fiscal revolution associated with the war transformed nineteenth-century commercial banking. In 1862, with species payments suspended, with
$400 million in greenbacks in circulation, and with only moderate success in
marketing war debt, a worried Congress decided to reorganize the union's
commercial banking system. The National Banking Act of 1862 would replace state charters with a uniform national statute. By making incorporation and the right to issue notes dependent upon the purchase of federal
bonds, Congress hoped to fill the union war chest.

A second national banking act passed in 1864 promised to provide the nation with a uniform currency, stabilize lending, and, following the Republican program for continental development, integrate east and west by providing a more secure currency on the frontier. Finally, in lieu of a central bank,
which might act as a lender of last resort, the National Banking Act of 1864
provided for a system of pyramid reserves centralized in New York City.
Though intended to protect against financial crises and to integrate regional
capital markets, its effect was quite the opposite.[18]

Having been mistrustful of central banking since the 1830s, Congress
identified New York City banks as the central reserve repositories for the national banking system as a whole. Moreover, the National Banking Act of
1864 designated eighteen regional reserve cities, where national banks might
hold a substantial portion of nearby country bank reserves. New York City
national banks, in turn, were empowered to hold no more than half of the regional city bank reserves. In theory, this pyramid organization, with its peak
in New York, would provide some central management to an otherwise decentralized and uncoordinated system. With the help of a central clearing as-

sociation, New York City bankers could engage in countercyclical reserve management. In practice, however, the pyramid reserve system exacerbated crises, as well as sectional and sectoral conflict, because funds flowed inordinately into the New York money market.[19]

Although the practice of pyramiding reserves in New York had been common before the war, it took on an all new character afterward. One reason for this was the heightened importance of the city's call-loan market. In theory, even by rule, this was a market for single-day loans, in which the borrower put up commercial paper or securities as collateral for short-term credit. In practice, call loans were rolled over from day to day, week to week, even month to month. Borrowers, in short, held extended lines of credit from commercial lenders. The practical limits of the call-loan market, then, were simply that lenders had the right to call an outstanding loan at any time. From the late sixties to the turn of the century call-loan customers were mainly securities brokers and traders on the New York Stock Exchange. One sign of the vastly more important position of the call-loan market after the war is the huge increase in demand by securities brokers. Before the war it has been estimated that there were only 150 permanent members on the Exchange; by 1873, there were well over 1100. The vast majority of those brokers traded in rails.[20]

Two factors encouraged hinterland savings to migrate to New York, where they drove interest rates down and fueled the railroad boom. On the demand side, since New York national banks could lend reserves on the call-loan market, they were able to offer out-of-town bankers substantial interest on their reserves. On the supply side, historian Richard Sylla has shown, country bankers, who typically faced little or no competition, could act as discriminating monopolists in their own captured markets. Lending a portion of their funds at relatively high interest rates in local markets, they would send the remainder to correspondent city banks or directly to New York. Admittedly, this was not new: state-chartered banks in New York had offered out-of-town correspondents interest on reserves prior to the war. Nor was the city's call-loan market a postbellum invention. Nevertheless, the practice exploded after the war. "In 1867 only twelve out of sixty banks who were members of the New York Clearing House explicitly paid interest on correspondent balances. By 1886 about half the members of the Clearing House directly paid interest on correspondent deposits."[21]

National banking's pyramid reserve structure had several results. It made interest rates relatively higher in the hinterlands than in eastern markets. It also funneled vast amounts of short-term loanable funds into the New York Stock Exchange, where they fueled a mania in longer term railroad investment. In 1874 the comptroller of the currency wrote, "Previous to the war the stock-board is said to have consisted of only one hundred fifty members and its organic principle was a strict commission business, under strict and conservative constitution and by-laws. The close of the war found the membership of the stock-board increased to eleven hundred, and composed of men from all parts of the country, many of whom had congregated in Wall Street, adopting for their rule of business the apt motto of Horace, 'Make money; make it honestly if you can; at all events make money.'"[22]

One other provision of the war's banking statutes helped to channel funds from the hinterlands to New York; namely, that national banks were prohibited from lending on real estate collateral. In theory, national banks were to be short-term commercial lenders, thereby assuring the solvency and flexibility of the system. In practice, city commercial banks provided resources for long-term corporate and public securities by lending to brokers, investment bankers, and merger and acquisition promoters, and by acquiring securities themselves. No such advantages, however, would accrue to western and southern borrowers. In these regions, where the primary, if only, asset was land, mortgage lending by national banks was prohibited. Consequently, agricultural borrowers in the hinterlands faced credit shortages and high interest rates. Moreover, the National Banking Act of 1864 required a minimum of fifty thousand dollars to secure a federal charter. This provision also biased incorporations toward larger cities in the Northeast and middle Atlantic states.[23]

Richard Sylla and Lance Davis have shown that other financial institutions —state banks and mortgage and trust companies—eventually took up the slack in the South and West, but they were slow in coming. State banks, for example, had been regulated out of existence, as Congress had increased the incentive to convert to a national charter in 1864 by placing a substantial tax on the state banks' currency issues. State banks were then hard-pressed to enter rural and small-town markets throughout the final decades of the century. Not until well after 1900 did intersectional interest rates begin to reach parity; that is, well after the railroads stretched across the country and secured their status as a dominant sector in Gilded Age economic development.[24]

Two final aspects of federal fiscal policy had equally profound effects on the flow of money and credit into the railroad corporation: greenback and debt retirement. It is well known that despite periodic calls to reflate at the trough of the business cycle, national policy makers maintained a relatively constant money supply during the three decades following the war. Under conditions of domestic economic and population growth, however, money remained tight and prices declined. Among other goals, this had the treasury's desired effect of making rescheduled Civil War bonds attractive to European and British investors. Tight money also encouraged enormous overseas investment in American railroad debt. Moreover, corporate debt had the added security of land and tangible property. When far-flung investors put down cash for American railroad bonds, they were assured not only of a fixed return and paid-in principal, but also, in the event of failure, of control over tangible property through the mortgage bond. Tight money made railway mortgage bonds seem particularly safe and profitable for overseas investors. By 1885 British investment in American railroads had outstripped investment in national debt; by 1890 the British had committed an estimated £300 million to American railroads.[25]

Federal debt policy also had the effect of funneling savings through the New York money market into railroads. Though Jay Cooke had distributed war bonds among many small holders, by 1875 refunding operations and secondary sales had concentrated bondholding considerably. Even though Americans disagreed over the method, they did agree that the war debt ought to be retired as rapidly as government revenues would allow. With this mandate, the treasury regularly flooded the New York open market with funds, as it called in nearly $2.8 billion worth of securities between 1871 and 1893. Thus, large holders—banks, corporations, wealthy investors—were routinely left with excess cash, which they promptly committed to the most liquid of available outlets: corporate securities. Like investment and commercial banking structure, then, postbellum fiscal policy also channeled unprecedented investment into the railroads.[26]

By the early 1870s the railroads had begun to digest the political reconstitution of American capital markets. In 1872 alone 7,432 new miles of tracks were built—well over twice the antebellum peak year of 1854.[27] This leap cannot be accounted for by the lumpiness of railroad technology or the nature of territorial competition unique to this industry. The railroad corporation was accorded a novel status by the rise of republicanism, the Civil War, and Reconstruction. Still, it was not merely the explicit policy to subsidize western development through this sector that accounted for the dramatic increase in postwar rail construction. Between 1860 and 1870 private capital markets had also been reorganized in ways that made the railroad corporation the leading sector in American industrialization. By design and unintended consequence, the New York money market became a magnet for domestic and international savings; and by far the largest portion of that credit went into the railroads. In sum, the pace of rail construction doubled after the war for politically contingent, not technologically necessary, reasons.

Instability, Credit Rights, and Reform

The reconstitution of capital markets in the Civil War transformed investment priorities in the American economy. The novel status of the New York money market, Robert Sharkey has written, ensured that "the creditor interest was dominant, large-scale instead of small scale enterprise was favored, and the East held the whip hand over the less developed regions of the country."[28] Richard Sylla concludes that the structure of late-century capital markets was a boon to American economic growth: by linking the open market for industrial investment to rural domestic and international supply, it shifted investment efficiently from its lower return in agriculture to a higher return in industry. And yet, not only hinterland farmers, who now seemed to be subsidizing industrial growth, were troubled by postbellum capital flows. Industry's beneficiaries—corporate entrepreneurs, bankers, and railroad managers—were much more ambivalent about the organization of Gilded Age capital markets than Sylla. For, although the pace of railroad investment doubled after the war, so did the magnitude of collapse: fully 30 percent of all railroad mileage in the United States failed and fell into receivership in the 1870s—twice the rate of bankruptcy experienced in the largest antebellum depression of the 1850s.[29]

On the one hand, railroad entrepreneurs and their allies in the banking community understood quite well that postbellum banking and fiscal policy had made abundant funds available for corporate investment: the New York investment community's sudden moderation on contraction and resumption in 1870 had signaled as much. On the other hand, railroad men complained more and more of overproduction, wild fluctuations in economic activity, price wars, and a profitability crisis as the century wore on. Their response to the Panic of 1873 showed early signs of this, but they would not organize a successful reform movement until well into the next decade.

Nonetheless, 1873 marked the beginning of a thirty-year cleavage between two money and banking reform movements. The ideological division between reformers did not fall neatly along partisan, class, or sectional lines. Moreover, the depression of the seventies, like the troughs of the sixties, eighties, and nineties, saw simple demands for reflation appear like clockwork. The Panic of 1873, however, spawned a more structural critique of the national banking system and federal financial policy from both the ranks of radical greenback farmers and workers and the corporate and banking community. Postbellum capital markets were shown to be not only politically constituted, but politically contested as well.

Three aspects of the politics of money and banking from Reconstruction to the turn of the century are critical to the conflict over American industrial order. Postbellum capital markets were economically volatile and politically fragile, that is, they generated economic instabilities and social conflicts affecting both beneficiaries and losers. Structural reformers, therefore, came from both camps. The two main lines of reform ideology—corporate administration and greenback decentralization—were remarkably similar to the cleavages in railroad politics explored in much more detail in the remainder of this book. Finally, until well after the crash of the nineties, a political stalemate kept the basic structural features of Civil War and Reconstruction capital markets intact. Therefore, the leading corporate sector and beneficiary of Gilded Age capital markets, the railroads, was forced to find sectoral solutions to problems financial reformers identified with the broader structural features of late nineteenth-century capital flows.

The Panic of 1873

Everyone seriously concerned with the Panic of 1873 and the long lean years following it grappled with the comptroller of the currency's official account of its causes and consequences. Surprisingly, reformers of opposing stripes agreed with the comptroller that the "present financial crisis may, in large degree, be attributed to the intimate relations of the banks of the city of New York with the transactions of the stock-board," and "by the [sudden] desire of the country banks," linked to the New York money market through "their city correspondents . . . to withdraw their balances from the city banks." In September of 1873, the comptroller explained, country bankers began to withdraw their reserves in order to finance the autumn harvest. Stung by cash shortages in the past, they "thought it safer to withdraw all their balances at once." Consequently, "when the reserves of the New York City banks became alarmingly reduced by the drafts of their country correspondents, the only resource left to the city banks was to convert their call-loans." But commercial lenders were stretched beyond their means in this market. Hence, their customers, "the numerous holders of . . . securities became alarmed . . . , the panic soon extended throughout the country," and "suspension followed." The "legitimate purposes of trade," concluded the comptroller, had been diverted into speculation on corporate debt, and when the fall harvest demanded commercial credit, national banking's pyramid reserve system was strained beyond its limits.[30]

Corporate leaders and greenbackers alike found the comptroller's explanation compelling. Even so, they drew quite different conclusions. In 1875, for example, prominent investment banker and railroad financier, John Murray Forbes, explained the panic to the House Committee on Banking and

Currency in much the same way. Speculation and personal extravagance, especially in "borrowing for the purpose of railroad building" resulted in a financial bubble, he said. By the fall of 1873 "the vicious system of lending the reserves of country banks to the New York banks had created an immense debt, then based largely upon railroad-securities of more or less doubtful value. This aggravated evil often exist[ed] just at the time when money [was] . . . needed by business men to move the crops on the fall trade." With credit extended to its breaking point from New York banks and with railroads overloaded with debt and built well "in advance of the needs of the country," plus farmers about to call in their reserves, "all the elements of a panic," Forbes concluded, were in place. "The failure of Jay Cooke [who had been unable to meet the debt requirements for his Northern Pacific Railway] merely set the ball in motion . . . The New York banks were unable to press their call-loans, for fear of ruining their customers, and thus becoming the owners of doubtful securities which they held. Their capital, needed for legitimate purposes, was thus practically lent out on certain iron rails, railroad ties and bridges, and rolling stock, *called* railroads, many of them laid down in places where much of it was practically useless. The banks probably did the most they could in temporizing their customers and their own creditors, but in the mean time the legitimate borrowers—the business men of the country—who were generally in sound condition, were made the victims."[31]

Forbes did not stop there. Hard money man that he was, he attributed speculation to the surplus of paper currency still in circulation. "Had [Congress] *carried into effect measures for resumption which they merely talked about or 'resolved,'* the surplus of currency for the several past years would not have gone into *premature* railroads and other wild enterprises, and the business wants of the country would have been amply supplied." Resumption, claimed Forbes, was the solution: a currency securely tied to gold would check inflation and the overinvestment necessarily accompanying it. Nevertheless, he echoed the New York Board of Trade's concern that it might be too rapid, resulting in a sudden and devastating contraction: "I would deprecate too early resumption as much as too great delay," he told the committee. Still, the gold standard alone would keep the nation from "gliding down the rapids of bankruptcy" so clearly exemplified by the events of 1873.[32]

Forbes's views were echoed by other prominent investment bankers. George Coe and Henry P. Kidder told the House committee that paper money had been responsible for the panic. Even Simeon Chittenden, who just five years before had been so sanguine about greenbacks, declared that the "'present amount of currency [was] beyond the requirements of all the legitimate business that would be done in 1874,' and it could be readily reduced without harm to business."[33]

Though Forbes's sense that railroad overproduction was the proximate cause of the Panic of 1873 was shared by many, others saw the underlying problems (and their solutions) differently. Western agrarians had suddenly become mobilized on "the money question" by the Panic of 1873. Many also blamed the panic on the relationship among national banking reserves, the New York call-loan market, and stock market speculation. "From all this," cried one greenback voice in Congress,

> it will be seen that our present difficulties are the result of an inordinate and uncalled-for expansion of the railroad system; a vicious custom of banks paying interest on deposits, thereby imposing on them the necessity of lending those deposits to brokers and speculators "on call;" certification of checks when no funds were on deposit, thus affording an improper credit to the drawer without any substantial foundation; and a resulting deficiency in the reserves so great that the slightest panic drove the banks into suspension for want of ready money to meet a run upon them. This was inflation, speculation, an expansion of the credit system to an unnatural extent, in short, a financial bubble; and when the credit of the great corporations and banking houses had been stretched to its utmost tension, and when the touch-stone of demand of payment came to be applied, by the withdrawal of country bank balances and merchants' deposits, the bubble collapsed and the distress we now experience ensued.[34]

Similarly, Bourbon Democrat John Rice Eden (Ill.), charged that "the currency driven through these artificial channels to New York, when needed by the producer to move his surplus, under the manipulations of Wall-street brokers, is absorbed in speculations, in watered stocks of railroads, to pay the interest on which additional carrying tolls are imposed on the people; and by its results raising the rates of interest, establishing excessive rates for transportation, depleting the legitimate avenues of trade, and making the stock gambler the competitor of the people for the use of money."[35]

Many westerners, however, disagreed with the hard money men on the deeper causes and solutions to the panic. Some, including several railroad men,[36] complained that the comptroller's analysis simply illustrated the inflexibility of the current system and demanded immediate reflation. Others called for loosening national bank incorporation laws to increase the distribution in the West and in small towns, or for free banking and tighter reserve requirements in the national banking system. Still others attacked national banking altogether and demanded public currency credit instead. In 1874, western Republicans, in alliance with well over half of western Democrats and two-thirds of southern Democrats in Congress, passed an inflation bill which increased national bank notes by $46 million and greenbacks by $18 million. The law also included a provision to tighten reserve requirements on country and regional correspondent banks, and thereby stem the flow of rural savings to the New York money market. In utter disappointment they watched the president cave in to hard money forces and veto the bill.[37]

Grant's action reverberated in the electorate: in 1874 the Republicans went down to defeat. For the first time since 1861 the House passed into Democratic control. Acting quickly, the lame duck Congress passed the Species Resumption Act, by which the treasury would exchange greenbacks for gold on the first of January 1879. Apparently a victory for hard money forces, a closer look reveals a compromise. On the one hand, the statute enacted free banking into law, with the proviso that new bank notes issued be offset by a smaller amount of greenback redemptions. This satisfied moderate inflationists. On the other hand, the treasury was to begin to accumulate gold in order to redeem the remainder of outstanding greenbacks in 1879. Moderate on both sides, the Resumption Act signaled more a stalemate, which would last until the turn of the century, than a compromise capable of solving the problems of late nineteenth-century banking and finance.

All of the institutional difficulties identified during the seventies remained. Investment continued to flow inordinately into the corporate sector, heavy industry, and railroads especially. The cycle of overproduction and collapse endured well after the economy rebounded in 1879, as did sectional inequalities in interest rates and the conflict between the seasonal demand for agricultural credit and the New York money market. Moreover, the politics of late nineteenth-century capital markets was left unresolved. Even though legislative managers and moderates thought they had negotiated a durable settlement, the experience of 1874–75 served to galvanize reformers on both sides of the debate. The Inflation Act sparked hard money intellectuals and corporate sector financiers to enlist the resources of the Social Science Association to their cause. Spearheaded by Forbes, the Association's "Financial Department" launched a weekly journal "intended as a Document for sowing seed among constituents."[38] By contrast, Grant's veto and the Resumption Act galvanized greenback forces to rally behind a structural critique of national banking and form a national third party. In the 1878 congressional elections, the Greenback-Labor party mobilized the labor movement in nearly every state, polled over a million votes, and sent fourteen representatives to the House.[39]

Here, then, was the genesis of a deep-rooted division between financial reformers which would become most clear in the late eighties and early nineties. Pluralist historians have long denied coherence to this cleavage. Self-interest and intellectual prejudice, on this account, multiplied cross-cutting cleavages on the money question that defy such order. Even so, unable to escape evaluating their subjects, these historians have concluded that not all reform proposals carried equal weight. Some proposals, rooted as they were among preindustrial groups—artisans, small farmers, and petit bourgeoisie—appear utopian in retrospect, or ultimately irrelevant to a modern industrial order. Everyone was self-interested, on this view, but some self-interest was more legitimate than others.[40]

Unfortunately, we are left with no criterion for legitimacy other than the test of success: some ideas were left to the dustbin of history, while others endured. Once we begin to see that such bedrock economic formations as capital markets and railroads were politically constructed, however, it becomes impossible to wrench the shape and direction that the American industrial order took in the late nineteenth century from the political struggles over its most elemental institutions. Therefore, by rejecting the notion that the form economic development took was determined by technological and economic necessity, the cleavage between structural reformers begins to become intelligible. We then see both greenbackers and corporate reformers for what they were: namely, groups for whom the money question became a constitutive issue in the politics of modern industrial order.

By greenback reformers, I mean all organized groups that made public, rather than corporate, currency and credit a centerpiece of their political program. From the National Labor Union in the 1860s to the Greenback-Labor party of the late seventies, the Knights of Labor in the eighties, and the People's party of the nineties, this remarkably diverse group of agrarian and labor reformers turned to the money question. Despite their heterogeneity in social and geographic origins, strategy, and timing, greenbackers were united by two consistent themes: republicanism and antimonopolism. On the one hand, their vision of a desirable political order was the classical one of a republic where widespread property ownership of small producers provides the basis for a virtuous citizenry capable of vigilantly checking society's tendencies toward economic concentration and political oligarchy. They understood themselves to be citizens in roughly such a republican order, with the natural duty to preserve and strengthen it. Nonetheless, the reformers perceived the government increasingly to be an instrument of certain economic actors, who gained "special privilege" and then used it to concentrate wealth in their hands and extend their political subversion of the republic.

This development offended the republican understanding of politics for two reasons: free citizens were being degraded into a poverty-stricken and dependent population unable to shoulder the burdens of citizenship; and the government itself was deprived of its proper character as an expression of the interests of the people as a whole.[41]

Cause and consequence of a nascent industrial oligarchy, fiscal and banking policy needed reform. In the 1870s grangers and western greenbackers denounced sectional inequalities in banking and credit as unfair in and of themselves. National banking and tight money, they complained, also caused excessive economic centralization, cyclical prostration, and the systematic and periodic collapse of agricultural prices. Workers also condemned postbellum financial policy. Drawing from antebellum monetary theorist Edward Kellogg and his postwar disciple, William Campbell, National Labor Union leader William Sylvis attacked the gold standard and corporate banking in the 1860s, as did Knights of Labor leader Terrence Powderly in the eighties. Separated by time, industrial origin, and political context, Sylvis and Powderly nevertheless agreed over fundamentals. Money was a public convention, not a god-given commodity. Therefore, the only reason to make a scarce commodity—gold—the standard of value was to make money dear, inflate interest rates beyond productivity growth, and thereby redistribute wealth from those who produced it to those who lent representations of it. The gold standard was, in effect, a fraud perpetrated upon all producers of wealth—workers, petty proprietors, and farmers. Similarly, the entitlement to issue currency had been stolen from representatives of the people—Congress—and delegated to corporate associations. This fostered scarcity and high interest rates, as national banks regulated the price of money by withholding notes and manipulating the price of gold. The result was only to further redistribute wealth from producer to nonproducer.[42]

The greenback solution, shared in its many incarnations from Alexander Campbell's 3.65 percent bond in 1864 to the Populist subtreasury plan in 1892, was to replace the gold standard with fiat currency and corporate rights to issue currency with public sovereignty. Diverse as they were, greenbackers were no mere inflationists. They shared Edward Kellogg's proposal that public currency be made interconvertible with interest-bearing government bonds at the will of the holder. The interconvertible bond, whose rate of interest would be set slightly below the expected annual rate of growth, would give currency the ability to represent augmented value associated with economic growth and productivity gains. As Kellogg had written, "The accumulative power is essential to the existence of money, for no one will exchange productive property for money that does not represent production."

The bonds would also provide a flexible currency capable of expanding and contracting countercyclically with the business cycle. If public notes were too numerous and in danger of fueling speculation and overproduction, the commercial rate of interest (made by private lenders) would be depressed below the public rate, and currency not engaged in productive activity would be converted into government notes. Conversely, when currency was able to accumulate value more rapidly in production and trade than in interest-bearing bonds, the latter would be converted.[43] As Wisconsin's 1878 Greenback-Labor party candidate for governor, E. P. Allis, said of the interconvertible bond, "If there is more currency today that can find employment at a reasonably greater profit than the rate of interest on the bonds, then to-morrow that surplus currency is swallowed up in the bonds. If the next day the legitimate demands of borrowers for trade or manufacture carry the rate reasonably above the rate of interest on the bonds, then the next day after the currency is out again." The beauty of this system was that "the whole people govern it [the value and volume of currency] and no man, or one set of men, can materially alter the result."[44]

Thus, credit issued at interest rates close to the annual increase in national wealth would assure that producers—farmers, artisans, petty manufacturers—rightfully retained the fruits of their labor. Agrarian greenbackers thus hoped to secure cheap public credit on future crops or real estate. In the West, this would translate into regional parity in interest rates. It would also give farmers a chance to withhold their harvest long enough to maintain prices. In the South, the Farmer's Alliance also hoped to secure credit on future harvests in order to support large-scale marketing and buying cooperatives designed to break the bonds of debt peonage.[45]

For labor, the interconvertible bond promised to dampen the business cycle and the tendency to gouge wages at the trough. It also promised to check the tendency to economic concentration during recessions, when savings and unequal access to credit secured by large manufacturers proved an unassailable advantage over their smaller competitors. Cheap credit would encourage labor mobility, as more skilled artisans were provided an opportunity to open their own shops or join together in cooperative ventures. Financial reform, then, would tend to encourage cooperation between employers and employees, thereby cementing the producer's alliance of labor and small business.[46]

Both labor and agrarian reform movements split over the ideology of republicanism and over the money question. Many western Populists and the American Federation of Labor ultimately rejected greenback doctrine and the reforms associated with it. Nevertheless, until the 1890s it was not at all clear what reform strategies would be most effective, nor what sorts of inter-mediate institutions were necessary to achieve agrarian and labor interests. Those who held to republican-antimonopolism tended to propose coopera-tives and regulatory institutions capable of supporting a regime of small property and republican self-determination. Thus, even though greenbackers were unable to effect institutional reform, they continued to address the is-sues that reformers of all stripes had recognized as early as 1874: instability, overproduction, sectional maldistribution of credit, and social unrest.

Of course, the same issues were interpreted quite differently by an emerg-ing class of corporate elites, investment bankers, and their intellectual allies. Like the hard money assemblies during Reconstruction, business associa-tions dedicated to financial reform re-emerged in the late eighties and flour-ished during the depression of the nineties. In part, this was in reaction to the re-emergence of greenback politics in the guise of the Farmer's Alliance and the People's party. But corporate elites also demanded reform for their own purposes. Paradoxically, they still suffered from the very organization of cap-ital markets that made their own enterprise possible.[47]

Heirs to the Social Science Association's Financial Department, first the Union for Sound Money, then the National Sound Money League, took up the banner of reform. Composed of America's leading corporate elites—rail-road officers and directors, prestigious members of the corporate bar, Amer-ica's first mass retailers, and the most prominent of urban commercial and in-vestment bankers—the Sound Money League criticized capital markets on grounds radically at odds with greenbackers. Despite the many subtle differ-ences among them, James Livingston has shown that corporate elites had come to agree over fundamentals. By the 1880s, they argued, industrializa-tion had fundamentally transformed the American economy, but capital markets had failed to keep up. Bankers, railroad men, corporate counsel to leading railroads and manufacturers, and national market merchants com-plained of a capital market out of control, that is, an excessively decentralized body in want of an administrative head. Overproduction, according to sound money leaders, issued not so much from large-scale expensive plant and equipment (though this was part of the problem) as it did from the many small-scale entrepreneurs enticed to enter the market during flush times. The result—redundant and relatively unproductive enterprise—inevitably caused price wars, profitability crises, waning investor confidence and ulti-mately collapse. Recessions had a purging effect, though, as marginal pro-ducers were pressed to the wall and as bridge loans were extended to the larger, more responsible and efficient firms. Still, capital markets desperately called for rationalization. For the boom-and-bust cycle had resulted in a long-term profitability crisis and unmanageable social stress.

This was abundantly evident in the national banking system's organization of reserve management. Like Forbes's complaints nearly two decades earlier, sound money leaders worried about the effects of the intimate association between country banks, the New York call-loan market, and the stock exchange. A market so subject to seasonal collapse might fail to maintain loyalty among new urban middle classes, the bulwark of small investors. Moreover, seasonal prostration in agrarian commercial credit caused by pyramid reserves came dangerously close to mobilizing western farmers to the Populist cause. The more support given to the cause of fiat money or free silver, however, the more volatile would economic activity become. For inflation inevitably led to indiscriminate lending and the sorts of unproductive investment that had resulted in regular crises throughout the late nineteenth century.

The solution lay in defending a sound basis for currency—gold—and a centrally administered reserve system. Unlike their predecessors in the seventies, National Sound Money League members had come to see the necessity for an elastic currency and countercyclical management. Careful to distinguish themselves from greenbackers or populists—"indiscriminate inflationists"—sound-money intellectuals argued that only a banking system with reserves pegged securely to gold and centrally administered by those who understood the investment and productivity dynamics of modern industrial capitalism would resolve the political and economic problems of American capital markets. Officially, the League favored privately administered reserves through branch banking and a more powerful national clearing house. But American banking was too decentralized at the turn of the century for the industry to accept such a scheme. In the nineties, then, corporate elites were satisfied to wage a public campaign against free silver. Thus, they took McKinley's victory as their own. Equally, the Gold Standard Act of 1900 was a triumph for corporate reformers; as such, it represented a break in the twenty-five year stalemate over money and banking reform. It also set the foundation upon which the Federal Reserve Act's central administration of reserves was built.

The Sectoral Politics of Industrialization

Industrializing America was conceived in civil war. Intentionally, the victors redirected national economic goals from Atlantic trade to continental development; unintentionally, entrepreneurs found novel opportunities in the new American landscape. The cumulative effect was to transform the priority capital markets accorded the railroads.

Postbellum Americans faced no dearth of resources—natural, technological, or ideological—to implement these goals. Steel rails linked one small town after another, as they coursed sparsely populated plains. Born in turbulence, late-century industrialization remained economically volatile. With the railroad industry as its marker, a boom-and-bust cycle touched Americans from all walks of life. In their search for practical solutions to economic instability, reformers tapped the wellsprings of moral conflict as old as the republic itself. Resourceful as they were, however, greenbackers and corporate reformers found neither the power to act nor the imagination to compromise. Though the reconstruction of American finance promised to relieve the periodic distress of the business cycle, it would have to wait until after the century's turn.

In the meanwhile, conflicts of societal scope were left to sectoral resolution. America's leading industry, the railroads, would become the locus of two conflicts of fateful proportion. The first—just how investment would be realized, given persistent overcapacity and excess debt—went a long way toward determining the financial and legal structure of the modern corporation. The second—how demand would be constituted once railroads were built beyond realizable remuneration—shaped the organization of twentieth-century market landscape and the nature of the administrative state. Thrust to the center of the politics of industrialization by conditions beyond its control, the railroad industry became the locus of a struggle whose outcome shaped twentieth-century American industrial order.

CHAPTER THREE

Reconstituting
Fixed Costs

Accorded leading sector status in postbellum capital markets, railroad building boomed. Between 1865 and 1900 mileage swelled fivefold, from 35,000 to 193,000.[1] Abundant supplies of capital fueled the construction of vast autarkic national systems as entrepreneurs sought to preempt rivals from controlling open territory. However, the long railroad expansion from 1870 to 1900 was also punctuated by routine collapse. Excess capital spurred construction so far beyond realizable demand that large portions of the industry periodically failed and fell into court-ordered receivership: over 30 percent of domestic mileage in the 1870s, 15 percent in the 1880s, and 25 percent in the 1890s.[2]

Until the 1880s, receivership was a routine practice by which railroads raised new money or were sold at auction. In that decade, it became evident to leading entrepreneurs that the very entitlement structure that enabled national system building now threatened its progress and their own authority. So convinced were the federal judges who oversaw receiverships that national systems needed protection, that they systematically reallocated extant rights within the corporation from creditors (bondholders) to incumbent managers. The result was not only to buttress bigness and ensure the separation of ownership from managerial control; it was also to disempower creditors, thereby enabling incumbent managers to reduce debt (fixed costs) on reorganized railroads on average by one-third.

By the turn of the century, twelve of the nation's twenty-eight largest railroads (accounting for well over one-third of all mileage in the U.S.) had emerged from such "friendly receiverships"—national systems intact, ownership subordinate to management, and fixed costs slashed on average by 27 percent. Thus, railroad fixed costs were politically reconstituted in order to buttress national systems from dismemberment. As such, they were much more malleable than conventionally thought. In other words, two defining features of the modern railroad corporation—the separation of ownership from managerial control and bigness—are better explained by the historically contingent choices of managers and federal judges than by optimizing behavior under the technological constraint of high fixed costs.[3]

Corporate Theory and Receivership Practice

In order to appreciate transformation in receivership practice after the 1880s, we need see its place in a broader clash over nineteenth-century corporate theory. The corporation in industrializing America was initially conceived as a public body, its rights and obligations carefully circumscribed by the state. In the first half of the century, then, state legislatures granted special charters to railroads, banks, canals, and insurance companies, in which they routinely restricted managerial powers, placed ceilings on capitalization, and carefully spelled out the legitimate geographic and business scope of the firm. In adjudicating *intra*corporate disputes, then, judges weighed management behavior against charter provisions, regarding all actions beyond the powers granted by the state *ultra vires*.[4] On this "grant theory," when a railroad failed to meet its financial obligations, management was ousted and courts of equity appointed a temporary and disinterested receiver so that the carrier could continue to meet its public obligations, while its finances were adjusted. Unlike later failures, those before the 1850s were typically seen as much as failures of promotion as they were of the railroad: usually subscribed capital was insufficient to complete a project promised by charter. Therefore, in order to meet construction costs, carriers took on excessive short-term or "floating" debt. There was also fraud involved, as inside managers used their dual positions on railroad corporations and independent construction companies to funnel paid-in capital to themselves. Such actions were deemed *ultra vires*, and incumbent managers engaged in double-dealing were routinely ousted in receivership.[5]

State legislatures, moreover, were often heavily invested in railroad equity prior to the 1850s. Consequently, receivership courts understood the problem of insolvency as a temporary one, in which new public as well as private sources of capital would be tapped to pay off floating debt and complete projects promised by charter. Moreover, debt still represented the smaller part of railroad finance. Thus the main problem for receiverships after the 1880s, reducing fixed costs, was not yet significant. As a result, few railroads that failed before the 1850s were brought to foreclosure. Instead, receivership kept creditors temporarily at bay; granted shareholders time to elect new management; and gave receivers the chance to raise new money by assessing shareholders, by initiating a public issue, or by borrowing from the state.[6]

Several factors shook the grant theory and the doctrine of *ultra vires* loose from their mooring. First, as early as the 1830s, the special privileges accorded to state-chartered corporations came under attack by Jacksonian Democrats. As a result, more and more states adopted the general purpose charter—purportedly available to all comers and issued more or less routinely by administrative, rather than legislative, bodies. Under this practice, the state-chartered corporation became subject to fewer and fewer regulatory restrictions. Furthermore, after the panic of 1857, state governments began to disinvest in railroads. As private investors took their place, legislatures lost their zeal to scrutinize corporate behavior. By the time railroad construction had resumed after the Civil War, the doctrine of *ultra vires* had little to hang its hat on. This is not to say it disappeared. As we shall see in Chapter 4, a grant or public theory of the corporation retained its hold on the imagination of the many who would regulate railroads by state or federal commission. By midcentury, however, the judiciary routinely defined the corporation in terms of its private, rather than public, purposes.[7]

Even so, the private theory did not result in a self-evident understanding of corporate legitimacy or receivership practice. In fact, by the 1880s two dramatically different private conceptions of the corporation clashed on the battlefield of railroad insolvency. The first, which emerged from the ruins of the grant theory in the decades surrounding the war, also saw the corporation as an artificially constituted entity. On this individualist or market theory of the corporation, its powers initiated not from the state, but from the will of its owners. Like the traditional partnership, the corporation was conceived as no more than the aggregate sum of its private investment contracts. The sovereignty of property and a will theory of contract reigned supreme. Consequently, management was expected to act in the interests of shareholders, with its authority derived from its fiduciary responsibility to owners. The corporation, in short, was to be run as a "trust fund" for its creditors.[8]

Nowhere was this more evident than in the mortgage "trust indenture," so indicative of the shift from equity to debt finance after the war. Encouraged by generous railroad land grants, deflation, and a burgeoning overseas market for railroad securities, debt surpassed equity for the first time in 1872. Seventeen years earlier it accounted for only 39 percent of all capital invested in railroads. By 1875 that proportion had swelled to 53 percent. "At the time of the panic of 1857," wrote Arthur Stone Dewing, "mortgage bonds were practically absent from the financial plans of New England and Southern railroads. They were comparatively rare among the roads of the middle states, and the exception, rather than the rule, among the roads then built in the western states."[9] Moreover, railroad mortgage bonds became especially attractive to far-flung foreign investors after the war, not only because interest was guaranteed, but also because, in the event of failure, they were legally tied to concrete parcels of property. Mortgage bonds assured distant investors control over the disposition of corporate property in the event of failure. Under these conditions, the courts began to look more and more to the terms of contract (the indenture) between the corporation and its creditors.[10]

On the trust-fund or market model of the corporation, when a railroad failed to meet binding obligations outlined in an indenture, ownership reverted to its unpaid creditors, management was ousted, and a temporary receiver was appointed at the initiative of owners. Receivership practice followed these procedures quite closely from roughly the 1860s to the 1890s. Insolvent railroads emerged from receivership in the black by mutual agreement among shareholders to assess themselves or by initiating new securities on particularly favorable terms. In this way, short-term or "floating" debt was retired, old debt renegotiated, and at least for a time, new sources of finance secured. Otherwise, the corporation was brought to foreclosure at the initiative of its bondholders, sold at auction, and its assets distributed to unpaid creditors. This is not to say the corporation was gutted. Indeed, often incumbent regimes recaptured the property at auction. Rather, it indicates that property (bondholders) took priority in the final disposition of the assets. The roads surviving receivership emerged solvent, with essentially the same financial structure and the trust-fund rights of shareholders and fiduciary obligations of managers intact. As one observer remarked looking back from the dramatic changes of the nineties, "Railroads which failed in the early seventies were not really reorganized — they were simply regalvanized."[11]

Perhaps the most cogent example of a "trust-fund receivership" was the early reorganization of the Erie Railroad. Notorious for the way speculators Jay Gould and Jim Fisk lined their pockets by saddling this road with excess debt, the insolvent Erie Railroad was pressed into receivership by its British bondholders in 1877. In a plan designed by the bondholders' protective committee, the Erie raised new cash and put off current debt payments by refunding old bonds and assessing preferred stockholders. Though it emerged in the black, the new Erie Railroad was burdened with even greater debt than before. Hence, within eight years it fell into receivership once again, only to repeat the trust-fund procedures of 1877.[12] A similar pattern of receivership without structural reorganization was followed on a number of roads in the 1870s and 1880s: the Philadelphia and Reading;[13] the Missouri, Kansas and

Texas; the St. Louis and San Francisco; and the Texas and St. Louis, among the most prominent examples.[14]

Beginning in the 1880s, however, the trust-fund receivership came under attack. For the same entitlement structure that fueled the drive to construct huge national systems now seemed to threaten their tenacity. Followed to the letter, the trust-fund receivership would oust their architects and grant mortgage bondholders the right to sell off regional divisions. So fearful of this prospect did incumbent managers become that they petitioned the federal courts for receivership prior to default. By doing so, they hoped to stave off creditor claims and protect their systems from dismemberment. Convinced that railroad systems had value—while their parts had none—federal justices acquiesced. Now creditors were routinely stripped of their rights in receivership, managers were appointed receivers of their own railroads, and corporations were thrown into the protective arms of the courts prior to default. Corporate jurists now began to rethink corporate doctrine. Less and less did they conceive of the corporation in market terms, the aggregate sum of its individual contracts. Instead, they began to reconceptualize the corporation as a natural entity, a body with a personality of its own, whose life plan was best devised by management. This "natural entity" or corporate liberal theory not only successfully fended off the challenges of creditors in receivership, but it also rebuffed the claims of the state in regulation. Still, the transformation of receivership law and corporate doctrine was strewn with uncertainty and conflict, its outcome not at all assured by technical necessity or the brute exercise of power. If the national railroad system emerged the victor and bondholders bore the cost, this was for historically contingent, not economically necessary, reasons.

The Wabash, St. Louis and Pacific Railway

On May 28, 1884 Jay Gould, president and controlling owner of the Wabash, St. Louis and Pacific Railway, sent his representatives into a federal district court in St. Louis with the brazen request that they be appointed receivers of the Wabash before it had defaulted on its financial obligations. In a widely acknowleged departure from precedent, Judge Treat acquiesced. Why were Treat and his peers on the federal bench convinced to depart from a market or individualistic theory of the corporation? In particular, what led Gould to pursue such an unorthodox legal strategy? And finally, how does this case illustrate the enormous uncertainty over what to do with huge insolvent railway systems and the way that courts systematically filled that void with the rudiments of a novel theory of corporate origins, entitlements, and legitimacy?

The Wabash neared collapse in 1884 because it had become the main pawn in Jay Gould's strategy to build a massive, self-sustaining interterritorial system from the eastern Great Lakes to the Far West and Southwest. But Gould was not alone: his competitors and imitators became interterritorial system builders in the eighties, and many of them found themselves in similar difficulties over the next decade. Following Gould's lead, they turned to the judiciary for help. By 1895 twelve major railroad systems (and key parts of others) petitioned the federal courts for the protective embrace of receivership. Thus, a better look at Gould's strategy will afford a window onto the nature of interterritorial competition, system building, and the role of the federal courts in the political construction of the modern railroad corporation.[15]

At the time of its receivership the Wabash system consisted of over thirty mortgages, representing nearly as many separate lines. Together, they formed a through route from Omaha, Nebraska, through St. Louis to Toledo, Ohio. Many small feeders served the trunk. From just east of Decatur, Illinois, an ancillary route fed the main line's traffic to Chicago. And from Chicago another route stretched east to Detroit. To the east the Wabash might exchange traffic with several large trunklines connecting the Midwest to the eastern seaboard. To the southwest it connected with the Missouri Pacific and to the west with the Union Pacific. Both of the western roads, like the Wabash itself, were controlled by Jay Gould.

The Wabash had grown to its 1880 proportions and complexity as a strategic pawn in Gould's grand scheme. Because of its critical midwestern location—sandwiched between the large eastern trunklines and Gould's western roads—it became a tool in a competitive fight for through traffic. By expanding the road east and west and forcing Wabash rates down, Gould hoped to divert long-haul traffic to his roads in the Far West, where there was little competition. In this way, he planned to skim regional profits from the West.[16]

Gould faced obstacles at both ends of the road, however. To the east was the Eastern Trunkline Pool. To the west was the Iowa Pool, which competed with the Wabash for connecting traffic in Iowa and Nebraska. In the East he faced a conflict. The Wabash competed with the western reaches of the eastern trunklines into Chicago, so Gould had to make the Wabash route west from Toledo to St. Louis more attractive. He needed trunkline cooperation, too, though, to secure access to the eastern seaboard. By threatening to cut rates on the Wabash's eastern divisions and by offering attractive traffic agreements with each of the trunklines individually, Gould hoped to play one road against another. To his dismay, the trunkline association held firm. Gould retaliated by expanding the carrier north to Chicago and east to Detroit, hoping to bypass trunkline traffic altogether. In a similar strategy to the West, Gould planned to divert traffic from the Iowa Pool to his own roads in the Far West by acquiring the Kansas City Railroad and then building an extension to Omaha.[17]

At both ends Gould eschewed cooperation for autarky. The success of this plan, however, rested on the Wabash's ability to divert sufficient traffic across Gould's western roads: the Missouri Pacific, the Texas Pacific, and (until he lost control of it in 1883) the Union Pacific. Once assembled, the midwestern carrier had to set rates sufficiently low to attract traffic in competitive territory. Without it, revenues would be lost in the West, and the whole system might collapse. The pawn in a systemic strategy, then, the Wabash mounted a rate war in the Midwest, but the more traffic it added by way of rate cuts, the worse its net profits became. In the short run, then, system building failed. Gould had misestimated demand and the tenacity of his competitors. Still, investors followed him onto the battlefield of interterritorial competition. In a deflationary economy, Wabash mortgage bonds remained attractive. Nevertheless, the more the carrier took on new debt, the more it became dependent upon increasing through traffic and the more vulnerable it became to rate competition and fluctuating demand. Unable to meet mortgage payments, Gould took on more and more short-term debt. This only worsened the situation; until late in 1883, just weeks before a large interest payment came due, he petitioned the court for help.

Historian Albro Martin has written that Gould had little choice in this matter.[18] Victim of the rate wars of the eighties, the Wabash had sought to protect its valuable property by proposing receivership. This interpretation begs the question, since Gould sparked the rate conflagration among pool members. By system building, he threw the cartels at both ends of the Wabash into disarray. Consequently, his request to place the Wabash in receivership prior to default must have appeared all the more audacious to Judge Treat. Explaining his capitulation to Gould before Superior District Court Judge David Brewer, Treat wrote, "The simple proposition submitted to this court was this: Here is a vast property, in a bankrupt condition,—whether through mismanagement or otherwise, was immaterial to this court . . . It was [my] duty . . . , under the circumstances presented, to take possession of this property, and conserve the interests of all concerned."[19] In this way, Treat not only justified preempting the rights of creditors, thus declaring bankrupt a corporation not yet in default, but he also justified the appointment of Gould's petitioners, Solon Humphries and Thomas Tutt, as coreceivers. Instead of bearing fiduciary responsibility, management was entrusted with authority to adjust its own obligations to shareholders.

With these powers in hand, Gould hoped to leverage concessions from Wabash security holders. The receivers would assess stock and bondholders for cash, exchange fixed interest bonds for securities contingent upon future profit, and issue new certificates on better terms than the old. The goal was to raise sufficient funds from existing shareholders to keep the system intact.

Bondholders, however, rejected the plan. Still worse, mortgage holders for the eastern division formed a protective committee and proceeded to challenge the St. Louis receivership. Illinois Federal District Court Judge Walter Gresham (whom the Populists would unsuccessfully attempt to recruit for their presidential candidate in 1892) listened sympathetically as petitioners criticized Gould. The creditors had not been consulted prior to the receivership, management had no right to legal standing, and most outrageous of all, Wabash representatives should have been removed, not appointed receivers. Like "the highwayman's clutch on our throat, the robber's demand 'your money or your life!'" We have been held hostage, they complained.[20] Judge Gresham concurred and appointed a separate receiver to the road's eastern division. Despite Treat's orders, Gould's worst fears were realized: his system was split in two.

But fighting did not remain confined to procedure. A substantive quarrel now split east and west. Gould and Treat in the West argued that the system was the only thing of value. If individual mortgages were allowed to press their claims, all property would become worthless. By contrast, eastern bondholders, now led by senior creditors from the Chicago division, held that unprofitable expansion and unfair ratemaking was at fault. The eastern divisions, they discovered, had earned profits sufficient to meet mortgage payments. Management had overissued junior securities to finance unprofitable expansion and then attempted to cross-subsidize weaker parts of the road with revenues from the sound divisions in the East. Equally wrong, argued the eastern bondholders in Gresham's court, it seems that the Wabash had been leased directly to the Iron Mountain Company, a subsidiary of Gould's Missouri Pacific. Wabash revenues had thus been funneled to the parent company in the West. There was ample revenue to meet Wabash obligations, had it not been siphoned off to subsidize other ventures.[21]

Though a minority committee held firm to these complaints, most eastern creditors capitulated. The St. Louis receivership, it seems, had so succeeded in preempting their authority that Wabash securities had become temporarily worthless. Under these conditions the western receiver's threat became compelling: "If they [the bondholders] did not accept" a permanent reduction in claims, "and attempted to foreclose their mortgages, the litigation would be long and expensive; . . . many intricate questions would arise as to the apportionment of the receiver's debts, the ownership of the rolling stock and terminal facilities; and . . . the payment of coupons would be deferred indefinitely."[22] Creditors relucantly agreed. "If 5 per cent interest is all the company can safely undertake to pay," remarked the dissenting bondholder's committee in 1886, "its bonds bearing such a rate would command a higher price in the market than bonds bearing a higher rate of interest."[23] On the defensive as a result of Gould's preemptive use of receivership, the bondholders agreed to trade their fixed property rights and guaranteed income for liquidity and trading value in the open market.

Even though Gould's autarkic strategy had failed in the short run, in the hands of a federal judiciary committed to protecting national systems, it succeeded. Not only had he preempted mortgage bondholder entitlements, he also sacrificed the Wabash to his western roads, the Missouri Pacific and the Texas Pacific. (By now he had lost control of the Union Pacific.) By depressing midwestern rates below fixed costs, Gould attained sufficient funds to skim monopoly rents in the West. Temporarily successful, this strategy could be sustained and institutionalized only if the federal courts were convinced that system integrity, cross-subsidy, and managerial authority necessitated protection from property owners.

The Wabash emerged from receivership intact in 1889 with Gould firmly in control. He had succeeded in accomplishing exactly what his Erie counterparts had failed to do a decade before, namely, to systematically scale back fixed obligations to anticipated minimum earning capacity. Under the trust-fund receivership bondholders had been too powerful. Unlike the Erie and roads like it, then, economic instability would no longer threaten management authority or system tenacity on the Wabash, at least for the foreseeable future. It was in this sense that Gould had used the protective arms of the courts to reconstitute fixed costs (and the rights attached to them) in order to meet the contingencies of interterritorial system building—not, as the prevailing interpretation has it, the other way around. Railroad capital costs, in other words, were inescapably distributive, and as such they were tied to a normative structure of corporate rights and obligations. By finding in favor of system integrity and management authority, the court had reasoned substantively: the interests of all claimants to revenues were best served by reconstituting the corporation's former contractual commitments. And when the precedent in Wabash was tested under appeal, the priority of the system over its trust-fund obligations was ratified.[24]

Challenge to Legal Theory

Wabash and cases like it alarmed trust-fund theorists of the corporation. A decade after the Wabash emerged from receivership, counsel for dissenting bondholders, D. H. Chamberlain, asked *Harvard Law Review* readers, "What proper suitor for redress or protection of the property interests of creditors, or of the state, was before the court when these [Wabash] receivers were appointed? Only the debtor, the defaulting, delinquent corporation." Just imagine this case generalized to other areas of the law, he went on. What "if a court . . . of its own motion [were] to assume to represent and act for the parties before it? . . . Is not the vista opened by such claims unbounded, as well as portentous? Who could wish it entered upon?"[25] Or just imagine a noncorporate debtor with Jay Gould's audacity, conjectured the editor of the *American Law Review*:

> Suppose . . . a farmer were to go into a court of justice with a bill in equity against his creditors, in which he should say to the court: "I have a farm here of my own, and I am the lessee of several contiguous farms. I have been unable to operate these farms at a profit. My own farm has certain mortgages upon it, and I have placed a consolidated mortgage upon my own farm and upon my leasehold interests in other farms. In attempting to carry on these farms I have issued a good many promissory notes and have incurred many floating debts, which I am unable to pay. These promissory notes have been indorsed by friends and agents of mine, who are interested with me in carrying on these farms, and some of them are about to mature. I want the court to appoint two of my agents to take possession of these farms and operate them for me until such time as an adjustment can be made between me and my creditors." Suppose that the court entertains this bill and appoints the farm bailiff of the plaintiff and another one of his creditors at arm's length. *Did any one, other than a railroad fixer and manipulator, ever have the hardihood to face a court of justice with such a bill in equity as this?* Has it come to be a principle of equity jurisprudence that a failing debtor can sue his creditors, and have his property impounded by a court of equity and managed indefinitely by such a court for his own benefit?[26]

"The courts," agreed Henry Wollman in 1894, now "appoint receivers for corporations on the flimsiest of grounds . . . but prevent the creditors doing anything, except to sit by and see the managers operate them [railroads] as they deem proper." It seemed the most elementary principle of jurisprudence, agreed these critics, that "the court must await the coming of the proper suitor before exercising its powers." "Once for all," charged Chamberlain, "let it be said, courts have no function except to sit still until they are moved by parties having legal rights to assert before them."[27]

Still worse were the results. The friendly receivership "opens the door to gross frauds upon creditors," cautioned Charles Beach in his 1887 treatise on receivers, potentially "enabling unscrupulous manipulators to use the power of the United States courts to stay the hands of creditors . . . and carry on the business of the road, while schemers force favorable compromises."[28] By the midnineties, Wollman complained,

> the larger number of receiverships [were] simply placing the strong arm of the court between the officers and the stockholders and the creditors. If the officers knew in advance that when their companies failed they would lose control, they would be much more conservative. When they know they will have to seek new positions, they will be less apt to study how to "freeze out" by a receivership the rank and file of stockholders and creditors. We would then have less "reorganization" schemes, which practically take the small holders by the throat and force them to accept the terms offered.[29]

Corporate property, concluded Wollman, affirming the private artificial-entity theory, "is a trust-fund, and should be administered for all creditors alike," not for inside shareholders, a corporate abstraction, or incumbent managers. "New fashioned receiverships," like other abuses of corporate power, he warned his readers in the midst of the Populist upsurge of the nineties, treated property unjustly, and encouraged "radically socialistic tendencies" among the public, "even the desire [for] the abolition of corporate franchises" altogether. As "absurd" as this was, it was understandable, since it appeared that "the judiciary of this country [was] . . . under the hypnotic charm of the officers of corporations." Only when corporation law and receivership practice were radically overhauled, he concluded, would such demagoguery subside.[30]

Judge Gresham cautioned the public and the bench against the dangers of "friendly receivership." When an Indiana district court appointed management for the Indianapolis, Decatur and Springfield Railroad receivers, Gresham protested: The company had simply used judicial power to shirk its obligations, that is, "to get out of paying [its] indebtedness for labor and supplies." Such candor prompted public praise. "At a time when every Department of the Government seems to be inspired by sordid considerations, or intimidated by the power of money," wrote the Evansville Courier, "it is reassuring to know that there are still a few men in public station, who, like Judge

Gresham, are uninfluenced either by the blandishments or threats of the Plutocrats." Even so, he won few friends in the Republican party or the Harrison administration. As Gresham's biographer has written, he saw it as an "ill-disguised rebuke" when the president appointed his arch-nemesis in Wabash, Judge David J. Brewer, to the Supreme Court. Indeed, Harrison's "[a]ttorney [g]eneral W. H. H. Miller, seemed to have Gresham in mind when he defended the new justice as one who had the 'courage' to decide in favor of 'wealth and power and corporation' when 'the law and justice of the case demand it,' . . . a 'courage of a kind . . . demagogues lack.' "[31]

Still, such protest went for naught. Brewer, not Gresham, was appointed to the Supreme Court. Moreover, because interterritorial railroad systems crossed state lines, virtually all receiverships landed in federal courts. Here judges had been appointed by the same national administrations that made huge land grants (the Union Pacific's was the size of New England), tight money, and national banking—that is, *continental development*—the pillars of economic policy. In this political atmosphere, and under the influence of an emerging elite and specialized corporate bar, Wabash became gospel. In 1898, when Congress re-enacted a federal bankruptcy statute (for the first time in over two decades), it did so on Wabash principles. A 1910 amendment to that law explicitly extended voluntary bankruptcy from equity law to statute. In so doing, it broadened the availability of voluntary receivership from railroads, utilities, and banks to a full range of industrial corporations.[32]

The same year, speaking for the Supreme Court, Justice Peckham looked back on the decade of friendly receiverships following Wabash.

> If judgement were obtained in many of these cases, or in any other of the cases where creditors were pressing their demands, it would result in disastrous consequences to the public, by a possible sale and dismemberment of the system under which the railroads then operated, and might result in sales of portions of the roads to different individuals or corporations . . . a sale of the roads would probably be for a sum greatly beneath their value . . . There are cases where in order to preserve the property for all interests, it is a necessity to resort to such a remedy. A refusal to appoint a receiver would have led in this instance [the Metropolitan Railway Company] almost inevitably to a very large and useless sacrifice in value of a great property, operated as one system . . . [and] to endless confusion among the various creditors in their efforts to enforce their claims.[33]

Whether the beneficiaries of corporate largesse were the shipping public, various classes of shareholders, labor, or management, the federal courts now granted system integrity first priority in a hierarchy of legal entitlements. Everyone would have to wait her turn in claiming revenues, especially when the corporate entity was in visible danger. This was a remarkable change in corporate jurisprudence. If the system had value, its parts none, then first-order entitlements rested neither with the state nor shareholders. The federal courts had initiated a novel theory of the corporation in receivership, namely, the idea that it was a natural entity, an economic body with a status prior to the individual or politics. Though corporate jurists would not develop this view fully for another decade, its seeds were set in the 1880s. Indeed, it is difficult to imagine the generalization of Wabash during the 1890s without the federal bench accepting the rudiments of a corporate liberal theory of the modern corporation.[34]

Although the courts responded to management's demands in Wabash and after, this was not merely the sort of instrumental or utilitarian logic that realist legal historians have long attributed to Gilded Age corporate jurisprudence. Best articulated by Willard Hurst, this view claims that over time the postbellum judiciary came to favor utilitarian over egalitarian ends. Judges tended to resolve intracorporate disputes, like those in receivership, on the criteria of productivity or effective capital mobilization, rather than on equity considerations.[35] Instrumental goals, however, were rife with uncertainty in the 1880s. Receivership courts were hard put to decide which utilitarian end —investor confidence or system integrity—to favor. After all, they were perceived in conflict, especially from the vantage point of the liberal, trust-fund conception of the corporation.

Even more uncertain, would intracorporate or intermortgage cross-subsidies restrain or advance productivity? If one believed high-volume through traffic was the only way to achieve transportation economies, then rate setting to maximize such traffic would attain priority, regardless of its equity effects. This was not, however, the only available criterion for transportation efficiency. Chapter 5, a study of the Chicago Great Western Railway, will show that an even smaller road could remain autonomous and serve primarily regional rather than interterritorial trade efficiently. In principle, then, eastern division creditors might have sold their property at foreclosure to an independent management or a regional carrier profitably and successfully. This possibility made Gould and those following him especially frightened of the trust-fund receivership. Thus, despite the claims of Gould, Brewer, and Treat, the practical outcome of the dispute over receivership was uncertain. For this reason system builders were compelled to make their best case, under admittedly favorable judicial circumstances.[36]

Moreover, even though the "friendly receivership" was justified on the grounds of system integrity, subsidiary divestment by an incumbent regime in receivership was not unknown. The Philadelphia and Reading, for example, would divest itself of two enormous holdings—the Lehigh Valley and the Boston and Maine—in its "friendly receivership" a decade after Wabash.[37] It is conceivable, then, that on both equity and efficiency grounds, Wabash bondholders might have made a different choice, had they retained the opportunities afforded by earlier receivership practice. Had the court failed to grant Gould preemptive powers, bondholders could have ousted the incumbents and brought the corporation to foreclosure, or agreed to put it back in the black under new management, whose only concern was the Wabash itself.

Wabash and the cases following it were not merely examples of interest group pressures upon the courts either.[38] Though managers had clearly gained the upper hand, shareholders were not bereft of choice. Constrained, to be sure, by management's preemptive action, bondholders nevertheless reconceived the carrier's future and their place in it. That is, like the courts, they became convinced of the need for system integrity, managerial authority, reduced financial claims, and a relatively marginal legal status accorded to property. Nor is this to say that Gould intended to transform corporate jurisprudence. (After all, ideally, he alone would have access to the friendly receivership.) In order to sustain his national system, he was compelled to convince, not merely coerce, courts and shareholders of its necessity.

It was in this sense, then, that Wabash and the cases following it were decided on substantive and ideological grounds. There were no easy solutions to receivership conflicts on utilitarian or instrumental criteria alone. It should not be surprising, then, that in Wabash two federal judges (both reasoning instrumentally?) came to opposite conclusions. Nevertheless, Brewer's decision was prophetic: in the decade following, courts of equity came to see the unitary corporate hierarchy in everyone's interest—management, investors, and the shipping public. This judgment, as legal historian Robert Gordon has written of the more general changes in corporate jurisprudence during the Age of Enterprise, is best understood as an ideological one. At once, it redefined mortgage bondholder entitlements and management responsibility within a frame that assimilated normative discourse to the idea that large-scale interterritorial systems were inevitable, efficient, and needed protection. In receivership, as in other areas of the law, the courts slowly but surely abandoned a market or contractual for a corporate liberal theory of the corporation. On the latter, the modern corporation was conceived as a natural entity, with an autonomous personality composed of more than the sum of its parts. Corporate managers, more than its shareholders, were best able to devise the firm's life plan.[39]

System Building and Collapse

If Wabash convinced federal judges and bondholders that large-scale interregional railroad systems were inevitable and needed protection, Gould also convinced other managers of the need for autarkic system building. His competitors and imitators pushed regional systems well beyond formerly accepted "natural territory," to build huge interregional systems in the 1880s. Gould goaded members of the Iowa and Eastern trunkline pools to defect from their associations and build self-sustaining systems. Long the most conservative of regional carriers in the Midwest, the Chicago, Burlington and Quincy pushed headlong in the Far West in response to Gould's challenge.[40] Among eastern trunklines, the Philadelphia and Reading, the Baltimore and Ohio, and the Rock Island also pressed beyond their natural territory, between the seaboard and the Great Lakes, into the Northwest and up and down the East Coast.[41] Moreover, prodded by Gould's western roads, the Atchison, Topeka and Santa Fe pushed eastward into the Midwest and west to San Francisco from its regional base in the Southwest.[42] Similarly, the Union Pacific and Northern Pacific pursued interregional strategies in the 1880s.[43] Finally, in the South, three unwieldy systems—the Richmond and Danville, the Richmond Terminal, and the East Tennessee, Virginia and Georgia Railroad—locked horns in a protracted struggle over southern territory. As a result, each attempted to preempt the other through interterritorial expansion.[44]

Chandler is absolutely correct to argue that interregional system building was the prevailing strategy of the 1880s. Yet it was no more than that, namely, a *particular strategy*, shaped not so much by the necessities of railroad technology (high fixed cost) and market size as by the background conditions of capital-market institutions, credit entitlements, and national-debt policy. Even though management and the federal courts cast system building in universal terms, it was a historically contingent strategy. It not only depended upon the pattern of property rights particular to postbellum capital markets and corporation law; there were other ways to structure capital markets, to conceptualize the corporation, and to realize transportation economies.

Moreover, without judicial protection, interterritorial system building failed. In the two decades following the Wabash, over one-third of all national systems collapsed as quickly as they had been constructed. In the 1890s alone, one-third of all railroad mileage in the United States was in receivership.[45] Indeed, system after system toppled under the weight of debt and declining demand. The Baltimore and Ohio; the Erie; the Philadelphia and Reading; the Southern; the Atchison, Topeka and Santa Fe; the Union Pacific; the Northern Pacific; the Norfolk and Western; the Rock Island and key parts of the Great Northern; the Chicago, Burlington and Quincy; and the Missouri Pacific were all subject to receivership and reorganization during the depression of the nineties. It was during this decade, then, that the financial, organizational, and legal principles first seen in the 1884 Wabash reorganization became generalized.

With the coercive machinery of the federal courts available to inside managers and their allies in investment banking, reorganization proceeded apace. Without the friendly receivership, reorganizers had learned that bondholders would throw their full weight in financial negotiation. Not only had receiverships before Wabash failed to bring debt down to levels that no longer threatened incumbent managers and system integrity, those systems which had attempted to reorganize without receivership in the late 1880s inevitably failed. For example, in-house reorganizations were unsuccessful on the Baltimore and Ohio in 1887, the Atchison, Topeka and Santa Fe in 1889, and the Northern Pacific in the same year. In each instance, without the legitimacy of the courts, bondholders blocked plans to permanently reduce fixed charges.[46] As a result, inside managers facing imminent default followed Gould's lead and petitioned federal district courts for "friendly receivership." By the 1890s most judges followed Brewer, not Gresham, and obliged.

Morganization: The Wabash Generalized

No one made more extensive use of the new-fashioned receivership in the decade following Wabash than the investment banking firm Drexel, Morgan and Company. Its reorganization of the Southern Railroad; the Atchison, Topeka and the Santa Fe; and the Reading railroads became paradigmatic cases for an industry about to undergo wholesale restructuring. During the 1890s Morgan virtually institutionalized the principles of reorganization pioneered on the Wabash.

Though inside managers routinely secured friendly receivership in the 1890s, unlike Gould they typically sought outside help from investment bankers for several reasons. In the first place, even though receivership bore heavily upon creditors, reorganized railroads returned to capital markets for new finance; therefore banker prestige and underwriting services often determined their success. Second, although the courts had rearranged rights and priorities within the corporation, as judges perfected the "friendly receivership," they called for a complicated show of consent for reorganization plans from outside shareholders. Finally, beginning in the 1890s, investment bankers made reorganization services a central part of their own market strategy, and as they did so, a specialized cadre of attorneys and financiers oversaw an ever more complex set of internal corporate negotiations.[47]

Of course, investment banking services to the railroads were not new in this decade. The fate of railroads had been closely tied to private banking since the war.[48] Merchant bankers to the railroads, many investment houses underwrote, negotiated, and marketed railroad securities in domestic and international markets during the 1870s and 1880s. In the 1890s, however, they became more and more involved in reorganizing corporate structure and overseeing financial management. In so doing, many prominent bankers altered their market strategy and the nature of their business alliances.

Morgan best illustrates this transformation. Throughout the late nineteenth century, three Morgan firms marketed railroad securities: J. S. Morgan and Company in London and Drexel, Morgan and Company in Philadelphia and New York. As merchant bankers, they negotiated security sales in New York and London for the Louisville and Nashville, the Baltimore and Ohio, the New York Central, the Union Pacific, and a number of other prominent roads in the 1870s and 1880s. J. S. Morgan placed more American railroad securities in the London market than any other investment banker in this period. Dominant in the international triumvirate, the London firm carefully followed the progress of their railroad clients and, as financial intermediary, represented the interests of British bondholders to American managers. In the 1870s, for instance, when a Morgan account, the Cairo and Vincennes Railroad, fell on hard times, the bankers successfully represented the bondholders' interests in the ensuing receivership and reorganization. And when, in 1870, J. S. Morgan learned that the Erie was placing a new bond issue that would depress the market value of an 1865 issue the bankers had negotiated, he threatened to withdraw from Erie accounts. Notoriously surly, the younger Morgan chided one railroad president during this period, "Your roads! Your roads belong to my clients!"[49]

A decade later, however, the Morgans shifted market strategy and, in effect, their national allegiance. As business historian Vincent Carosso writes, "In the 1870s much of Drexel, Morgan's railroad business was as a participant in London-led accounts, in the 1880s their roles were reversed."[50] Likely hastened by the elder Morgan's death in 1890 (on holiday in southern France, his carriage was overturned when the horse was frightened by a passing locomotive.), J. P. Morgan began to steer the company's focus from London to New York. But, it was only once he began to make use of the friendly receivership in the 1890s, that Morgan shifted the bank's main business from securities sales and representing British bondholders to reorganizer (and temporary manager) of America's largest railroad systems.[51]

The younger Morgan's interest in reorganizing and bringing stability to American railroads began the decade before. In 1889, he attempted to use his leverage to enforce agreements between the eastern trunklines to limit competitive building and ratemaking. But Morgan the peacemaker still played both sides of the fence—while using his influence to dampen competition, he was also partaking in Gould's syndicate to finance competitive expansion on the Union Pacific. Indeed, just as the banker chastised management for overbuilding and rate wars, managers chastised him for "sponsoring overcapitalized lines that could not weather recessions because of their heavy debt load." In the 1890s, however, Morgan fused efforts to stabilize the industry with corporate reorganization into a novel market strategy.[52]

His first major project of the decade was the Southern Railway. This railroad went into receivership under three separate corporate identities: the East Tennessee, Virginia and Georgia; the Richmond Terminal and Warehouse Company; and the Richmond and Danville Railway. Tenuously linked through interlocking directors, intercorporate shareholding, and personal ownership by directors and officers, this vast system was riddled with debt. Not only had interterritorial competition and protracted fighting over corporate control inflated debt on each of these roads and their subsidiaries, but interlocked as they were, they became subject to managerial opportunism. Utilizing their joint positions on several boards for personal gain, corporate officers had saddled the costs onto subsidiaries and minority shareholders. By the late 1880s, then, all three roads faced imminent default and petitioned the court for receivership. Having successfully fended off creditor claims, they still faced the more intractable problem of resuscitating insolvent corporations. Together, then, management for the Richmond Terminal, the Richmond and Danville, and the East Tennessee asked Morgan to manage a joint reorganization.[53]

In this, the first of Morgan's reorganizations, he developed the principles that had been laid down by Gould in the Wabash. He agreed to serve the southern carriers only if a majority of their shareholders placed their voting rights in trust with the House of Morgan for the duration of the receivership and for some time after. Like Gould, Morgan used the power of the court to wring substantial concessions from bondholders: as a whole, debt was slashed by over one-third. All three corporations were consolidated under a single holding company: the Southern Railway Company. Finally, Morgan estimated the minimum future earning capacity of the railroad and reduced annual fixed charges (interest and principal on debt) to the lowest level of projected annual revenues. This feature ensured that downturn in the business cycle would threaten neither solvency, nor system tenacity.[54]

Morgan applied the same principles in the reorganization of three more national systems—the Erie, the Reading, and the Northern Pacific—as well as the subsidiaries of many others. His specialized cadre of financiers and attorneys—Francis Lynde Stetson, Charles Coster, and Charles Tracy—reshaped American railroads at the turn of the century. Moreover, other prominent investment houses of the era—Kuhn and Loeb; Morton, Bliss; Kidder Peabody; August Belmont; Winslow, Lanier; and the Seligman Brothers—followed Morgan's lead into railroad reorganization. When nearly one-third of the industry emerged from receivership, the bankers found themselves deeply entrenched in railroad financial management.[55]

Externalizing Costs: Hierarchy and Scale Institutionalized

By the turn of the century, twelve of the nation's twenty-eight largest systems had come out of friendly receivership and Morgan-style reorganization: the Baltimore and Ohio; the St. Louis and San Francisco; the Southern; Atchison, Topeka and Santa Fe; the New York Central; Union Pacific; Northern Pacific; Denver and Rio Grande; Missouri, Kansas and Texas; the Wabash; Erie; Norfolk and Western; and the Chesapeake and Ohio. Together, they accounted for approximately 34 percent of all railroad mileage in the United States. Following Gould's and Morgan's lead, the financial result was to slash fixed charges (debt) on these systems by an average of 27 percent. In sixty-eight leading companies reorganized between Wabash and 1897, fixed charges were reduced on average by 34 percent (see Table 1). Fixed costs, as it turned out, were not so fixed on the railroads.

The cost structure of railroad technology is an unreliable parameter by which to explain two defining characteristics of the modern railroad corporation: its huge size and the separation of ownership from managerial control. To the contrary, fixed costs were adjusted to meet the contingencies of large size. Moreover, the separation of ownership from managerial control, at least at moments of crisis, was not a necessary consequence of railroad size. Before the federal judiciary rearranged the rights of property in receivership, security holders were hardly as "passive" as the conventional wisdom suggests. In fact, the scope of railroad reorganization went well beyond the temporary reduction of fixed costs to systematic effort to externalize the cost of economic uncertainty and instability onto outside shareholders.[56] By exchanging obligations fixed by law for those payable at the discretion of

Table 1. Fixed Charges: Sixty-seven Leading Company Receiverships, 1885–1897 (in thousands)

Railroad	Fixed Charges before Receivership	Fixed Charges after Receivership	Percentage Change
Allegheny Valley	1,783	1,866	+6
Atchison, Topeka, & Santa Fe	9,536	4,529	−53
Atlantic & Danville	297	75	−75
Baltimore & Ohio	153	132	−14
Buffalo, N.Y. & Philadelphia	1,505	500	−67
Central Branch, U Pac.	236	100	−58
Central RR & Banking Ga.	1,552	1,454	−6
Central Wash.	129	62	−52
Charleston, Cincinnati & Chicago	367	625	+70
Chattanooga, Rome & Columbia	112	27	−76
Chesapeake & Ohio	673	530	−21
Chicago & Atlantic	390	400	+3
Chicago, Peoria & St. Louis	192	211	+10
Choctaw Coal & Ry	630	274	−57
Cincinnati, Jackson & Mackinaw RR	175	192	+10
Colo. Midland	831	372	−55
Denver & Rio Grande	1,952	1,550	−21
Des Moines N & W	111	117	+5
Des Moines, Osceola & S	62	0	−100
Detroit, Bay City & Alpena	150	116	−23
Detroit, Lansing & N	315	195	−38
Duluth & Winnipeg	115	60	−48
E Tenn., Va. & Ga. RR	1,435	1,072	−25
Evansville & Richmond	70	10	−86
Findlay, Ft. Wayne & W	72	60	−20
Ga. Midland & Gulf	66	50	−24
Ga. S & Fla.	205	200	−3
Grand Rapids & Ind. RR	690	357	−48
Green Bay, Winnipeg & St. Paul	125	0	−100
Ind., Decatur & Springfield	320	204	−36
Kanawha & Ohio	336	59	−82
Kansas City & S	133	0	−100
Kansas City, Wyandotte & NW	182	175	−4
Louisville, N Albany & Chicago	1,020	955	−6
Louisville, St. Louis & Tex.	249	105	−58
Louisville S	250	150	−40
Memphis & Little Rock	218	163	−25
Minneapolis & St. Louis	591	581	−40
Mo., Kan. & Tex.	2,819	1,677	−41
Mobile & Birmingham	225	78	−65
N.Y., Chicago & St. Louis	1,243	800	−36

(continued)

Table 1—*continued*

Railroad	Fixed Charges before Receivership	Fixed Charges after Receivership	Percentage Change
N.Y., L Erie & W	9,400	7,550	−20
Norfolk & W	3,214	2,230	−31
N Pac.	9,494	6,053	−36
Ogdensburg & L Champlain	253	220	−13
Orange Belt	42	50	+19
Oreg. Ry & Navigation	1,185	901	−24
Oreg. Short Line & Utah N	2,789	1,853	−34
Pecos Valley	117	140	+19
Philadelphia & Reading	10,035	9,317	−7
Pittsburgh & W RR	338	379	+12
Pittsburgh, Akron & W	182	125	−31
Quincy, Omaha & Kansas City	88	15	−83
St. Joseph & Grand Island	420	80	−81
St. Louis & San Francisco	2,530	1,994	−21
San Antonio & Arkansas Pass	459	840	+83
Sav., Americus & Montgomery	219	255	+16
Seattle, L Geo. & E	340	223	−34
S Jersey	43	60	+40
S Central	190	80	−58
Toledo, Ann Arbor & N Mich.	386	280	−28
U Pac.	6,694	4,000	−40
Wabash	80,762	78,000	−4
Wash. & Columbia River	209	100	−52
W N.Y. & Pa.	1,195	715	−40
Winona & SW	127	58	−54
Wisc., Minn. & Pac.	194	0	−100
		Average Change in Fixed Charges =	−34

Sources: Poor's Railroad Manual, 1900, lxxxiii (Baltimore & Ohio), lxxxiv (Wabash), and cvi (all other roads).
Note: Fixed charges = total debt.

management, reorganizers ensured that for the foreseeable future corporate integrity would no longer be threatened by the business cycle. The corollary to this goal was to augment management authority over corporate finance.

The courts and bondholders were not without influence over such plans. For one thing, as the corporate bar and the federal judiciary perfected receivership practice after Wabash, judges demanded a formal show of consent from organized shareholders.[57] Though rarely able to block a reorganization plan, bondholders routinely exploited their minimal powers to wring compensation from the corporation. The result of such "consent receiverships" (as they came to be known) was to exchange old fixed obligations for new contingent securities.[58] As the *Wall Street Journal*'s railroad editor told the national Industrial Commission in 1901, "What Morgan did in all his reorganization [sic] was to estimate the minimum earning capacity and take care to get fixed charges down to that, but when he came to charges that were not fixed, or to securities dependent on future prospects, people could pretty much help themselves."[59] If railroad capital costs remained high after the turn of the century, at least they would no longer threaten the status of the corporation, the tenacity of the national system, or the discretion of management.

Morgan's reorganizations were typical in this regard. In nearly every major reorganization of the 1890s capital stock was increased to compensate for reduced fixed charges and cash assessments made on bondholders. A sample of fifteen major reorganizations between 1886 and 1898 shows that eleven resulted in higher equity. Indeed, contingent securities were increased on average by 21 percent (see Table 2). In addition, nine of fifteen reorganizations resulted in higher total capitalization (debt plus equity) than they began with. The mature consent receivership, then, resulted in scaling down fixed costs to meet the projected trough in railroad revenues and inflated promises to unsure future revenues.[60]

Table 2. Changes in Capitalization Due to Reorganization (per mile)

Railroad	Receiver Apptd.	Foreclosure	% Change in Debt	% Change in Equity	% Change in Total Cap.
Atchison, Topeka & Santa Fe	1893	1895	−28.85	+109.31	+13.84
Ga. Central	1893	1895	−27.17	−65.16	−26.22
E Tenn.	1885	1886	−23.84	+29.00	+9.59
Minn. & St. Louis	1888	1894	+7.50	+27.55	+17.80
Erie	1893	1895	−9.54	+15.39	+3.59
Norfolk & W	1895	1896	−64.92	−8.45	−35.61
N Pac.	1893	1896	−1.84	+56.89	+20.64
Oreg. Ry. & Navigation	1893	1896	−29.73	+28.75	−2.4
Oreg. Shortline	1893	1897	+17.87	+4.96	+13.42
Southern	1892	1894	−31.37	+3.63	−10.30
St. Louis & San Francisco	1893	1896	−7.15	−5.16	−10.36
St. Louis & SW	1889	1890	−14.65	+58.13	+15.40
U Pac.	1893	1898	+10.15	+122.83	+56.85
Colo. & S	1893	1898	−35.18	+15.22	−.44
Central Ga.	1892	1895	+40.71	−66.35	+6.86
	Average =		−13.24	+20.7	+4.84

Source: Poor's Railroad Manual, 1900, lxxi–cvi.

Among those promises, reorganizers invented new classes of securities unthinkable in an earlier era, such as nonvoting stock and the income bond. The former, typical of Morgan reorganizations, ensured that newly ensconced managers would remain in power, even if they failed to pay stock dividends for a period of time. The latter—the income bond—was a contradiction in terms on the old trust-fund theory of the corporation. Like mortgage bonds, these instruments had a fixed duration after which they were to be paid off and retired. Unlike mortgage bonds, which promised property ownership in the event of default, income bonds obligated the corporation to no fixed interest schedule. Like stock dividends, interest would be paid only at the pleasure of management.

One final innovation of receivership and reorganization ensured the railroad corporation against insolvency and divestiture: corporate surplus. This was a safety fund drawn from the cash assessments levied on shareholders during reorganization. In theory, corporate surplus was to be an ongoing account which could be expanded and contracted with the business cycle. As such, it would provide yet another buffer against economic instability. Morgan, especially, made the establishment of a surplus account a necessary condition for his participation in a reorganization.[61]

It had become clear to managers and investment bankers by the 1890s that corporate financial structure was the best instrument available to ensure the stability of large-scale interregional railroad systems. They only needed to look at the systems that weathered the depression of 1893 successfully in order to drive home this lesson. The Wabash, for example, avoided receivership by suspending payment on its new classes of preferred stock and tapping its surplus account for six years in the midst of depression (see Table 3). Similarly, a 1906 study comparing carriers that survived the depression of the 1890s with those that failed found the former had a much more extensive financial margin, which could be cut off before interest on fixed obligations was endangered. Moreover, this margin was not the consequence of low operating costs generated by hierarchy and economies of scale; rather, it was the result of low fixed charges. In fact, operating expenses were, on average, higher for the railroads that survived the depression of the nineties than for those that failed (see Table 4).

Four factors, then, fell into play in the railroad reorganizations of the 1890s. First, the courts revolutionized receivership practice and corporate doctrine by severing their mortgage or trust relationship between investors and the railroad corporation. By doing so, they made judicial powers available to managers intent upon buttressing financially unsound railroad systems. Second, mortgage bondholders (especially those overseas) paid an

Table 3. Wabash Accounts during the 1890s Depression (in thousands of dollars)

Year	Dividends on Preferred Stock	Net Surplus
1890	210	238
1891	210	36
1892	210	91
1893	210	38
1894	000 (strike)	−671
1895	000 (strike)	−543
1896	35	32
1897	000	28
1898	000	401
1899	000	148
1900	210	210
1901	210	93

Source: Wabash Railroad Company, Annual Reports, 1891–1902.

enormous price to maintain system integrity, as railroad fixed costs were systematically matched to historically low levels of demand. By 1901 the financial columnist Edward Sherwood Meade concluded that despite their name, "general mortgage bonds were claims upon profits, and not, in the real sense of the term, claims to fixed rates of return. In flush times, their interest could be paid. In periods of depression, the company must default on its . . . mortgages, and, fearing foreclosure, go into the hands of a receiver until the real status of its various securities could be determined." The friendly receivership, another contemporary observer concluded, had made "obsolete" the "distinction between owner and creditor."[62]

Third, the rash of receiverships in the 1890s saw international investment bankers, like Morgan, switch market strategy from merchant banking to active financial management, allies from bondholders to inside managers, and national loyalties from Britain to the United States. In fact, it was during the railroad receiverships of the nineties that Americans first saw the enormous repatriation of capital, as British shareholders unloaded railroad securities en masse. It has been estimated that by 1901, one-fourth of American securities theretofore held in Britain and Europe had been repurchased and brought back to the United States.[63] Finally, emerging from the machinery of receivership in the nineties, reorganization managers designed a series of financial and legal buffers against the vicissitudes of the business cycle. Contingent, rather than fixed, securities, corporate surplus, investment banker participation, and the judicial separation of ownership from control all served to buffer the large-scale multidivisional railroad from legal challenge and divestiture.

Table 4. Financial Condition of Railroads in the Depression of the 1890s (percentage of gross income)

	1893			1892		
	Operating Expenses	Fixed Charges	Surplus	Operating Expenses	Fixed Charges	Surplus
Principal bankruptcies						
Baltimore & Ohio	66.89	24.27	8.83	67.68	24.55	7.76
Erie	64.91	32.12	2.96	66.46	31.85	1.68
N Pac.	59.25	43.55	0.00	53.71	36.34	9.94
Reading	57.04	45.41	0.00	52.64	33.91	13.44
Richmond, Danville & E Tenn.	73.49	25.63	0.12	68.79	31.15	0.00
U Pac.	59.66	43.18	0.00	51.91	36.42	11.26
Atchison, Topeka & Santa Fe	77.47	24.96	0.00	77.16	21.59	1.24
Principal successful railroads						
Chicago, Burlington & Quincy	64.66	23.12	12.41	65.17	20.86	13.96
Chicago, Milwaukee & St. Paul	65.95	20.78	13.26	64.00	22.36	13.63
Chicago, Rock Island & Pac.	71.72	13.31	14.96	69.88	19.83	10.28
Great N.	50.44	34.54	15.01	52.66	32.98	14.34
Ill. Central	61.92	25.84	12.23	64.58	23.99	11.12
New York, New Haven & Hartford	72.31	16.07	16.36	73.36	8.77	17.86
New York Central	68.79	20.84	10.36	68.46	21.53	9.96

Source: Stuart Daggett, *Railroad Reorganization* (Cambridge: Harvard University Press, 1908), 342–43.

The Corporate Person in Modern Industry

Hived off into the judicial realm of private law, the national politics of over-production were temporarily relegated to sectoral resolution. Though the scope of conflict over entitlements to credit in industrializing America had been narrowed, the contest over railroad receivership was no less an example of constitutive politics. It was resolved by the members of a legal community who made choices among genuinely ambiguous options. Where judges sat in the nineteenth-century political division of labor did not determine where they stood on receivership. They disagreed fundamentally over whether corporate doctrine allowed managers to reconstruct unilaterally intrafirm entitlements in the name of system integrity.

Nor was the transformation of receivership practice merely the private affair of managers, bankers, and shareholders. Its public consequences were profound. Wabash and its children acquainted Americans with a defining feature of the modern corporation: the legal separation of ownership from managerial control. Moreover, railroad reorganization in the 1890s set new standards for the industry.

Although many prominent systems avoided receivership, they now competed with firms whose fixed costs had been written down on average by 27 percent. Finally, the influence of leading reorganizers spread throughout the industry. Morgan, Harriman, Vanderbilt, Jay Gould's son George, and others used their new-found influence to knit together America's largest railroads into seven huge working groups. Interlocked through a complex pattern of intercorporate shareholding, these "communities of interest," as Morgan called them, exercised substantial influence over competition in rate making and construction on fully two-thirds of the nation's mileage.[64] By 1905 the reconstitution of corporate entitlements had transformed American railroads.

Part II REGIONAL REPUBLICANISM

CHAPTER FOUR

Regional Republicanism in Policy

Regulated Competition

National system building and ratemaking to ensure long-haul, high-volume bulk freight were two sides of the same strategy. We have seen, for example, how Gould set rates to maximize through, rather than local, traffic on the Wabash. This strategy—I shall call it national-market ratemaking—was typical of the huge systems that labored to organize demand in relatively large-scale centralized markets. The result was a national rate structure in which the short haul became proportionately, even absolutely, dearer than the long, the small shipment than the large, and the mixed commodity than the homogeneous. Furthermore, the effect of rates upon market landscape was dramatic. An 1895 study of the Upper Midwest, for example, found 331 retrograde townships along a corridor served by the Chicago, Rock Island and Pacific and the Michigan Central railroads. "For five hundred miles," its author wrote, "in a straight line through four States [Iowa, Illinois, Michigan, and Indiana], some evil influence is at work to arrest the growth and destroy the prosperity of all the groups of population which are too small to resist it . . . [Y]ear after year they have seen their hopes deferred, their business dwindle, their young industries starved out, their most enterprising citizens depart until dilapidation seems their natural condition, and public spirit dies away. It is not surprising to find that when the people move away they close up their shops and mills; or probably it would be more accurate to say that, being compelled to abandon their means of livelihood, they went elsewhere in search of that employment their own communities denied them."[1]

Such rate discrimination not only threatened many an American's livelihood but also offended their republican sense of economic justice. Having turned public powers to private ends, the railroad corporation had corrupted the state and steadily undermined the material conditions necessary to cultivate citizenship. The result was an urban landscape and a regulatory order in which vast gulfs in wealth and power generated a widespread sense of instrumental selfishness, inhospitable to the demands of self-government. This worldview better explains popular agitation for railroad regulation from the Granger Laws of the 1870s to the Interstate Commerce Act of 1887 than conventional interest-based interpretations. In the more prosaic language of urban geographers, Gilded Age fighting over regulation was not so much over the distribution of wealth and advantage (the politics of power) as it was over the constitution of the "urban pyramid" (that is, the ranking of American cities by size).[2]

Admittedly, political scientists and historians have long recognized that rate discrimination was the paramount force behind societal agitation for nineteenth-century regulation. At one point or another, scholars agree, nearly all shippers protested their competitors' rate advantages. If debate has persisted, it is over *who*, among the array of economic groups got *what, how,* and *why?* More often than not, however, the answer has rested upon an ephemeral notion of interests. For despite conceptual differences over the source of interest—class, market geography, sector, or some finer distinction within—scholars agree that where actors sat in the salient division of labor is the best predictor of what they wanted from regulation. Interests defined in this way, however, are inescapably ambiguous. Farmers, merchants, and manufacturers were hard pressed to identify their interests from a division of labor itself up for grabs in the politics of regulation. Given genuine uncertainty over the economic outcome of politics, they had little choice but to picture an industrial order within which they could locate an ongoing place for themselves. At most times that image remained dim and imprecise. However, at constitutive moments of acute conflict, when it became necessary to enlist allies and identify adversaries, the regionalist worldview was made explicit and its regulatory program carefully articulated.[3]

This was equally true for state actors, for whom the economic outcomes of politics were just as uncertain and interests just as ambiguous. At critical junctures of opportunity and conflict, politicians, judges, and would-be public administrators were compelled to make explicit their assumptions about property, the corporation, railroad economy, and regulatory design. And like societal actors, their positions on these issues cannot be explained by where they sat within the state (that is, within the political division of labor). We shall see that similarly situated state actors can be found on both corporate liberal and regional republican sides of the conflict over railroad regulation.

To be sure, not just any model of industrial order was relevant; nor was any regulatory architecture possible. Like group interests, regulatory policy was ambiguous, not infinitely plastic; both were subject to economic constraints. Any successful policy had to come to terms with the problems of overcapacity, cost recovery, and excess competition. This said, however, constitutive questions about citizenship, corporate entitlements, economic efficiency, and market landscape were left wide open. In particular, whether the state would encourage railroad concentration and then supersede competitive ratemaking (that is, regulate monopoly) or subject competitive behavior to strict regionalist norms (that is, regulate competition) was open to conflict well within these constraints.

The Interstate Commerce Act of 1887 and its first decade of implementation were a limited, but quite real, victory for the advocates of a regional republicanism. Their model of regulation—regulated competition—was also successful on the new institutionalists' criteria for effective administration: the early ICC mediated conflicts among economic groups and served the general interest in the ongoing health of the industry. At the same time, however, it achieved the Interstate Commerce Act's regionalist goals. Still, administrative success alone did not ensure regulated competition's longevity. For nowhere was the constitutive struggle between the practitioners of regional republicanism and corporate liberalism more fateful than in judicial review. So incommensurate would the Supreme Court and the Interstate Commerce Commission come to perceive their approaches to regulation that only one would fully survive.

The Granger Laws

Popular agitation against railroad rate discrimination swept through the Upper Midwest after the Civil War. Within a decade of Appomattox, Iowa, Illinois, Wisconsin, and Minnesota had enacted the Granger Laws—a set of statutes characterized by the authority they delegated to regulatory commissions to enforce rate schedules designed to grant parity to intraregional trade. Though they failed to check the centralizing power of national market ratemaking, the Granger Laws galvanized the alliance of merchants and farmers which first articulated the regionalist vision that would undergird the Interstate Commerce Act of 1887. Failure in the states only escalated the conflict. Once in the national arena, some of the most articulate spokespeople for regional republicanism issued from the Grange states.

Like the scholarship on federal regulation, our understanding of the Granger Laws has been burdened by an excessively reductionist notion of economic interest.[4] Historians have disagreed over whether to credit farmers or merchants with agency. Neither attribution is correct: a farm-merchant alliance was responsible for the Granger Laws. Alone, this observation might be trivial. However, seen through the analytical distinction between constitutive politics and the politics of power, it takes on a different cast. The act of alliance, I contend, was constitutive; as such it shaped regulatory interests.

True, merchants had long been out front in the fight against rate discrimination in the Upper Midwest. From Mississippi River towns, St. Paul, and smaller markets throughout the region, merchants complained of rate advantages granted to Lake Michigan and seaboard markets. Even the privileged of Chicago complained of discrimination in favor of St. Louis commerce. From 1867 to 1872 merchants sent representatives to state assemblies throughout the Midwest, where they introduced no fewer than a dozen bills outlawing rate discrimination. However, all but one—a weak Illinois law, overturned in court in 1868—failed without agrarian support. Not until the meteoric rise of the Grange after 1872 were merchants able to secure rules against rate discrimination and regulatory agencies designed to ensure compliance.

What united farmers behind the regional merchant's demand for rate parity? After all, many farmers saw merchant "middle men" as their natural enemies—no more than parasites preying upon the toil of "producing classes." Some contemporaries argued that the national railroad, not the merchant, was the Granger's natural ally. In 1870 trunkline managers told the Iowa Assembly that national-market "rate schedules were prepared in the interests of farmers, and they pointed to the fact that low through rates to Chicago were the only means whereby the inland farmers could compete in the eastern market. As far as discrimination against trade within the state was concerned, they insisted that long experience had shown these distinctions to be both necessary and just. The differences in rates were simply the result of variations in traffic and costs. The proposed legislation [outlawing rate discrimination] would be extremely burdensome and would probably necessitate the abandonment of through-freight service."[5]

Seen in retrospect, this appeal is quite consistent with the findings of new business historians. If national railroads offered lower rates for long-haul, high-volume trade to centralized markets, this merely reflected lower costs. Hence, by favoring bulk grain shippers, rate discrimination served both the farmer and the consumer. That is to say, discrimination allowed the welfare advantages of scale economies to be passed on to shippers and consumers. In fact, midwestern farmers were not without sympathy for this position. In the 1860s, for example, many joined eastern merchants in a public call for cheap transportation. Moreover, the Grange routinely demanded low rates to seaboard markets.[6]

Nonetheless, by 1872 Grangers supported merchants in their struggle against national-market ratemaking. It was not until the fabulous growth of the Grange in 1872 and 1873 that legislative initiatives were successful. Within two years, Iowa, Illinois, Wisconsin, and Minnesota had enacted antidiscrimination laws and established independent regulatory agencies to enforce them.[7] But why did the Grangers join regional merchants in their fight for regulation? Did farmers and merchants simply logroll their interests, trading the support for cheap transportation for antidiscrimination rules? I think not. In the first place, despite their differences in assigning agency, Granger Law historians Solon Buck and George Miller agree that the intent of regulation was antidiscriminatory. Second, Granger antimonopolism was not a redistributive ideology, pure and simple. Oliver Kelley, founder of the Grange, had long championed the "promise of the Mississippi Valley as a distinct region"; North and South bound together by the "great river" along whose shores *every crop can be raised and everything manufactured.*"[8] But Kelley was not alone. "There were many," Miller writes, "who believed that the valley . . . had become too dependent upon outside markets and thus it should be allowed to develop its own economic destiny . . . This spirit of regionalism remained and was an essential part of the Granger movement in the Middle West." The staunchly proregulatory and antirailroad *Industrial Age* echoed Granger sentiment well. There was no reason why "Iowa, Wisconsin, and Illinois should not make all the clothes they need, as well as their boots and shoes . . . The Northwest abounds in iron and coal, and has the skilled labor to make almost any implement or article made from iron. Why not do it and save the heavy freights from the East?"[9]

In 1873 Illinois Grangers sponsored a regional conference in Chicago under the auspices of the Northwestern Farmers Association. In addition to the Grange states, delegates hailed from Indiana, New York, Michigan, and Pennsylvania. At the top of their agenda, farmers called a federal law against charging more for the short haul than the long under any circumstances. They also demanded that the federal government replace subsidies with public ownership and operation of selected railroads. By doing so, they argued, the state might set competitive standards for the remaining private carriers. Finally, the Grangers resolved that rate schedules should promote "home manufactures" in developing regions, thereby lessening the costs of transportation altogether. Through regulation and public ownership the state would ensure that "one industry would not be protected at the expense of another," and that all shippers would have equal access to improved transportation.[10]

By 1872 Grange state merchants and farmers came to share the rudiments of a regionalist vision of economic development. Midwestern regionalism, however, should not be confused with sectionalism. This was not merely a conflict between the frontier and the industrialized Northeast, that is, between an intranational "metropole" and its "semiperiphery." In a sophisticated but incorrect application of world systems theory to domestic politics, Elizabeth Sanders has recently explained the development of national railroad regulation in sectional terms. Farmers in the "peripheral south" and the "semiperipheral Midwest," she argues, were responsible for regulation, from the Interstate Commerce Act to its early twentieth-century reforms. It was they who suffered at the hands of railroad rate discrimination; and they alone had sufficient numbers in Congress to usher regulation into law. The evidence, however, belies this interpretation. The political economy of sectionalism, like the pluralist and class interpretations of public policy it is intended to replace, mistakenly derives agrarian preferences from an uncertain geographic division of labor. That midwestern farmers came to support the demand for parity for short-haul and less-than-carload freight had more to do with their vision of regional development than their fixed interests in one or another rate structure. This is not to say that they chose *against* their interests; only that they envisioned a secure place for themselves in a relatively decentralized and balanced regional economy. If Grangers rejected rate discrimination, they also rejected their region's status as a mere primary products tributary to eastern and overseas markets. Though the relationship publicly drawn between economic regionalism and regulation was still rough in the seventies, it would develop into a more coherent picture over the next decade—one which its proponents would articulate in favor of national rate regulation.[11]

Regionalism and sectionalism often coincided on the railroad question. Most midwestern trunklines were financed in New York and Boston. Therefore westerners fingered absentee ownership from the East when they attacked discriminatory rate practices. Even so, the battle cry of sectionalism and rate discrimination were not one and the same. In the 1870s and the decade that followed, by contrast, regionalism and the commitment to antidiscrimination law were.[12]

Granger Laws Challenged: The Origins of Constitutive Debate

By 1874 farm-merchant alliances in all four states had set their embryonic regionalism into practice. Subtle in their differences, the Granger Laws nevertheless shared these provisions. All four states outlawed unreasonable rate discrimination and established regulatory commissions to formulate and revise detailed intrastate rate schedules, graduated by distance and classified by freight. No sooner were regional republican norms written into law, however, than they were attacked on corporate liberal grounds. From the most intransigent of railroads and their allies among America's new intellectuals came a concerted effort to shift the terrain of debate from the construction of market landscape to the distribution of income. Here, then, were the seeds of a two-decade constitutive conflict between the advocates of regulated competition and of regulated monopoly.

Though decidedly hostile, not all railroads attacked the Granger Laws from their inception. Officials for the Chicago, Burlington and Quincy, the Illinois Central, and the Rock Island initially indicated a willingness to lower intrastate rates to the level demanded by Granger schedules and to make up the difference by raising unregulated interstate levies. This would have gone some distance toward achieving the intent of the Granger Laws, namely to proportionalize long and short, or intraregional and interregional rates, according to distance. Hopes for cooperation were dashed, however, as the most uncooperative carriers announced their intention to force repeal of these unconstitutional statutes.[13]

No sooner was the ink dry on Wisconsin's Potter Law, than officials for the Chicago and Northwestern and the Chicago, Milwaukee and St. Paul declared they would disregard the Iowa and Wisconsin statutes and await challenge in court.[14] The Potter Law, Milwaukee and St. Paul President Alexander Mitchell told Wisconsin Governor William R. Taylor, "arbitrarily deprive[s] [the] company of its property, without due process of law. It is confiscation"—a breach of contract by the state which had granted the corporation the right to set its own rates. Hence, officers and directors, he concluded, "believe it their duty to disregard" the Granger rate schedules.[15]

Others followed Mitchell's lead and were promptly challenged by attorneys general in state courts. But, unlike their receivership experience in the federal courts during the next decade, the midwestern carriers found no relief from regulation before the bench. Supreme courts in all four states declared their respective statutes enforceable at law and enjoined the railroads to comply.[16] Still hopeful, however, the Granger roads appealed to the Supreme Court.

Swamped by kindred petitions in 1876, the high court consolidated the Granger cases in a single hearing. Still, the carriers found no more sympathy in Washington than in Madison or Springfield. In the leading case of the era, *Munn v. Illinois*, the Court declared that all businesses "affected with a public interest" were legitimately subject to the state's police power. As Justice Bradley explained a year later in the Sinking Fund cases, "When an employment or business becomes a matter of such public interest and importance as to create a common charge or burden upon citizens; in other words, when it becomes a practical monopoly, to which the citizen is compelled to resort, and by means of which a tribute can be exacted from the community, it is subject to regulation by the legislative power."[17] Railroads and grain ware-houses, the Court added, "stand . . . in the very 'gateway of commerce' and take toll from all who pass," and therefore "exercise a sort of public office." So "affected with a public interest" are they that the power to establish rates is the legitimate right of state legislatures. True, added Justice Waite, that "power . . . may be abused; but that is no argument against its existence. For protection against abuses by legislatures the people must resort to the polls, not the courts."[18]

Munn did not pass without dissent. On the Supreme Court, it initiated a corporate liberal challenge that eventually transformed judicial doctrine. In society, it mobilized many among America's emerging middle-class professionals to a principled attack upon the excesses of democracy. Supreme Court Justice Stephen J. Field, for one, condemned the Granger Laws as confiscatory: they deprived railroads of their property "as effectively as if the legislature had ordered its forcible dispossession."[19] This was but the first of Field's attack on the "affectation doctrine." But, as Charles McCurdy has shown, Field was no mere apologist for corporate power; he worried legitimately that Munn had opened the door to unlimited police power. Since the Court made no effort to distinguish business "affected with the public interest" from any others, virtually all activities might fall into this category. Thus, not only were the consequences likely to be obnoxious, the Court's imprecision played havoc with the prized liberal distinction between public and private. Absent doctrinal guidance, there was no telling the legislative excesses the judiciary might condone. For Field, then, the problem was how to distinguish an inviable boundary between legitimate public regulation and the protection of private property. This was, he thought, essentially an empirical problem; therefore, it was the duty of the corporate jurist to distinguish empirically verifiable parameters of the public sphere from those of the private. For this reason, we shall refer to Field's method as "liberal positivism."

On the private side of the equation, Field argued, property was a presocial right, an entitlement that inhered naturally in the individual. Such rights, he said, always "required protection from the vagaries of government." Only an immutable boundary drawn between public responsibility and private right could protect individuals from unjust confiscation by the state. But how and where to draw the line? This was Field's mission. In the first place, it was quite clear that some economic activities were not affected with the public interest. These were "ordinary trades," where market transactions governed and contract best prevailed. Naturally, other economic activities, Field conceded, were affected with the public interest. Some, like railroads and highways, necessitated public easements in order to ply their trade. Others necessarily involved the public health, safety, and morals of the community. But these were criteria inherent to the economic activity itself. As such, they were observable and universally applicable.

But what of the corporate franchise, which held both public and private functions? Surely this was a more ambiguous case. Like the distinction between "ordinary trades" and those "affected with the public interest," Field thought it possible to identify autonomous standards by which to separate the public from the private aspects of the corporation. He conceded that railroads were devoted to "public use" and "recognized that state legislatures had generally reserved the power to alter rates fixed in corporate charters." It was one thing to acknowledge the public aspects of railroad activity; it was quite another to infer that railroad corporations were mere "agents of the state." The majority in *Munn* had erred in "converting *private concerns with public duties into wholly public corporations.*"[20]

The railroad corporation's reliance on private investment capital, Field said, privileged the private sphere. For without investment, neither public nor private interests would be served. If railroads remained at the mercy of "hostile legislatures," he charged, investment would cease. The duty of the Court, then, was to "define the limits of the power of the State over its corporations . . . so that, on the one hand, the property interests of the stockholder would be protected from practical confiscation, and on the other hand, the people would be protected from arbitrary and extortionate charges."[21] Since the proximate interests of the state and the corporation were antagonistic, it was the Court's duty to assure that, on this criterion, regulated rates were "reasonable."

Though alone on the Supreme Court, Field found a sympathetic (corporate liberal) assessment of the Granger Laws among many of America's most cosmopolitan journalists and intellectuals. Indeed, as the carriers took Justice Waite's advice and turned from the courts to the ballot box, they also found ready allies among the most prominent students of the railroad problem: E. L. Godkin, Charles Francis Adams, Jr., Arthur Twining Hadley, and a number of seaboard journalists.[22]

Editor of the mugwump journal *The Nation*, Godkin condemned the Granger Laws in no uncertain terms. "The Potter Law," he wrote, "is simply a mild way of doing what a mob law does when it burns a station or tears up rails or throws locomotives off the track." This was no more than the "brigand way of dealing" with the railroad problem. Should these low rates persist, he predicted, it would mean "the absolute ruin of the companies."[23] Perhaps no one, however, articulated this view with more influence than Charles Francis Adams. The architect of the Massachusetts Railroad Commission and soon-to-be president of the Union Pacific, Adams was the paragon of the republic's cosmopolitan intellectuals. "The wild utterances" of the Grangers, Adams wrote in *The Nation*, "took the form of yet wilder laws." Wisconsin's Potter Law was the "most ignorant, arbitrary, and wholly unjustifiable law to be found in the history of railroad legislation." Reducing tariffs by as much as "twenty to fifty percent," Adams wrote, it "seemed designed as practical confiscation of the many millions of foreign capital invested in the public improvements of that state . . . If ever a problem called for wise legislation, founded upon careful and patient study, this one certainly did. The Granger legislatures, however, went at it like so many bulls at red rags."[24]

Others joined in. "The depressing fact," wrote journalist J. W. Midgely, is that under the Granger Laws, no railroad in the region "is in a position to earn a dividend . . . In compliance with popular demand, a crushing blow has been struck. Beneath it a mighty industry lies prostrate." The deluded Granger, added W. W. Grosvernor, had seen himself the "toiler" under the thumb of the "bloated" capitalist. As a result, "he turned communist" and the "spoliation" of property ensued. But nothing could be further from the truth, added Grosvernor. No one, especially the Grangers themselves, was served by laws that "entirely ignored the right of the stockholder to hope for any return on his investment." It is no wonder "capital took fright . . . and the crash of September, essentially a railroad panic," followed. This was the "immediate" and sure "effect of [the] Granger legislation."[25]

More reserved but no less critical, Yale University president and economist Arthur Twining Hadley reached similar conclusions in his influential 1885 treatise, *Railroad Transportation*. The Granger schedules, he wrote, had been "unremunerative"; their inevitable result to suspend investment and construction altogether. "The laws of trade," Hadley reasoned, "could not be violated with impunity." There were limits to redistribution, but more to the point, antidiscrimination law distorted efficiency, since discrimination in favor of long-haul, high-volume freight achieved scale economies.[26]

By decade's end, managers and their allies among intellectuals had succeeded in shifting the terrain of debate over the Granger Laws from regional republican to corporate liberal norms; that is, from a debate over how rate structures ought to shape market landscape to one over the distribution of income within an industry presumed to be naturally constrained by the requisites of private investment. Smarting under the strain of the depression, falling grain prices, and tight credit, one after another state legislature caved in. Railroad lobbyists were especially effective in Wisconsin and Minnesota, where they mobilized legislators from districts still ill-served by railroads to their cause. By 1880 all four states had repealed their rate schedules. Only hollow oversight commissions were left, empowered, like Adams's "sunshine commission" in Massachusetts, to collect and disseminate data and publicize the most egregious of rail abuses.

As it turned out, the opposition alliance of railroads and intellectuals was not monolithic. Indeed, perhaps the most careful and sympathetic assessment of the Granger Laws came from one who was both a railroad manager and an intellectual: A. B. Stickney, president of the Chicago Great Western Railway. Like the farmers who allied with aggrieved merchants against the midwestern trunklines, Stickney pegged his private interest to a public vision of balanced regional development. Although a sore exception among Grange state railroad men, he would become both market and political ally to agrarian, mercantile, and manufacturing regionalists. In politics, he became a staunch advocate of antidiscrimination law. In business, he formed market alliances with moderate-scale intraregional shippers by building and operating a genuinely regional railroad. Chapter 4 will explore the viability of railroad regionalism in practice by comparing Chicago Great Western operating, ratemaking, and financial practices to the huge national systems that came to dominate the Plains and the Upper Midwest. The feasibility of regionalism, however, depended upon more than alternative business practice. Like interregional system building, it turned on a supportive institutional environment. This was a lesson Stickney well understood—the battle for economic place would be won not on the field of rate and service competition alone. Rule and custom in capital markets and regulation would serve to lock railroad development into one or another pattern of institutional practice. After the collapse of the Granger Laws, then, Stickney turned his boundless energy to regulation and by the mid-eighties he laid out his position in *The Railroad Problem*.

Looking back on the Granger experience, Stickney saw an early, but missed, opportunity for the carriers to cooperate with regional shippers. Both, he reasoned, had legitimate claims: the railroads to a fair rate of return on their investment, the Grangers to fair and nondiscriminatory rates. Contrary to many of his peers in the industry, Stickney thought the Granger Laws had established just such a foundation for cooperation. Carefully assessing the Granger rate schedules, he showed in some detail that the intent of the laws had been to grant parity to the intraregional short haul, not, as management and their apologists protested, to redistribute net revenues from railroads to shippers. "The uprising of the people of the Western states," he wrote, "was not against the aggregate amount of rates which were being collected by the railways, but against the discrimination they were practicing in collecting their revenues. This fact should be thoroughly mastered by every mind which desires to comprehend the meaning of the so-called Granger Legislation."[27]

Also, the Granger Laws had provided the railroads the flexibility to meet the challenge of the regionalists and their constant capital costs. While Granger rate schedules had placed strict upper limits in the less favored short-haul, small-volume carriage, they also tended to leave long-haul, large-volume freight rates alone. For one thing, the latter were mostly interstate and therefore unaffected by state schedules. For another, the intent of the laws was to check discrimination against intraregional trade. Once the carriers were forced by law to stop cross-subsidizing long-haul competition with monopoly rents from short-haul traffic, Stickney reasoned, they would have no choice but to raise long-haul rates to compensate for regulated losses. In other words, although Granger rate schedules were rigid in regulating the short haul, they were flexible in the discretion they accorded managers to raise long-haul rates in order to assure average revenues sufficient to cover costs.

Stickney reprimanded his fellow managers for not cooperating with Grange state shippers. Instead, bringing their case to the public and the courts, they had distorted the intent of these laws beyond recognition. Regulation would so depress revenues, management had protested, it would drive the carriers to bankruptcy. But, as Stickney pointed out, management always failed to adjust long-haul rates upward when making such doomsday predictions. To be sure, Burlington, Illinois Central, and Rock Island executives initially agreed to comply by raising long-haul rates at competitive terminals. But, once their competitors—the Milwaukee and St. Paul and the Chicago and Northwestern—mounted an assault on the Granger Laws, the others followed. Alexander Mitchell, Stickney charged, had been especially guilty of crying wolf. Failing to adjust long-haul rates upward, he had estimated that Wisconsin's Potter Law would drive the Milwaukee's revenues down a full 26 percent. Assessing the same rate schedule, Stickney concluded that average revenues would have remained virtually the same. (His calculations were corroborated by the Wisconsin Railroad Commission, which estimated a loss of less than 5 percent for the year 1873.)[28]

But we need not take the estimates of partisans as the final word on the Granger Laws. A 1903 study by Charles Detrick concluded that the decline in midwestern railroad profits, investment, and building could not be attributed to regulation. Freight rates on the two most contentious of the Granger roads, the Milwaukee and St. Paul and the Chicago and Northwestern, declined regularly from 1865 to 1885, with no marked decrease during the period that the Granger schedules were in effect.[29] When compared to carriers in regions without regulation, Granger state railroads performed virtually the same, or in some cases slightly better. For example, during the peak years of Granger regulation, 1874 to 1875, railroad mileage increased 6 percent in the Granger states compared to 4.1 percent in four western states, 5.9 percent in six middle states, 2.4 percent in ten southern states, and 5.5 percent in the United States as a whole. In order to control for regional differences, Detrick included in the category "western states" Indiana, Michigan, Nebraska, and Missouri, all of which were similar in geographic position, area, population, industrial development, and railroad mileage.

In addition, between 1873 to 1876 the average net earnings for railroads in the Grange states held their own with the middle and southern states. More dramatic, though, earnings increased three and one-half times faster in the Grange states than in the comparable four western states, where regulation was absent. Earnings and investment declined in the Grange states, as they did throughout the nation in the 1870s. But overall, concludes Detrick, "the Granger Acts appear in fact to have had little effect on railroad building and railroad receipts, because of the overshadowing influence of the financial panic of 1873 and the depression which lasted till 1879."[30]

But the struggle over the Granger Laws would not be won on the empirical merits of the case. Many other intellectuals—armed with quite different premises about railroad economics and regulation—reached dramatically different conclusions. And even though this debate continued well into the 1890s, the first round had been won by the least cooperative of the railroads and their corporate liberal allies. The Granger roads' threat to sustain a capital strike in the midst of depression was compelling: it mobilized voters from

Table 5. Increased Railroad Mileage, 1870–1890 (by regional states and %)

Regional States	1860–1870	1870–1888	1880–1890	1871–1873	1874–1875	1876–1877	1876–1878
Four Granger	133	96	50	44.5	6.0	5.5	10
Four Western	100	90	74	45.5	4.1	5.6	9.1
Six Middle	64	45	35	24.4	5.9	4.8	6.9
Ten Southern	115	33	72	16.2	2.4	3.9	5.5
Total U.S.	74	74	79	33	5.5	6.7	10.4

Source: Charles Detrick, "The Effects of the Granger Acts," Journal of Political Economy 11 (Mar. 1903): 250.

Table 6. Increase of Average Net Earnings Compared with Average Net Earnings for
Two Years, 1871 and 1872 (by regional states and %)

Regional States	1874–1875	1873–1876	1873–1879
Four Granger	29	31	44
Four Western	15	9	30
Six Middle	40	33	25
Ten Southern	32	34	23

Source: Charles Detrick, "The Effects of the Granger Acts," Journal of Political Economy 11 (Mar.
1903): 252.

districts not yet served by the railroads and weakened the case for antidiscrimination laws throughout the Midwest. Still, regional republicans were
only temporarily subdued by the depression. And counter to those who have
interpreted the Granger Laws as redistributive in intent, the demand for regulation did not die down with the return of prosperity. As the worst of times
lifted, regional republicanism went national.[31]

The Interstate Commerce Act

Complaints of railroad rate discrimination were scarcely limited to the
Grange states. Looking back on the long struggle for regionalism and regulation from the new century, Wisconsin Senator Robert LaFollette pointed out
that in their efforts to centralize trade in a few dominant locations, the railroads had generated a protracted struggle with interior markets throughout
the country. "From the Southwest to the Northwest the complaints come;
and from the Northeast to the Southwest. In every locality it is the most important industries and lines of trade that are attacked and suffering. . . . There
is Danville in Virginia; Atlanta in Georgia; Nashville in Tennessee; St. Louis
in the Mississippi Valley; Denver on the Great Plains; and Spokane in Washington. They simply represent types," LaFollette concluded.[32]

Unable to remedy the centralizing effects of national market ratemaking
in the states, then, midwesterners joined other regional complainants in a
drive for a federal antidiscrimination law. Though the source of shipper grievances varied from region to region—meatpackers, farmers, and merchants
in the Midwest; farmers and merchants in the South; independent coal and
oil producers in Pennsylvania and Ohio—a national pattern of rate discrimination became evident as early as the 1870s. Congressional leaders hailed
from all three regions: William McCrary and James Wilson from Iowa, James
Hopkins from Pennsylvania, and John Reagan from Texas.

The first stirrings for federal regulation began well before the Granger

Laws were defeated. In 1868 alone, three separate resolutions to regulate rail-roads were introduced in Congress, and over the next five years several com-mittees were formed to consider its constitutionality. In recognition that state laws had no authority over interstate discrimination, Representative William McCrary (R. Iowa) introduced a Granger-style bill in 1870. Though it squeaked by the lower house in 1874 (121 to 116, 53 not voting), the Mc-Crary Bill, like ten others introduced between 1872 and 1875, died in the Sen-ate, where national railroad sympathies ran high. Appointed by state legisla-tures well into the twentieth century, many senators eschewed popular opposition to national market ratemaking. Stalwart Republican leaders in the upper house would frustrate antidiscrimination initiatives for another twelve years.[33]

Iowans were not alone. The most stirring call for federal action in the sev-enties issued from Pennsylvania, where Standard Oil had colluded with the Erie Railroad to monopolize the trade in crude oil. The oil giant, the public learned, had secured secret rate rebates from the railroad, thereby assuring it critical cost advantages unavailable to its smaller competitors. In 1876 Pitts-burgh representative James H. Hopkins brought the plight of the oil indepen-dents to the attention of Congress. Joined in the popular press by Henry Demerest Lloyd, whose *Atlantic* articles made Rockefeller and Flagler house-hold names, Standard Oil became the model case for regionalists. So dra-matic was this case that it remains the subject of historical debate over the causes and consequences of industrial concentration in the American econ-omy. Some have seen Standard's tactics as the paradigm of ruthless competi-tion, intended to drive its opponents to the wall. In 1871, the story goes, Standard organized the South Improvement Company, whose sole purpose was to use its control over crude oil to play one railroad against another. Bowing to Standard's monopsony power, the Erie Railroad granted South Improvement rebates not only on its own oil, but on the independents' as well. Coupled with industrial sabotage and strong-arm tactics, Rockefeller and Flagler used rebates to gain control of over more than 90 percent of the industry by 1890. Judged at the time, or in retrospect, this case illus-trates predatory rate discrimination at its worst. And even though the oil giant was punished for antitrust violations in 1911, divestiture left it large and powerful.[34]

New business historians have defended Standard's growth strategy and market share, if not all of its tactics. Railroad rebates, they argue, though un-fair to the independents, were efficiency-motivated and ultimately served the consumer. Like railroads, the oil industry faced enormous economies of scale and speed. This was especially true after the early 1870s, when Standard centralized its refining capacity in Cleveland. In order to capture the economies of high-volume throughput, inherent in refining technology, Standard needed to assure a large and steady stream of crude oil. It did so by securing a long-term contract with the Erie Railroad: the carrier agreed to grant Standard reduced rates in return for minimum regular oil shipments. Since the Erie also faced scale economies, the deal served it well. More important, rebates reduced average costs for both railroad and oil company. Assured of steady, high-volume oil shipments, the railroad could afford to pass its cost savings on to Standard in the form of rebates; while Standard could pass its lower costs of production on to consumers. Despite public outcry, rate discrimination was in the consumer's, hence the public, interest.[35]

This argument is problematic for several reasons. Railroad managers, for example, were not of a single mind on economies of scale in shipping oil. Alexander Cassatt, president of the Pennsylvania, waged a nearly quarter-century battle against Standard's market power. So too did the Reading. In fact, Hopkins's first bill in 1876 was a collaborative effort by the Pennsylvania oil independents and the Reading Railroad.[36] Moreover, the independents claimed other economic advantages. Located close to the well head, they were able to avoid a great deal of double-shipping to market. They also had ready access to existing seaboard refineries and overseas ports. Perhaps the most compelling defense in their favor lay in their efforts to organize among themselves. In 1878 Pennsylvania's independents formed the Petroleum Producers Union, whose initial goal was to control overproduction and periodic price wars. Within a year, however, the Union had incorporated the Tidewater Pipeline Company, which built and operated the first successful oil pipeline across the Alleghenies to the Atlantic Coast. For the moment Standard's rebate advantages were lost. More important, by sharing transportation and collectively regulating the flow of crude to seaboard refineries, the independents claimed external economies equal to Standard's internal economies. Only once the latter had forced the independents to abandon their pipeline did it regain control over the industry.[37]

It is impossible to know whether Standard Oil could have attained its dominance without rebates or other forms of "unfair" competition. The 1901 *Report of the Industrial Commission on the Petroleum Industry* concluded in the negative.[38] Either way, the evidence indicates that neither Standard nor the independents could exercise unqualified autarky. Like small-town merchants in Iowa, oil producers needed market and political allies in order to advance their project. This was not simply a case of free-market allocative efficiency either, where profit-maximizing shippers and railroads chose among the best contractual partners. These were longer term collaborative transactions—what institutional economists and industrial sociologists call "relational contracts." Whether railroads pledged scarce resources to a particular strategy depended upon mutual commitments by shippers. But the contractual terms of collaboration between carrier and shipper had come under public scrutiny and dispute. For example, would Congress and the courts condone Standard's long-term relationship with the Erie Railroad in the name of free contract or scale economies? Or would this case and others like it illustrate how national market ratemaking undermined constitutional sensibilities of fairness and the moral economy of regionalism? Neither side would win the battle over railroad and industrial organization on the battlefield of market competition alone. The outcome would be determined in politics, mediated through Congress, the Interstate Commerce Commission, and the Supreme Court.[39]

In Congress, James Hopkins found innumerable allies among representatives of independent regional shippers. In his own state, he said, unfair rebates had deprived anthracite coal, iron, glass, and flour producers of locational and other cost advantages. A movement against discrimination, he added, has arisen "from all sections of the country. In Wisconsin, a political revolution was wrought upon this question. In Illinois it was regarded so important that the right to control railroads and prohibit discriminations was incorporated into the State constitution." Pennsylvania, Massachusetts, "and other states have sought in various ways to accomplish the same end, . . . the prevention of discriminations."[40]

Before he could muster sufficient support to pass an initiative, Hopkins's powerful adversaries turned him from office in 1876. The same election, however, elevated Texas Representative John Reagan to chair of the House Commerce Committee, where he led a decade-long battle for regulation. In 1878 and 1880 Reagan ushered two bills through the House, only to watch them die again in the Senate. Regulation had become deadlocked. Both houses retreated to committee, where they held extensive hearings and redrafted legislation. By 1885 the heirs to McCrary and Hopkins had developed a much more universal justification for antidiscrimination law. No longer was it sufficient to list constituent grievances. In their efforts to enlist allies, the architects of regionalism were compelled to make explicit their notions of citizenship, corporate entitlements, cost recovery, and market landscape. Despite itself, Congress deliberated.[41]

Regionalism and Regulation

After endless hours of registering complaints against rate favoritism, regional republicans posed a disturbing picture to their colleagues in Congress. In the

Senate the battle for antidiscrimination law was led by Iowa's James Wilson; in the House John Reagan continued to use the chair of the House Committee on Interstate Commerce as an advocacy pulpit. Although many in Congress expressed outrage at the market consequences of rate discrimination, Wilson was likely their most articulate spokesperson. As the government's representative on the Union Pacific's board from 1874 to 1882, he had witnessed at close range the contradictory powers of railroads. He knew quite well what vast engines of national economic growth they were, and he saw how management autocracy could unfairly dominate trade and development.[42]

In 1885 "Jefferson Jim" put the regionalist's case before Congress. As a first-term representative in 1866, he said, he had joined hands with radical Republicans to enact an interstate commerce law whose intent was to assure that no privileged person or community would lawfully connive to monopolize and control the lines of transportation and trade in the United States. This statute made it unlawful for the states to collude with their own railroads to block entry by interstate carriers. Such practices, Wilson pointed out, would neither conserve constitutional ideals, nor transportation efficiencies made possible by "abolishing unnecessary changes, delays, breaking of bulk, and attendant wastage, cost, charges, and loss of time."[43]

Unfortunately, historians have all too often confused the opening of national markets and strengthening of the national state during Reconstruction, favored by Wilson and other radical Republicans, with the inevitability of dominant city urbanization. From this vantage point, many Gilded Age political struggles—regulation just one of them—centered on town versus country, community versus society, localism versus cosmopolitanism, or to put the matter another way, the ideology of a passing order versus prophecy of the new.[44] But from the worldview of the regionalists in Congress, railroads presented not so much a threat to an old order as an opportunity to better realize the material conditions necessary to cultivate the republican ideals of a virtuous and independent citizenry. If harnessed correctly, the revolution in transportation could go a long way toward achieving the vision nineteenth-century economist Henry Carey described as "a society of 'little town and cities,' each a local center of manufacturing serving the surrounding countryside, and providing a market for its industrial produce."[45]

This picture was rapidly being thwarted by the railroads. Transportation had become the "master of commerce," when, by right, railroads must be "public servants." "To give [the railroads] artificial life and perpetual existence, to give them the power to condemn private property of the citizen for their use, and to give them exclusive control of the highway for their vehicles," protested Senator Vance of North Carolina, "and then to permit them to go uncontrolled as absolutely as though they were private citizens in the management of their business would be a monstrous proceeding indeed. It would be the story of Frankenstein converted into actual fact."[46]

Such corrupt behavior was neither necessary nor just, for once Congress and the railroads had broken down interstate trade barriers, Wilson argued, "each locality, industry, and person should be entitled to receive a fair proportion of the advantages that were expected to result from the improved transportation facilities authorized by [the Act of 1866]."[47] "What the people want," echoed Senator Camden of West Virginia, "is an approximate uniformity in rates. They do not care to the same extent about what the [level of those] rates are."[48] The national commitment to *free* interstate trade, in short, intended a promise to *equal* interstate trade.

Equal access to proportional shares of improved transportation, however, contradicted the carriers' favored ratemaking principle of disproportionality. Perhaps the clearest statement of this policy in practice came once again from the president of the Chicago Great Western Railway, A. B. Stickney. As a rule, he argued in *The Railway Problem*, his colleagues had simply failed to conceptualize ratemaking in proportion to cost and service. Instead, they had spared no effort to secure long-haul traffic at virtually any price. Stickney conceded that there were cost advantages to the long-haul; its lower ratio of terminal to hauling costs made it cheaper per mile than the short haul. But the primacy management had accorded long-haul traffic—and to building up markets at the ends of their lines—Stickney argued, was based on an illusion. Armies of freight agents were instructed to offer rebates, special favors, and virtually unremunerative rates to secure long-haul traffic. In other words, management had come to see the advantages of the long haul in *absolute*, not *proportional*, terms—and they set rates accordingly. The result was perverse: wild competition at connecting terminals often drove revenues well below cost, and whatever proportional cost advantages long-haul, high-volume freight might have had quickly vanished. Still worse, Stickney added, the railroads incurred the wrath of local shippers, who concluded not only that they were paying rates disproportional to distance and cost, but they also reasoned that the depressed rates per ton-mile on the long haul were remunerative and therefore represented fair standards for short-haul traffic as well.[49]

By 1885 the effects of this ratemaking logic on settlement and trade became quite clear to federal policy makers. Once more Wilson stated the case most cogently: the railroads had colluded with major shippers to establish an "abnormal system of forced combination and centralization . . . a vast concentration of capital and work, and workers in the ponderous cities."[50] Having corrupted the public weal, added Senator Beck of Kentucky, the railroads "can build up or tear down towns and villages, even cities, just as they please."[51] The effect was to drive "population and business enterprise from the country and the towns to the cities and the centers of railroad competition, and of creating for one section over another section commercial advantages which no power ought to be permitted to exercise," echoed Senator Camden.[52] The carriers had seized a power unto themselves, Congressman Reagan told the Senate, "which no government of a free people would dare to exercise . . . , and yet the railroad companies demand and insist on the right to exercise this vast and dangerous power. And under it they are impoverishing some cities, towns and communities, without any fault of their's, and enriching others having no other merit to this favor than the arbitrary power of the transportation companies."[53] This "tendency to drive manufacturing industries and all who employ and are employed therein to a comparatively few localities . . . [does not] conserve the public interests, whether we regard them from the standpoints of moral, material, or political consideration, singly or combined. The system is repressive and unjust," Wilson bluntly concluded.[54]

Management autocracy had not only biased economic development, it also distorted interests. Many western farmers and miners, Wilson pointed out, had become reluctant to give up their long-haul rate advantages to eastern markets. This was the result of a contrived alliance, dominated by the carriers, in favor of national market ratemaking.

> While it [the policy of charging less for the long than the short haul] remains the low rate is the only door through which the West and far interior can reach distant markets at the points of centralization. It is not the abolishment of the low rate on the long haul that is the immediate need of these great regions of our country lying distant from the dominant market centers. The thing most needed is a change of the system which keeps producers and consumers of both agricultural and manufactured goods so far apart, forcing the great volume of our interstate commerce to be transported over great distances, thereby rendering the low rate on the long haul a necessary element in the freight traffic of the country.[55]

Shipper interests, Wilson noticed, were not fixed. The development of the regional market town, which would spawn local processing and ancillary industry, would better serve agrarian interests.

The core of the problem lay in management's perception that rate setting was a private right, for which, like any commodity, the price of service ought to reflect "what the traffic would bear." This notion seemed absurd to the regionalists. One might as well think of the production and distribution of air in this way, Stickney argued. For rail transportation had become the "oxygen of trade," cut off from it one simply could not survive. As such, added Wilson, it ought to be the "great conserving force of commerce," and this it would be, if management would give up its drive to "forced centralization" by which they bind the industries of the country. If management could not be made to see its obligation to conserve the lines of commerce voluntarily, they should be forced to do so by law.[56]

Once in place a nationally uniform antidiscrimination law would go a long way toward freeing commerce from its current centralizing tendencies. Sanguine about regulation, Wilson told his fellow senators that "a diffusion of industries will multiply such communities (energetic, self reliant, and prosperous) and this diffusion will transpire whenever the shackles shall have been stricken from the willing limbs of communities now impatient of the restraints which hold them to inaction."[57] "If small shippers were charged no more than the larger," added Congressman George of Mississippi, "the expense and delay of shipping to the great cities and thence distributing to the consumer would be avoided. The producer and the consumer would be brought nearer together; . . . the producer would receive more and the consumer would pay less."[58] No longer, added Senator Camden, would "manufacturers and shippers" at disadvantaged terminals "be . . . compelled to remove their business to the cities of competitive railroad centers," or simply quit the trade altogether. Of course, the regionalists did not "mean by this [to] legislate so cities will cease to grow; but . . . that the practices of the transporting companies whereby abnormal growth is forced upon a few cities at the expense of the equal rights of other communities shall cease by voluntary action or be reformed by law."[59]

The problem was not only unequal access to interstate transportation. The effect of discrimination on the market landscape was even more disturbing. It transgressed the republican ideal of a society of small producers, located in a network of moderate-size cities, engaged primarily in regional trade. Only the federal police power over interstate commerce would ensure that privileged shippers and communities did not turn temporary bargaining advantages into permanent dominion over market size, location, and the flow of national trade.[60]

All other issues, then, would be subordinated to the principles of proportional access and regional markets. Consider the critical question of railroad pools. Many managers and prominent intellectuals like Charles Francis Adams argued that only publicly enforced railroad pools could equalize long-

and short-haul rates. As the president of the Southern Railway and Steamship Association, Albert Fink, put it, unrestrained competition at national terminals had depressed long-haul rates, often below cost, and forced the carriers to make up losses through high rates on noncompetitive traffic. The object of the pool, he claimed, was precisely to dampen such competition. Rate agreements were unstable, however, and when cartel members secretly defected, Fink and other pool managers had no recourse at law. Only legalized and enforceable cartels, he told Congress, would do away with destructive competition on long-haul traffic and bring regional markets into parity.[61]

Until the great railway mergers at the century's turn there was substantial support for legalized pools among railroad managers—if not to check discrimination, at least to moderate rate competition. It was this opinion that Gabriel Kolko sampled in his pathbreaking study.[62] Kolko's thesis that management was responsible for railroad regulation has since been criticized for ignoring counterevidence, and rightly so. Still, Kolko and his critics share equally in their economic reductionism. Even though he remains correct to argue that railroad management hoped to subdue internecine competition, Kolko systematically underestimates the means available for doing so: cartels, regulation, intercorporate ownership, holding companies, and communities of interest. The choice among means inevitably confronted management with ends. For a project this ambitious necessitated allies in the market and in politics, and which turned out to be the best among the options available depended upon who railroad managers learned to count on. Although they found ample support for state-enforced pools in the Senate, it became clear that the costs of public enforcement were high: Congress would place substantive restraints upon ratemaking that flew in the face of many of the interregionals' national market strategy. By contrast, railroad system builders found in investment bankers and the federal courts durable allies, aligned in support of corporate consolidation and national market development. Therefore, intercorporate ownership or "communities of interest" emerged from the turn-of-the-century merger wave as the most viable means to dampen competition.[63]

If Kolko has been criticized, he has also been turned on his head by those who argue that state-supervised pools would have served public, not private, interests. Following Fink and Adams, Albro Martin and Stephen Skowronek argue that only publicly enforced cartels could have solved the dual problem of discrimination and profitability. On this view, House opposition to pools was at best unwise; at worst, it was irrational, rooted in a "deep-seated mistrust, hatred and fear of large, insulated aggregations of power," public or private—an attitude, Martin writes, "which has always rested at the heart of

American equalitarianism." Such sentiments led John Reagan to ignore the obvious relationship between discrimination and competition and blindly serve constituent interests in redistribution.[64] Some in Congress opposed pooling for just such reasons, while others were convinced by Fink and Adams. Many regionalists, Reagan and Wilson among them, were unconvinced that pooling would equalize rates; experience had taught them to mistrust this claim. They had observed too many examples where pools had simply published existing rate schedules and then attempted to enforce them, or still worse, where they had explicitly devised discriminatory schedules. For example, cartels in livestock, oil, and anthracite coal, Reagan charged, had colluded with railroad pools to provide secret rebates to their members. The result, not surprisingly, forced independent producers to the wall.[65]

These complaints have been corroborated for the South by an exhaustive historical study of freight rates by William Joubert. Under Fink's presidency, Joubert concludes, the Southern Railway and Steamship Association (SRSA), left its members with a "virtual monopoly over local rates." The cartel sanctioned "high local rates," remained "deaf to the pleas of shippers in small communities for reductions and forcefully opposed all efforts to effect such reductions."[66] The pool's "basing point system" also favored national market development. The SRSA established key cities as basing points and then made rates to all other locations in their designated districts by adding the through rate to the basing point to the local rate from the basing point to a final destination.[67] The result, complained one wholesale grocer from Atlanta, was to give Nashville, an SRSA basing point, systematic advantages over its neighbors. Shippers from Charleston, Richmond, and Montgomery levied similar charges.[68]

In principle state-supervised pools could have achieved regional republican goals. That is, a regulatory commission empowered to enforce pooling agreements and to ensure that rate schedules were consistent with the principles of equal access could have dampened rate competition and granted parity to regional shippers. Prior to his tenure as the first Chair of the ICC, Thomas McIntyre Cooley had argued this point. So too did the head of the ICC's Statistics Department, Henry Carter Adams.[69]

Regional republicans saw the gulf between words and deeds as insurmountable. Experience had taught them to mistrust the advocates of pools among the intellectuals. Fink and Adams, especially, were seen as Janus-faced: though advocates of parity for the smaller scale regional shipper in theory, they had both practiced the most egregious sorts of discrimination as pool managers. As Henry Hudson wrote in attacking the weak Massachusetts-style commission, "The power [of the railroads] which has converted the Charles Francis Adams of 1875 [critic of Jay Gould] to the Charles Francis Adams of 1885 [advocate of pools] cannot be conquered by any body of 9 men at salaries of $7500 each."[70] Only the strict use of constitutional police power would solve the discrimination problem.

Of course, railroad pools were not the only culprits; the same evils might result from other private methods of controlling competition, such as interlocking directorates or intercorporate shareholding. Stickney put the matter this way: he, for one, had "little confidence, in the present crisis of railway affairs, that the proposed remedies of consolidation, pools etc. will be efficacious, if the plain principles of equity in the construction of tariffs are ignored."[71] Unless management was forced to reconsider its obsession with long-haul bulk freight, no organizational strategy to dampen competition would resolve the problem of financial stability or the fight between Congress and the railroads.

In practice, a strict law against rate discrimination, argued Wilson, would solve the very problem pool advocates had identified. If traffic at noncompetitive points bore the undue burden of cross-subsidizing rate wars at competitive locations, this would be impossible under a regime that outlawed charging more for short haul than long haul. But more important, like Stickney's account of the Granger Laws, it might provide grounds for cooperation. "It will serve the true interests of the railroads," Wilson said, "because it will prevent the foolish, wasteful, and demoralizing rate wars; for no railroad company will grant a less than remunerative rate for through freight if it can not unload its loss on the local stations along its line. It will serve the interests of the people whose business goes to and from local stations, because it will assure them at least as reasonable rates as are given to others . . ."[72] Antidiscrimination law strictly enforced would serve to regulate competition as effectively, and more justly, than state-enforced pools.

Although the latter were politically impossible in 1887, so too were Granger-style rate schedules. Stickney, for instance, argued that only a federal commission empowered to make, revise, and enforce a detailed national rate schedule, graduated by distance and calculated on the basis of average revenues, could serve the interests of regionalists in fair trade and the railroads in a reasonable rate of return. The call for public ratemaking powers, however, fell on deaf ears for nearly two more decades. In 1886 a compromise, short of both pooling and public ratemaking, seemed imminent. Even though the Senate had found an antidote to Wilson in the conservative chair of the Interstate Commerce Committee, Shelby Cullom, it could no longer hold back the clamor for antidiscrimination law. According to the Cullom Committee Report:

The [railroad] policy which has been pursued has given us the most efficient service and the lowest rates known in the world; but its recognized
benefits have been obtained at the cost of the most unwarranted discrimination, and its effect has been to build up the strong at the expense of the
weak, to give the large dealer an advantage over the small trader, to make
capital count for more than individual credit and enterprise, to concentrate business at great commercial centers, to necessitate combinations
and aggregations of capital, to foster monopoly, to encourage the growth
and extend the influence of corporate power, and to throw the control of
the commerce of the country more and more into the hands of the few.[73]

Discrimination, the report concluded, was at the very heart of the railway
problem. The "universal complaint has been made to the committee as to
the discriminations commonly practiced against places, and as to conspicuous discrepancies between what are usually termed 'local' rates and what are
known as 'through' rates."[74]

In principle, then, the Senate Interstate Commerce Bill (stamped with
Cullom's name) made all forms of rate discrimination unlawful. Yet it remained decidedly weak on the issue of charging more for long- than short-
haul carriage: the bill allowed for unnamed exceptions, claiming only that
like charges ought to be enforced for transportation under similar circumstances. Further, the Senate bill neither outlawed nor legalized railroad
pools. It did, however, provide for a five-member commission to investigate
and then remedy violations of the law. Though ambiguous in its definition of
reasonable rates and in exceptions to discriminatory practice, the mark of regional republicanism was clearly upon the Senate's proposal. Cullom's committee itself said that

the provisions of the bill are based upon the theory that the paramount
evil chargeable against the operation of the transportation system of the
United States as now conducted is unjust discrimination between persons,
places, commodities or particular descriptions of traffic. The underlying
purpose and aim of the measure is the prevention of these discriminations,
both by declaring them unlawful and adding to the remedies now available for securing redress and enforcing punishment and also by requiring
the greatest practicable degree of publicity as to the rates, financial operations, and method of management of the carriers.[75]

By contrast to the Senate, Reagan's House Bill on Interstate Commerce
specified unlawful forms of discrimination in some detail. For example, in a
strongly worded clause, it declared that under no circumstances should there

be greater charges for short-haul freight than for long-haul freight. Further, the House Bill declared pools illegal, and, in lieu of a commission, left enforcement to the judiciary. Once more Reagan guided his legislation through the House, where in April of 1886 it passed with ease (192 to 41).[76]

The Interstate Commerce Act of 1887 emerged from conference committee a compromise: railroad pools were made unlawful, the long-haul–short-haul clause was qualified, and Reagan agreed to a five-member Interstate Commerce Commission empowered to investigate and prosecute violators. Though a middle course, regional republicans had won a limited victory: in principle the law granted parity to the smaller scale, regional shipper. However, since the Interstate Commerce Commission had no authority to enforce rate schedules, nor to oversee pools, a large burden would be placed on the cooperation of the carriers. Would they fall into line with the intent of the law, raise their rates on competitive traffic and lower them for noncompetitive carriage? As with the Granger Laws, this remained to be seen.

The Interstate Commerce Commission

The Interstate Commerce Commission earnestly tried to rid the nation of rate discrimination. Its failures were not for lack of a coherent theory of regulation. Nor were they because the ICC was stillborn with an inherently contradictory mission, namely, enabling legislation that outlawed discrimination but venerated its cause, competition, by proscribing pools.[77] Admittedly, the problem of competition at some terminals and monopoly at others remained to be solved. The Interstate Commerce Act was equivocal on this and other important policies. Nonetheless, under the sure hand of its first chair, Thomas McIntyre Cooley, the commission faced these issues squarely and elaborated a practical doctrine consistent with the republican and geographic premises of the regionalists in Congress.

Thomas McIntyre Cooley

The ICC could have found no better chair for this task than Judge Cooley. Free Soiler in his youth, Cooley was committed to antebellum republican ideals—free soil, free labor, free education—and thus predisposed to regional republican goals: market decentralization, substantive equality, and widespread proprietorship.[78] More important, Cooley had long tackled the constitutional issues germane to his task on the commission, namely, the limits to legislative power and corporate theory. Author of the influential treatise *Constitutional Limitations*, justice on the Michigan Supreme Court, and receiver for the eastern division of the Wabash, Cooley had established a cogent, if an increasingly heterodox, position on these critical issues in Gilded Age political economy. While Field's corporate liberalism gained an ever-larger following on the federal bench and the Supreme Court as the century waned, Cooley became more and more willing to use the state to achieve substantive ideals. Like his Jacksonian mentor, William Leggett, he was instinctively cautious about the use of the legislative power in service of regulation or special privilege. This antebellum reluctance to use the state was not so much rooted in a liberal commitment to the prepolitical sanctity of property and contract (laissez faire), but rather was a pledge to substantive equality. Like Leggett, Cooley thought the state had been captured all too often by private power. He had seen how legislation was used repeatedly to secure and to institutionalize class privilege.

No more egregious example could be found than the special corporate charter. For Cooley and the radical Jacksonians it had become a threefold assault on republican principles. First, those granted special charters had surrendered their independence to the state. Second, once small numbers attained corporate privilege, the many became dependent upon the few. Such class legislation, in other words, doubly corrupted: the privileged lost their independence to the state and the disadvantaged lost their independence to the privileged. In neither case were such individuals able to shoulder the burdens of democratic citizenship. Finally, the special charter corrupted the state as well by thwarting its rightful purpose to represent the people as a whole.[79]

As late as the 1870s, Cooley complained of the abuse of corporate charters in Jacksonian language. On the Michigan bench he attacked land grants to railroad corporations as an example of "illegitimate," "unjust," and "corrupt" surrender to the prejudices of a class. "The state," he said, "can have no favorites. Its business is to protect the industry of all, and to give all the benefit of equal laws."[80] Like regionalists and greenbackers, as the century wore on, Cooley became more and more willing to use the legislative power to achieve republican ends: widespread property ownership, decentralization and equality before the law. Perhaps the most profound indication of this lay in his changing conception of the corporation. By 1883 he conceded that the state's franchise power had been routinely used to advance public, not private, ends since the Civil War. Nonetheless, Cooley faced Field's problem, namely, how to place limits on franchise powers. Approaching the problem from republican, rather than liberal, foundations, he articulated a remarkably different conception of corporate jurisprudence (and by implication, regulation).

Industrialization and urban growth, Cooley wrote in 1883, had expanded the domain of legitimate public needs—in public health, safety, communications, and transportation. Although government provision of public goods "apparently is most consistent with republican institutions, for it grants no favors, and does not complicate individual with governmental affairs, . . . in practice it is found subject to very serious objections."[81] The cost of many public projects, like railroads, was well beyond the public will to tax. Besides, experience had shown that more often than not huge public projects suffered from patronage. The play of partisan politics, he went on, failed to recruit the expertise necessary to manage "railways, lighting works, the telegraph or the telephone." The public franchise, then, proved a better option.

Nevertheless, "to grant such a franchise is to give special privilege which presumably has pecuniary value . . . [and] to prefer some citizens . . . over citizens in general." Railroad corporations, especially, "have the aid of eminent domain," tax breaks, and subsidies. "All of these special favors which they receive from the State . . . enable them to set up and carry on with profit their businesses as common carriers; and the inducement—if not the right—to grant them must be found in the fact that they are created to *subserve* public ends."[82]

Once the franchise had been granted, the corporator secured a vested interest in its privileges, hence the right to due process. Vested interests, however, were no more than rights sanctioned by the community. As such they were open to periodic evaluation and revision. The charter, then, did not vest the corporation with unassailable property rights. Nor did it bind the state in a contract whose "sacredness [was] supposed to inhere in public compacts and treaties." Customary and conventional as franchise rights were, legitimate only for public purposes, Cooley argued that the state always retained the right to repeal or revise the terms of charter. Otherwise, it would have "bartered away a large part of its ability to be useful to the people."[83]

This did not mean that the state could arbitrarily repeal a charter or take corporate property; the corporation, like the individual, was subject to due process. Cooley's idea of due process, like his notion of property, was sharply at odds with corporate liberals like Field. For them property was a presocial right, "given," as Justice Brewer put it, "not by man to man, but granted by the Almighty to everyone: something which he has by virtue of his manhood, which he may not surrender, and *of which he cannot be deprived*."[84] Due process, on this view, meant that individuals had natural rights which required protection, as Field put it, "from the vagaries of government." Public takings of property, whether by eminent domain or regulation, were only justified when judges found property invested in public use. Private property —"ordinary trades"—must always be protected by due process from encroachment by the state (or, for that matter, by other private interests). In the more complicated case of "private concerns with public duties," it was the court's responsibility to identify an empirically observable boundary between the public and private aspects of the economic activity in question. Once accomplished, corporate property rights would be protected from public takings.

By contrast, for Cooley all rights of any meaningful determinacy in practice were political and historical: hence, subject to collective evaluation and revision. Property was no exception. "Strictly speaking," he wrote, "there are no rights but those which are creatures of the law." Though charter entitlements were vested, they were neither natural nor perpetually locked in by contractual commitment. Subject to due process, corporate property could not be *arbitrarily* deprived. By due process, however, Cooley meant something quite different than Field: "No man shall be deprived of life, liberty, or property," he wrote *"except by those established principles which govern him alike with every member of the community."*[85] Cooley "dismissed those who spoke of natural rights which government must recognize by doubting whether 'nature had indicated any clear line which the human intellect and conscience would infallibly recognize.'"[86] His was a broad, historical and conventional view of both property and due process.

As Cooley saw it, the corporation was a public entity, which vested its private beneficiaries with rights of due process. Though nonarbitrary, vested rights were neither absolute nor presocial entitlements. Like the terms of the public franchise itself, the rights of the corporation were both historical and social. This was not to imply that the task of pinning down corporate and state obligations with some precision was hopeless. To the contrary, Cooley thought good legislation, whether drafting charters or regulations, would define sharp boundaries to acceptable behavior for both parties. Still, within the confines of legitimate state and corporate behavior, it was possible to locate grounds for cooperation. For ultimately, Cooley wrote, "the charter is granted for the *mutual benefit* of the State and the corporators."[87]

This was a remarkably different picture of business-government relations than the one drawn by Field. While both saw the public-private distinction along a continuum, Cooley pictured it as a moving one, changing over time, and subject to collective redefinition. For Field, the continuum was fixed in natural right and the empirical characteristics of economic activity. And while Cooley thought that convention—even legislation—could define the outer boundaries of legitimate state and corporate behavior, Field thought courts could only discover empirically verifiable parameters by which to draw a bright line between public and private rights. Moreover, given the inherent conflict of proximate interests between state and corporation, according to Field, it was for the court to draw the line. For Cooley, by contrast, once the outer bounds of obligation were drawn, the task was to locate the mutual interests of state and corporation that lay between.[88]

Regulated Competition

Cooley came to the commission in 1887 fresh from his tenure as receiver for the eastern division of the Wabash. Like the judge who had appointed him, Walter Gresham, Cooley had been passed over for a Supreme Court appointment in favor of laissez-faire liberal (and Field's nephew) David Brewer. (Predictably, Gresham and Cooley had proposed one another for the high court.) If Cooley's differences with Brewer and Field were profound in principle, on Court and commission they clashed in practice. Under Cooley's guidance, the ICC elaborated the doctrine of regulated competition, which not only subjected private ratemaking to strict public norms but also located terms upon which the regionalist's claim to parity and railroad's claim to cost recovery could be mutually served. But state-grown cooperation between regional shippers and railroads was short-lived. Scrutinizing the Interstate Commerce Act through Field's liberal positivism, the Court denied legitimacy to regulated competition, and in so doing, animated the most adversarial elements in the industry.

Nowhere was this story more telling than in ICC policy on the fourth section of the Interstate Commerce Act, which outlawed the practice of charging more for the short haul than the long haul over the same line. Herein lay a cornerstone to the smaller shippers' entitlement to parity and the potential to institutionalize intensive intraregional trade. Nevertheless, the long-haul–short-haul clause was not without ambiguity. Under Senate pressure, the Interstate Commerce Act provided for exceptions to the law strictly enforced. In principle, the statute declared that all charges ought to be alike under similar circumstances. What, then, constituted dissimilarity? Under what conditions could the carriers depart from the fourth section and still achieve "just and reasonable" rates?

For railroads who chose to challenge the long-haul–short-haul rule, the answer lay in the law broadly interpreted. Cost differences and competition, pleaded the Louisville and Nashville Railroad, were sufficient reasons to charge proportionately less for through traffic. It might be that higher costs "support a greater charge" for the short haul, the ICC admitted, but this was the exception, and railroads would carry the burden of proof. Competition, on the other hand, was not generally a "dissimilar circumstance." To hold otherwise "would create the disparity of rates . . . the statute seeks to prevent."[89]

While Congress, Cooley wrote, had intended to preserve competition (after all, this had been one reason to outlaw pools), it had also meant to *regulate* it. As he saw it, the problem for legislators and regulators alike was to distinguish "legitimate, open and fair competition" from that which was "equally destructive of public and private right."[90] Though the former had recognized competition as the "life of trade," they had also learned that "the common abuses . . . [of] rebates, drawbacks . . . and favoritism between places and communities were the result of violent competition." When unrestrained competition resulted in the common practice of carrying traffic below cost and foisting the revenue gap onto noncompetitive traffic, this "ceased to be legitimate." "Fair and reasonable competition," Cooley added, "is a public benefit, excessive and unreasonable competition is a public injury," or, to put the point another way, "*competition is to be regulated, not abolished.*"[91]

If competition alone was to be considered a legitimate dissimilarity of circumstance, he wrote in 1893, "any railroad might by its action absolve a competitor from its obligation, and be itself absolved in return," thereby making "the rule of the statute ineffectual."[92] Only when regulated carriers faced competition from unregulated transportation—foreign railroads or water carriers—would the ICC agree to relax the long-haul–short-haul clause. Otherwise, regulated competition would rule.

True to his public, yet mutualist, theory of the corporation, Cooley pleaded for cooperation from the carriers. Privately, he wrote, "The great need of the day was to reform the railroad managers"; publicly, he pleaded that antidiscrimination law would be in the railroad's, as well as the shipper's, interest.[93] Regulated competition "tend[s] very greatly to the maintenance of steadiness in rates," he wrote, "and in that respect renders it of great advantage not only to the public at large but . . . to the carriers themselves."[94] It "would benefit the[ir] revenues . . . not deplete them; it would make all traffic more evenly remunerative, and at the same time [relieve] very much traffic from the weight of burdens which were before relatively unjust."[95] As regionalists had long argued, the long-haul–short-haul clause had "important possibilities as a restraint upon reckless rate wars. The reduction when such wars are in progress has generally been made . . . at competitive points a considerable distance apart," Cooley explained, "and when a reduction of rates at such points involves also the reduction to or from a great number of intermediate points, a resort to a cutting of rates that goes beyond the warrant of *legitimate competition* becomes unlikely in proportion as it would be injurious to the party inaugurating it."[96] The fourth section strictly enforced would serve both the claims of regionalists to parity and those of the railroad to a legitimate return on investment.

ICC efforts to cultivate cooperation were not limited to its interpretation of the fourth section alone. In particular, the commission looked broadly at the antipooling clause of the Interstate Commerce Act. Not until 1898 did the ICC move against railroad pools—and then, only once it was under attack by the Supreme Court and intransigent carriers. In the meanwhile, Cooley looked on benignly as cartels adjusted their policies to meet the letter of the law. The Trunkline Pool, for instance, abandoned its practice of predesignating shares of tonnage to its members as a clear violation of the law. Instead, it would attempt to achieve the same ends through the price mechanism, now made official and public by the Interstate Commerce Act. Any member losing market share could now petition the Trunkline Pool's executive committee for a price adjustment, which, once granted, would be registered publicly with the commission.

Under Cooley's guidance, regulated competition went a long way toward achieving mutual gains and eliciting cooperation from the carriers. In 1887 the Trunkline Pool's executive committee agreed to a general strategy of compliance to the fourth section: members would adjust most local rates down and some through rates upward to "establish rough comparability with . . . average local rate[s]."[97] Taking the lead among the trunks, the Pennsylvania Railroad announced an array of rate changes on its local and through classifications between Chicago and New York. The Lake Shore and Michigan Southern, the New York Central, and other trunklines followed. In the South and West, as well, a number of roads signaled their intention to "increase long haul or through rates" in order to comply with the fourth section of the law.[98]

By 1890 the ICC proudly announced it "is pleasing to be able to state . . . that the carriers, looking only to their own interests and the satisfaction of the general public, are moving steadily in the direction of bringing their rates into proportionality [and] uniformity with those generally prevailing."[99] At the end of its first decade, the commission proclaimed that the most obnoxious cases of rate discrimination had been nearly eliminated. The regionalist goals of the Interstate Commerce Act, it seemed, had been achieved.

Moreover, true to Cooley's appeal to cooperation, regulated competition also served rate stability and railroad revenues. Paul MacAvoy's elaborate study of trunkline competition from 1871 to 1899 shows how early ICC policy increased the cost of cheating on official rates, thereby moderating the periodic rate wars that devastated the industry. Since all rates were registered publicly with the commission, secret rateshaving became unlawful in practice under the Interstate Commerce Act. Moreover, in order to comply with the fourth section, "any rate cut that was 'just and reasonable' had to be extended to all traffic." Consequently, rents gained from cutting long-haul rates had to be "accompanied by lower profits from the required cutting of local rates." Also, since all discounts were to be announced, this "reduced the length of time in which the disloyal firm received larger profits."[100] MacAvoy concludes that by increasing the cost of cheating on public schedules, the ICC effectively stabilized trunkline rates between 1887 and 1893. Even when a minor rate war erupted during the depression of 1893, it was shallower and shorter-lived than those of the previous decades. Although subsequent studies have qualified MacAvoy's conclusions, none has found that strict enforcement of the fourth section harmed long-line railroads during the first decade of regulation.[101]

Nevertheless, business-government cooperation was short-lived. So too were the regional goals of the Interstate Commerce Act, as the doctrine of regulated competition came under scrutiny by a federal judiciary steeped more and more in Field's corporate liberalism. As early as 1892, the federal courts began to chip away at the doctrine of regulated competition. In a series of cases concerning ratemaking across connecting, but legally independent, lines, the court struck down the ICC's method of utilizing joint long-haul tariffs to calculate violations to the long-haul–short-haul clause. For such purposes, the court said, the ICC had to consider all joint tariffs as "separate but independent."[102] This position, the commission complained, made *all* connecting roads, which cooperated in making joint through rates, exempt from section four of the Act to Regulate Commerce. As such, it would license "open defiance" to the law and give "character and force to the opposition against the [fourth] section."[103]

The ICC was prescient: the federal courts had opened a gash in the law through which the least cooperative of the railroads now mounted a relentless offensive. By 1897 they had won. In *Alabama Midland* the Supreme Court gutted ICC doctrine on what constituted a "dissimilarity of circumstance." Not only joint ratemaking, but competition itself, the Court declared, justified a departure from the law strictly enforced. This case involved a southern carrier who had charged a substantially higher absolute rate from Florida to Troy, Alabama, than to Montgomery, even though the former was en route to the latter. In overturning the ICC's ruling against the railroad, the Court held that greater competition at Montgomery justified the lower rate. Besides, added Justice Shiras writing for the majority, traffic managers for the Alabama Midland Railway had not personally discriminated against shippers in Troy, Alabama, in favor of Montgomery. They had merely responded to the workings of the market.[104]

Twenty years had passed since *Munn* v. *Illinois* and Field's distinction between ordinary trades and those affected with the public interest now flowered on the high court. Competition, the Court suggested with weighty persuasion, made ratemaking in Montgomery a private affair. Therefore, the carrier was entitled to overlook the rule. Market competition, in other words, made ratemaking an "ordinary trade," better regulated by contract than command. The Court, however, did not stop there; it also reconsidered the facts. Although it eventually agreed to limit review, in principle, to procedure, the high court was compelled to examine substance.[105] How else would it realize Field's liberal positivist mission to identify the empirical boundary between public and private? After all, from this vantage point establishing "just and reasonable" rates was no more than an empirical question.[106]

This said, the Court and the commission weighed different facts. From a liberal positivist perspective, regulated competition was unintelligible, an oxymoron. If some aspects of ratemaking were ordinary market transactions, competition would guarantee a just price. If property was protected, railroad and shipper would devise mutually advantageous contracts. Had the carrier, on this view, intentionally discriminated against shippers in Troy, it would be in violation of its public function—an obligation to serve all customers without prejudice. In the former case, competition best regulated rates, in the latter the state best regulated rates.

The Court was equally muddled from the commission's perspective. Recall Cooley's thinking on the subject: since property rights were social conventions, "ordinary" market transactions were a fantasy. Contract was the inescapable subject of common law norms. It was precisely on this logic, Cooley argued, that Congress had introduced a parity rule for competition into the Interstate Commerce Act. Section four (the long-haul–short-haul clause) delimited railroad property rights and provided a uniform standard for all shipping contracts.

By 1898 the Supreme Court and the Interstate Commerce Commission talked past one another. "To hold that . . . competition might be shown as creating a necessary dissimilarity which would take the case out of the fourth section," the commission said in response to the *Alabama Midland*, "would be to hold that the very same thing which it was intended to prohibit by . . . statute might be shown as an excuse for violation of the statute." If so, "there is nothing left for the section to act upon."[107] That is to say, by declaring that "railway competition between carriers . . . creates a necessary dissimilarity of circumstances and conditions, [the court] necessarily overturns the procedure of the Commission under that section up to the present time, and virtually nullifies the section itself."[108] This was, however, to conclude the absurd, namely, that Congress had "enact[ed] a law and . . . at the same time [guaranteed] that it should be of no effect."[109]

Still, the Supreme Court insisted the ICC's logic was fallacious: "It confounds cause and effect," Justice White wrote in 1900. "For, if the preference occasioned in favor of a particular place by competition there gives rise to the right to charge the lesser rate to that point, it cannot be that the availing of this right is the cause of the preference." Competition meant that ratemaking fell to the private side of the distinction. Of course, "there might be cases where the carrier cannot be allowed to avail [itself of] the competitive condition because of the public interests," but this was not one.[110]

Taken together with the rulings on railroad receiverships, the high court seemed to be saying that as long as the corporation was deemed a natural entity, it was vested with rights prior to the state. Those rights, however, were not derived from individual proprietors, but from the corporation's status as an organic entity. If the large-scale incorporated railroad system had a natural status derived from economic necessity, so too did the market (or what was left of it). So in the first instance—the law of receiverships—the economic necessity of system integrity overrode the individual contractual obligation of the corporation. While in the second, market competition—not management "incompetence" or "bias of personal preference"—determined rates. In neither case was management exercising arbitrary, self-serving, or particularistic powers over individuals (shippers or shareholders). Field's liberal positivism, it seems, had successfully assimilated the large-scale railroad system and the Interstate Commerce Act to its natural entity theory of the corporation. Corporate liberalism had triumphed.

Only Justice Harlan made sense of Cooley's architecture and the doctrine of regulated competition. In *Alabama Midland,* he forcefully reminded the majority of the regional republican intent of the law and the consequences of its ruling.

> Taken in connection with other decisions defining the powers of the Interstate Commerce Commission the present decision goes far to make that commission a useless body . . . The acts of Congress are now so construed as to place communities on the line of interstate commerce at the mercy of competing railroad companies engaged in such commerce. The judgement in this case . . . proceed[s] upon the ground that railroad companies, when competitors for interstate business at certain points, may, in order to secure traffic for and at those points establish such rates that will enable them to accomplish that result, although such rates may discriminate against intermediate points. Under such an interpretation of the statutes in

question, they may well be regarded as recognizing the authority of competing railroad companies engaged in interstate commerce—when their interests will be subserved thereby—to build up favored centers of population at the expense of the business of the country at large. I cannot believe that congress intended such a result, nor do I think its enactments, properly interpreted, would lead to such a result.[111]

From this point on, the ICC began to rethink its mission. Under attack from intransigent carriers and the federal courts, the commission abandoned regulated competition and cooperation. It signaled as much by reversing its position on pools: either they should be legalized and regulated as natural monopolies, the ICC now argued, or broken up under the Sherman Antitrust Act and competition enforced. If the cost of the former was to monopolize the industry, then so be it. The commission no longer considered it competitive anyway. The "railroad," it declared in 1898, "is essentially a monopoly."[112] The trouble as the ICC now saw it was this: since monopolization remained incomplete, the remnants of competition caused rate wars and discrimination. Regulatory reform, then, ought to "exclude the idea of competition" altogether. Instead, the state should grant the carriers monopoly status, encourage and enforce the organization of pools, and regulate maximum rates. In other words, "if [the railroad] is essentially a monopoly, then it must be [price] regulated. The two things," the ICC concluded, "of necessity go hand in hand."[113]

The prospects for legalized pools and regulated monopoly were politically remote before the turn of the century. Therefore the commission informed the Justice Department that the trunkline's Joint Traffic Association was likely in violation of the antipooling provisions of the Interstate Commerce Act and the newly enacted Sherman Antitrust Act.[114] By the time the dust had settled from *Alabama Midland*, the Supreme Court had declared both the Trans-Missouri Freight Association and the Joint Traffic Association in violation of the Sherman law. Thus Field's liberal distinction between ordinary trades and those affected with public obligations had triumphed. Regulated competition—a doctrine which acknowledged the inherently political nature of property and contract, and the need to cultivate cooperation between corporators and the democratic state—would become less and less accessible to public policy. Only enforced competition or regulated monopoly respected the bright line the high court endeavored to draw between public and private.

The effects on the industry were predictable. "Within five days from the reading of the decision of the Court [in *Alabama Midland*], the Trans-Missouri Freight Bureau filed schedules to raise rates at intermediate points on over 100,000 square miles of territory."[115] Parity for regional trade was no longer secure. Nor was rate stability. Notwithstanding the trunklines' success in containing a depression-induced rate war by early 1896, demoralization resumed in 1898.[116] With the ICC's authority to enforce section four, rectify "unjust rates" and maintain public schedules for extended periods of time defunct, the penalties for ratecutting disappeared. Regulated competition no longer served either regional shippers or the carriers.[117]

Relative rate stability did re-emerge after the turn of the century, when wholesale mergers and intercorporate shareholding forged "communities of interest" among many competitive carriers. Management turned to investment bankers and a judicially furnished reorganization technology to secure what it could no longer get from regulation. Legal parity for regional trade, by contrast, would await another decade before Congress expunged the phrase "under similar conditions" from the long-haul–short-haul clause in the Mann-Elkins Act of 1910. Regionalism's moment had all but passed by then. Settlement and trade remained extremely sensitive to national market ratemaking. By the First World War, railroads had become the backbone to a national landscape we have come to associate with the modern corporation and mass production. Dominant firms, like Swift and Armour in meatpacking, Standard Oil, U.S. Steel, and American Tobacco were able to centralize production in Minneapolis, Chicago, Durham, and New York City. As Chandler has pointed out, the structure of twentieth-century American industry was virtually in place by 1917. Many of the largest firms on the eve of war were the same firms that remained more than a half century later.[118]

Regionalism became a faded memory in the twentieth century, as it fell more and more to the margins of debate. The commission admitted as much in its first general policy statement on short-haul discrimination after Mann-Elkins went into effect: *Arlington Heights Fruit Exchange* v. *Southern Pacific*. Ruling on blanket rates for citrus fruit from California east, the ICC conceded that it could find no legal or policy reason to replace the existing rate structure, which charged the same for all mileage east of the Rockies, with one graded by distance. At the same time, the regulators noted the intimate relationship between rate structure and market landscape with marked ambivalence. The ICC's authority to rule on section four, admitted Commissioner Lane, "involves a question of the highest national importance. What is to be our policy with respect to the movement of traffic? Shall the country be treated as a whole for commercial purposes, or shall it be infinitely divided?"

For the railroads, "there is no uniform policy, even upon the same lines or systems." As Lane saw it, the choice among possible "ratemaking systems" was a political one:

> The people may say (1) that railroad rates shall be made so as to carry all products into all markets within the four lines of the country; or (2) that after a certain narrow limit is passed the whole of the land shall be one zone; or (3) a system of rates that will keep producers and consumers as near together as possible and eliminate waste in transportation. These are national questions. They go to the very future of our industrial life. Upon their determination depends the character of the farm products and the nature of the industries in various sections of the country.

Lane had no memory of the twenty-year debate leading up to the Interstate Commerce Act of 1887. "Perhaps," he speculated, "the United States will one day declare a policy of its own in this regard." The substantive intent of the 1887 statute had become unintelligible. Although he well understood that regulation could not create a level playing ground, the choice among ratemaking principles—each of which was discriminatory—seemed arbitrary. Therefore, concurring in a unanimous opinion, Lane capitulated to the status quo. "Without any expression of policy from Congress," he concluded, "we accept the policy which the railroads themselves have made"—namely, national market ratemaking.[119]

From Regional Republicanism to Pluralist Theory

Standing before Congress in 1905, a first-term senator from Wisconsin recounted the long struggle for regionalism from the Granger Laws to *Alabama Midland* and beyond. Robert LaFollette reminded his colleagues that

> [t]he experience of the American public in its effort to secure fair treatment at the hands of the railroads has been a record of bitter disappointment . . . There is nothing in the record of railway domination of the industrial development of this country which should deter us from taking that domination "out of the hands of the railways." On the contrary there is much to demand such an action. The mainspring of the railway policy that decides which centers shall succeed and which shall fail, is the selfish interest of the carrier. It has no concern in the promotion of commerce in the public interest. The *social economy* of serving a given territory from the center which would serve it best and cheapest, the economy of the multiplication of convenient centers of trade and industry, of the building up of

many small cities well distributed over the country, is disregarded. It does not suit the schemes of the traffic managers. Their aim is the long haul, the big tonnage, the large revenues, and the dividend. To these considerations all else is sacrificed.[120]

The effect of railway rate policy, LaFollette added, had been to centralize the "bulk of the country's commerce . . . at four points across the continent, the Atlantic coast, the head of the great Lakes, the Missouri River, and the Pacific coast." All interior points were left fighting for residual trade. When any citizen came to realize the "tremendous influence upon the economic and social life of the people with all its consequences to this generation and generations to come, he will be shocked that it should be left in the hands of the traffic managers of railroads." "The control of commerce," LaFollette argued in the tradition of the public theory of the corporation, ought to "go to the upbuilding of the state, the nation. It must be controlled unselfishly, controlled with the highest patriotism, upon a broad national policy."[121]

Nevertheless, LaFollette's memory of the *public* spirit of regional republicanism was rapidly fading from public memory. The ICC acknowledged as much well before Arlington Fruit. By the time Congress debated regulatory reform in 1910, many Americans believed that the struggle over rate discrimination had never been anything more than a clash of private interests. Arguing against the initiative to strengthen the long-haul–short-haul clause in 1908, the Senate's sponsor of the 1910 statute, Stephen B. Elkins (D. W. Va.), was prophetic.

What is satisfactory to one community does not satisfy another. Every railroad tried to build up the communities which are situated on the road. There is always rivalry between railroads in that respect and jealousy between communities . . . Now you cannot satisfy all shippers and all sections of this country. Shippers always want lower rates and always will; they will never be satisfied . . . You can not, by legislation, possibly settle the rate relationship between communities. What [those who propose to strengthen section four] want is to confer a power upon the commission which they can not exercise—to adjust the rates between communities. One community that is not as well favored naturally says, "I want the same rate that some other community gets," or "I want a better rate; I am not being treated right." It is not the fault of the railroads that a man lives in Los Angeles, San Francisco, or Chicago, and therefore has more advantages than a man living in Salt Lake. He went to Los Angeles and these great centers because of these great natural advantages. These are conditions against which you can not legislate . . . Do not try to reverse the laws of Providence, but move out and go to those cities, and then you will have perfect satisfaction. You can not live and do business in Utah and Montana and at the same time enjoy all the advantages of living in the great cities I have named, and no act of Congress can make the advantages equal or the conditions the same.[122]

Elkins and like-minded politicians lost the proximate battle over the long-haul–short-haul clause. But their worldview triumphed over LaFollette's. If the ICC recognized the need for a universal ratemaking principle in 1911 but was at wits' end to choose among the candidates, as time wore on every general rule seemed to mask private interests. By midcentury, this corporate liberal perspective had become fully internalized in pluralist political science and interest group history. In the scholarship on railroad regulation, Earl Latham's classic 1952 study of the politics of the basing point system, *The Group Basis of Politics*, and Lee Bensen's 1955 study of railroad regulation in New York concluded that all politics was group conflict. The problem for political science, therefore, was to explain who got what, how, and why.[123]

Recent studies of American political development have made great strides beyond the pluralist scholarship of the 1950s. In particular, two recent bodies of work have challenged the genesis amnesia of intellectuals at midcentury. Historians of nineteenth-century republicanism and the state-centered new institutionalism have gone a long way toward challenging the idea that all politics is simply "partisan mutual adjustment" among private interests who agree over the rules of the game. The first body of work has gone a long way toward recovering ideological conflict between producer-conscious workers, farmers, or petty proprietors and corporate elites. The second has shown in some detail how autonomous state institutions shaped societal interests and the trajectory of political (under)development in twentieth-century America. Still, as far as these two research programs have gone, the full extent of institutional alternatives in state and economy have remained largely inaccessible to them.

In the first instance, though new social and labor historians have found the republican ideology of cooperation, civic humanism, or class fluidity functional in the eighteenth- and early nineteenth-century world of small towns, artisanship, family farms, and simple commodity production, they conclude it was overwhelmed by the hardened class and factional conflicts of industrial society.[124] Similarly, although state-centered scholars have recovered constitutional struggle over the nature of the state in the twentieth century, more often than not they have misconceived the politics of statebuilding as an adaptive, rather than constitutive, enterprise, responding with varied success to exogenous changes in economy well beyond the will of democratic influence.[125]

In both cases, then, institutional alternatives to corporate liberalism have remained invisible. For as far as these scholars have gone beyond the pluralist and consensus schools of the 1950s, they tend to capitulate to the same underlying notions of economic development as their predecessors. As a result, the claims of nineteenth-century regionalists to parity in rate structures, like those of greenbackers for access to credit, are typically seen as expressions of private interests, rooted in one or another version of an advancing division of labor. Absent a genuinely constitutive account of the modern corporation and redistributive regulation, social historians and state-centered scholars have tended to read these movements as anachronistically as their mid-century predecessors would have read Senator Elkins.

CHAPTER FIVE

Regionalism in Economic Practice

The Chicago Great Western Railway, 1883–1908

A. B. Stickney, critic of management, ally to Grangers, and advocate of regulation, was also a regional railroad builder. The Chicago Great Western, at times embattled, at others troubled, nevertheless endured. From its inception as the Minnesota and Northwestern Railway in 1884 to its acquisition by the Chicago and North Western in 1968, it carved out a unique place in its region and the industry.

It would be surprising if Stickney, the rogue in regulation, was not so in the industry. This might lend credence to the view that ideology was superfluous: had Stickney spoken in support of regionalism, and yet capitulated to national system building, we might add one more piece of evidence to the view that technology and markets determined railroad and corporate form. If the Chicago Great Western had failed altogether, we might conclude that regionalism was economically inviable. The first was not the case: in form and operation, Stickney's railroad remained a regional carrier for seventy-five years. While on the second criterion, success or failure, the results were ambiguous. By some criteria, the Great Western succeeded during Stickney's presidency and well beyond. By others, it failed. The test, however, is not merely whether a firm profits and endures, since even the most thriving national systems depended on financial, legal, and regulatory privileges. Hence, when we consider that regional republicanism was defeated within the chambers of the state, the fact that the Chicago Great Western was successful by any economic criteria indicates that railroad regionalism was a practical alternative to nationalism.

The counterfactual question, then, is not why, if the Great Western was efficient, did regional carriers fail to outcompete their larger competitors on the battlefield of economic productivity. Rather, what were the constitutive elements of practical productivity associated with regionalism; how did they differ from those instantiated in the dominant model; and what institutional practices beyond the firm might have moved the Great Western from the status of alternative to history's center stage?

Maple Leaf Morphology

In an 1889 public relations scheme management for the Chicago, St. Paul and Kansas City (the Great Western's ancestor) asked the nation's station agents to participate in a contest to design a trademark for the carrier. From more than two thousand entries, a Wabash employee's depiction of the road as a maple leaf—its lines shown as veins radiating from Oelwein, Iowa—was chosen. Throughout Stickney's tenure, the maple leaf logo graced the road's engines and tenders, timetables, and advertisements. Renamed the Corn Belt Route in 1910, the Great Western, nevertheless, retained its maple leaf form for nearly three-quarters of a century after its naming.[1]

Like its modest size, the Great Western's shape distinguished it from the interregional lines that coursed America's plains. While the Chicago, Burlington and Quincy, the Atchison, Topeka and Santa Fe, and the Chicago, Rock Island and Pacific grew like the centipede—lengthy trunklines with many miles of short feeders—the Great Western grew primarily as a trunkline road, connecting regional markets through a hub-and-spoke system. Railroad form, we shall see, was intimately tied to function. But we shall also see how form followed strategy—and how strategy emerged not merely from the pressures of technology and competition, but from a vision of regional development homologous to the one codified in the Interstate Commerce Act.

Even so, it is not at all clear that Stickney envisioned a maple leaf at the Great Western's birth in 1884. His earliest ventures as an independent railroad promoter indicated that he might become another speculator, a spoiler, who used a short line's competitive leverage to inflate its price at auction to the region's established carriers. When Stickney acquired control of a paper corporation, the Minnesota and Northwestern, in 1884 and announced plans to build from St. Paul 110 miles south to Mona, Iowa, many observers saw not the birth of a regional carrier, but one more financial syndicate which lined its pockets through an independent construction company. Having learned of Stickney's plan to build into the Windy City, the press conjectured that the Illinois Central, "the Chicago, Burlington & Quincy, or the Chicago Rock Island & Pacific might swallow up the infant carrier" for its access to the twin cities and Chicago.[2] Stickney's prior ventures led one editor to conclude, "Of the many railroads he built, not one of them did he build with the intention of operating them as independent lines, but built them for speculation, and he has made money by doing so."[3] The St. Paul to Chicago line would be no different. This was, after all, the era of system building.

Stickney must have changed his mind, if not his tactics, because the opening of the St. Paul to Mona line under the Minnesota and Northwestern banner was the first leg of what would become, by 1903, a 1,467-mile regional system. Also, in the midst of building a tripod between Chicago, St. Paul, and Kansas City (the Maple Leaf's second corporate name, from 1887 to 1892), Stickney found time to work out his views on regionalism, market landscape, and regulation in *The Railway Problem* (1890). Though it was a decade before he had to articulate those views before the ICC and market allies in Nebraska, by 1890 his commitment to regionalism was evident.

Stickney moved deftly while the route to Mona was under construction. First, he negotiated a joint project with Dubuque, Iowa, businessmen: they would construct a line into Chicago, and he would extend the Minnesota and Northwestern southeast to meet them in Dubuque. The Maple Leaf added two more veins before its completion in 1903: a southern route to Kansas City in 1888 and a western division to Omaha in 1903. Like the Chicago line, the former was constructed through an alliance with an existing short line: the Wisconsin, Iowa and Nebraska Railroad. Stickney also began negotiations in 1893 to acquire James J. Hill's Mason City and Fort Dodge Railway, which he planned to build north to the St. Paul-Chicago line and southwest to the Missouri River at Omaha and Sioux City. Unfortunately, the depression of the 1890s stalled the Omaha project until 1903 and killed entry into Sioux City altogether.[4]

At each step of the way, Stickney rejected interterritorial projects and deepened his commitment to regionalism. In 1885 he explored but scrapped an extension into Dakota Territory. Several years later a similar plan to build west to Denver fell by the wayside. By contrast, circumstance, not plan, forced Stickney to abandon two regional projects: the Sioux City division and a fifth vein running southeast from Marshalltown, Iowa, to St. Louis. Unlike the former, the Maple Leaf did secure temporary access into St. Louis through Stickney's control over the Central Iowa Railway and a brief alliance with a connecting line. An 1888 advertising map boasted service to Chicago, St. Paul, Kansas City, and St. Louis. But Stickney's control over the Central Iowa Railway was short-lived. By 1890 the southeastern vein had disappeared.[5]

One last project—a loop serving southeastern Minnesota—completed the Maple Leaf Route. Though the railroad's only departure from mainline service, the "Mankato Loop" would not become a mere feeder. Providing local service to regional market towns, it also linked them directly to Chicago and St. Paul.

By 1905 the Chicago Great Western had grown to its final size, 1,467 miles, and to its hub-and-spoke form. Though Stickney might have begun as a speculator or national system builder, he ended up a regionalist. Just as he wrote on the advantages of decentralized regional development and the injustices of rate discrimination, he labored to construct and operate a viable regional carrier in a territory coursed by huge national trunklines. Radiating from its hub at Oelwein, Iowa, distinguished by a unique central triangle linking its veins, the Maple Leaf Route would attempt to carve out a unique place in this highly competitive territory through innovative service, low cost, and aggressive rate competition.

Hub City Reorganization

With lines radiating from northern Iowa to Chicago, St. Paul, and Kansas City in service, and a fourth division to Omaha and Sioux City on the drawing board by the early 1890s, the Great Western had made a final commitment to a regional hub-and-spoke form. However, the road's organizational and locational structure lagged behind strategy. The Chicago Great Western was still a St. Paul railroad. Its officers and directors hailed from the Twin Cities; corporate and operations management were located there, as were its main repair shops and master mechanics. Traffic gravity, however, pulled the road's center steadily south to the point where its four divisions connected in northeastern Iowa.

Nowhere was it more evident that the locus of operations and maintenance had moved south than in Great Western efforts to economize during the depression of the 1890s. More and more, traffic managers rerouted disabled motive power and bad car lots from St. Paul to makeshift facilities at the nexus of the road's three divisions in Oelwein, Iowa. Consequently, in 1894 Stickney proposed a formal reorganization of Great Western operations and maintenance in the hub city. The offices of both the assistant general superintendent for the whole system and of the road's master mechanic, he suggested, should be relocated from St. Paul to Oelwein, as should the Great Western repair shops.

Like the Omaha division, a tight money market stalled the Oelwein project. Not until late in 1898 did construction begin in earnest and a full-service repair shop did not become operational until after the turn of the century.[6]

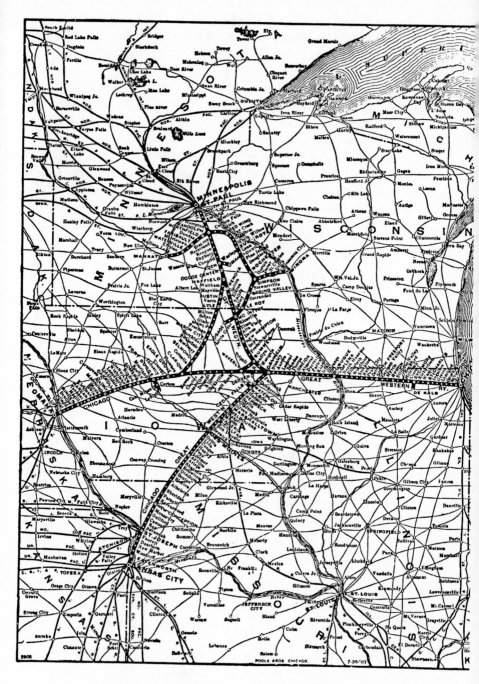

Figure 1. Chicago Great Western Railway and Proprietary Lines. A. B. Stickney, *Nebraska's Opportunity to Increase the Prosperity of Her Farms* (St. Paul: The Pioneer Press, 1904).

The long wait, however, did not belie quality. The Oelwein shops were the first in a long line of Great Western innovations in railroad service and technology. First to abandon steam or water power in favor of electricity, the Maple Leaf exploited the new technology to fundamentally redesign the repair shop. An electric motor, driven by a single coal-fired power plant, allowed the company to arrange separate repair departments, independent of the single power shaft which had driven all equipment in previous shops. Above two long rows of repair stalls, linked by a huge transfer table, were rows of specialty shops: "an electricians' room, an air brake instruction room, an air hose work room, a lubricator and injector room, a cleaning room, . . . brass trimming rooms, a tin shop, a copper shop, . . . a dye room, an upholstery shop, a cabinet shop, a varnish room and offices." An electric freight elevator and several huge electric cranes facilitated the movement of parts and equipment between machine stalls below and among specialty shops above. Electricity, generated from a single power plant, also provided ancillary steam to be used for heat, hot water, and compressed air, as well as electric light and power.[7]

Contemporaries marveled at the Oelwein plan. Nearly a decade after the shops were in service, one engineer wrote: "The history of 'modern' locomotive repair shops may be considered as beginning with the use of what has been called the 'electric drive'. One of the first shops to make use of the electric motor for both individual machines and groups of tools, as well as the electric crane, and central power plan, was the Oelwein Iowa shops of the Chicago Great Western put in commission in 1900. Since that date there have been over 70 shops either built entirely new or modernized from existing plants."[8] The young Walter Chrysler, who came from the Fort Worth and Denver City Railway in 1904 to supervise the Oelwein operation, wrote in his autobiography that these were the biggest, most unusual shops he had ever seen. Oelwein not only advanced the efficiency of maintenance and repair, it became a design shop in its own right. Later administrations called on skilled mechanics and sophisticated equipment to redesign, customize, and rebuild motive power and freight cars in-house.[9] Such expertise became indispensable to a railroad which chose to compete as much on service as rates.

Oelwein, Iowa, also became more than the home of sophisticated machine shops. In 1897 managers reorganized the carrier's division of labor to complement the relocation of the traffic department from St. Paul to Oelwein. Guided by Stickney's son, Samuel (who had recently returned from his engineering studies at M.I.T. to become general manager), the Great Western adopted an unorthodox operating structure in order to exploit its hub-

and-spoke form. Following standard organization practice in the 1880s and 1890s, prior to reorganization the Great Western had three line supervisors, one for each separate spoke. These division superintendents were located in Chicago, Des Moines, and St. Paul, their jurisdiction running approximately the full length of each line. Below the division superintendents, agents at the largest stations were given jurisdiction over each station yard, its yardmen, and enginemen. Station agents would communicate either directly with the general superintendent in St. Paul or more typically through their division superintendents.

Once the operational center of the Maple Leaf had been moved to Oelwein, General Manager Stickney questioned the effectiveness of this hierarchy. Following his father's suggestion, the superintendent of transportation was relocated from St. Paul to the hub city, and the offices of the division superintendents were dismantled. The Oelwein office would now "have entire charge over the movement of trains, supplying cars and, in fact, all matters relating to transportation proper on the entire system." Moreover, all chief dispatchers would be relocated from their separate locations in Chicago, St. Joseph, and Oelwein to a new department under the authority of the superintendent of transportation. Under the new arrangement, division dispatching would be handled by means of overland wire from Oelwein to Kansas City, Des Moines, St. Paul, and Chicago.

Since the divisional offices were abolished, station agents would now report directly to the road's general superintendent in St. Paul, where the working hours of train and enginemen would be kept and, with the exception of large terminals, station payrolls would be made. Also, under the new plan, the superintendent of transportation in Oelwein took on four assistant train supervisors. These men, selected from the ranks of skilled mechanics, were to perform the duties of traveling engineers. Constantly on the road, they would make recommendations concerning train and engine service, as well as station, yard, track, and signal improvements and repair.[10]

Chicago Great Western organization now differed from that on virtually all of the national railroads. Although the manner in which traffic departments were integrated into the organizational structure of larger carriers followed two patterns, they were invariably broken into regional subdivisions. In some cases, as with the Great Western's competitor, the Chicago, Burlington and Quincy, regional traffic departments were part of a general divisional office, which also included legal, accounting, and purchasing departments. On most others, separate divisions sat below a central, systemwide traffic department. Prior to reorganization, the Great Western fit the latter pattern.

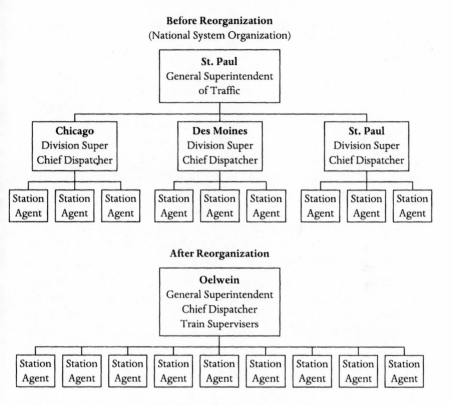

Figure 2. Chicago Great Western Operating Organization

By abolishing its separate divisions the regional carrier broke ranks with its larger competitors altogether.[11]

Just when the prevailing orthodoxy among the interregional carriers was to thicken their managerial hierarchies by adding layers of mid-level traffic management, the Maple Leaf flattened its hierarchy and attempted to open new lines of communication between the top and the bottom of the organization. Agents at larger stations gained new levels of discretion over station, yard, and terminals, formerly allocated to division superintendents and their staff. All station agents now communicated directly with the transportation superintendent in Oelwein on traffic matters, and the road's general superintendent on matters of personnel and payroll. Chief dispatchers in Oelwein communicated directly with terminal dispatchers, each other, and the traffic superintendent in Oelwein, rather than through separate division superintendents. Finally, roving train supervisors, staff to the superintendent of transportation in Oelwein, communicated directly from the field to the transportation department in the hub city.

Sociologists of organizations have long recognized that the effectiveness of bureaucratic hierarchies depends upon environmental stability and certainty.[12] Only when product markets are relatively stable and predictable are bureaucratic features—a high division of labor coordinated by a hierarchical command structure, fixed by clearly delineated duties and rules—effective. Two factors made bureaucracy less effective on the Chicago Great Western. First, in their efforts to rationalize the flow of intraregional freight, managers realized that the Maple Leaf could best exploit its hub-and-spoke form by a complex system of networking traffic through Oelwein. Also, committed as Stickney was to regionalism and dispersed market development, the Great Western faced the complex problem of hauling heterogeneous traffic—long- and short-haul, carload and less-than-carload lots of freight. The following section will show how the carrier managed to successfully integrate rather than specialize this diverse mix of freight. A highly complex and uncertain task, it necessitated substantial discretion among station agents, dispatchers, and freight handlers. There was simply no way to fully predict the freight mix and traffic flow on any given day. Therefore high levels of divisional specialization, top-down control, and formal rules became dysfunctional on this regional hub-and-spoke railroad.

If the extent of hierarchy in the nation's first big business, the railroads, depended upon predictable, large-scale markets, then the divisional organization of traffic administration in the larger interregionals also depended upon long-term relational contracts with large-scale, long-haul shippers. It is little wonder, then, that they found antidiscrimination laws onerous. For once national systems had committed themselves to a high division of labor and extensive operational hierarchies, the regional shippers' demand for parity became costly. By contrast, in an effort to make the best of on-line, heterogeneous, unpredictable markets, the Great Western flattened its operational hierarchy and redistributed discretion from its administrative center to its operational periphery.

Operations for Economies of Scope

In reorganizing its traffic department the Great Western signaled its commitment to achieving economies of joint production or what industrial organization economists call "economies of scope." These are cost reductions resulting from the use of technologies or processes within a single operating unit to produce more than one product. In transportation, economies of scope are achieved by mixing and networking, rather than segregating, heterogeneous traffic distinguished by class and destination.[13] The Chicago Great Western achieved such economies by integrating, where possible, long- and short-haul traffic; by networking traffic through its hub city and other key nodes throughout the system; and by mixing carload and less-than-carload freight.

Contrast Great Western management with the ideal mode of operations on the national trunklines. Though they did not ignore small lots of regional freight (as common carriers they were legally obliged to serve all), the interregionals endeavored to achieve economies of scale by maximizing relatively homogeneous, long-haul freight between national markets. Chandler has described this strategy well. In order to ensure control over high-volume through traffic (and so the benefits of scale), organizational entrepreneurs consolidated end-to-end lines into vast autarkic systems. Similarly, by offering mass producers, like Standard Oil, rate rebates in return for guaranteed high-volume freight, the interregionals were readily able to offset lower revenues per unit of freight with lower average costs. Nevertheless, we have seen how national system building and ratemaking was no more than a particular strategy, driven by the politically contingent organization of capital markets rather than the high fixed costs of railroad technology.

In principle there were cost advantages to long-haul, bulk freight and Stickney acknowledged them: the ratio of terminal to hauling costs was lower on the long haul, and high volume resulted in longer and heavier freight trains. Nonetheless, relatively short-haul and small-scale freight—or to use the vernacular of the trade, "way station" or "way freight" and "less-than-carload"—was not beyond efficient management. In 1905 Stickney explained to the Minnesota Railroad and Warehouse Commission how the Great Western achieved economies of scope by integrating its long- and short-haul traffic. In theory, he maintained, where there was sufficient through traffic, it was cheaper and more profitable to integrate through and way freight, instead of providing specialized service for each. In practice,

> generally speaking, all local freight . . . [on the Great Western] is carried one day one hundred miles or less on a way-freight-train, and the balance of the distance on a throught-freight-train (sic). To illustrate: the local freight which is received at its St. Paul station to-day by the Chicago Great Western Company, destined to local stations between St. Paul and Hay-field (Hayfield being the end of the way-freight run) is loaded into a car, carried and peddled out on the way-freight-train. All such freight as is destined to stations between Hayfield and Oelwein (Oelwein being the end of

the next way-freight run) is loaded into another car and carried from St. Paul to Hayfield on a fast through-freight-train, and at Hayfield it is taken by the next way-freight-train and peddled out by it at the stations between Hayfield and Oelwein. All such freight as is destined to stations beyond Oelwein is loaded into still another car and carried on a fast through-freight-train to Oelwein; and at Oelwein it is taken by the next way-freight-train and peddled out at the stations between Oelwein and the end of the next way-freight run. And this process of expediting the movement of such freight is repeated as to the way-freight runs beyond.[14]

From this illustration, he concluded, it could be seen that virtually all local freight was carried less than one hundred miles (the distance between through terminals) on a slow moving way-freight train. The results were both to achieve economies of scope and to "give better despatch (sic) to local freight which is carried long distances."[15]

Put differently, Stickney told the commission that the *joint costs* of hauling way-station and through traffic were lower than those of segregating service. Even though in principle it was more costly to run two or more one-hundred-mile way-freight trains than a single carrier devoted to local traffic, these costs were more than offset by two factors. First, the one-hundred-mile maximum assured that way-station trains would be light-loaded (toward the end of the run) for shorter distances. Second, the Maple Leaf gained a competitive edge from prompt way-station deliveries and thereby from a larger local market. (As we shall see, given its high proportion of competitive traffic, this turned out to be critical.) Traffic managers had found that regional markets were served more efficiently by expanding the scope of operations; by mixing local and through freight to intermediate traffic nodes, rather than providing specialized local service, the Maple Leaf reduced joint costs and provided better service.

A second technique to achieve economies of scope involved networking all long-haul traffic through the Great Western hubs in Oelwein and Clarion. Instead of providing specialized long-haul service between its four end terminals, dispatchers stopped incoming through traffic at the hub, where freight was broken down and recombined. Even though this resulted in higher terminal and switching costs, as well as some loss in traffic due to lost time, such costs were more than offset by the lower costs associated with heavier and longer trains entering and leaving the hub. Thus, unlike its larger competitors, who achieved scale economies by increasing speed or "throughput," the Great Western realized networking economies by stopping and remixing freight in Clarion and Oelwein.[16]

Although these techniques made the best of long- and short-haul traffic, careful attention to way station or regional markets introduced the added burden of hauling small lots of heterogeneous freight. Once again Stickney acknowledged its disadvantages: "The most difficult business to manage so as to get a new dollar for each dollar of out-of-pocket expense, is the transporting of less-than-car-load (lcl) lots for short distances, or even for long distances, for that matter." After all, when payload was calculated by the total weight carried, gravel and grain was bound to be more profitable than machinery and ceramic pipe. Nevertheless, lcl lots were not beyond rationalization and profitable service. Like way station freight, they could be mixed with carload lots where there was sufficient through traffic or warehoused until such time as heavier loads were gathered. Though the latter became common practice on the Great Western, Stickney pointed out that country and jobbing merchants were often willing to pay the higher price associated with smaller lots in order to have "prompt and daily delivery."[17] By paying careful attention to loading and dispatching less-than-carload lots according to size, shape, station order, and destination, Stickney boasted, the Great Western had increased its average less-than-carload weight from 3,000 to 4,000 pounds to 7,393 pounds in the span of a few short years.[18]

Given the Maple Leaf's relatively high proportion of local traffic, all of these methods were critical to its success. Though systematic data comparing local and less-than-carload to through and carload freight is unavailable, fragmentary evidence indicates the Great Western's mix. In one sample of freight carried from the Twin Cities during the first twelve days of June and October in 1905 (both peak agricultural seasons), the Maple Leaf hauled 306 cars of local freight, each carrying an average payload of 7,400 pounds, and 405 cars of through freight, each carrying an average payload of 50,960 pounds. By weight, local and less-than-carload freight was a relatively small proportion (about 10 percent) of the total. Measured by cars, however, approximately 43 percent was local and lcl traffic. Moreover, in 1905, of the 15,134 freight cars allocated to livestock, only 1,537 (or 10 percent) were carried between the road's western terminals at St. Paul, Omaha, or Kansas City and its easternmost point in Chicago.[19] Served as they were by a carrier committed to regional development, local markets prospered. As Vice-President Ansel Oppenheim told the finance committee in 1906,

> the last year or two [the traffic of local territory] has developed a manufacturing growth heretofore entirely unknown. Thus Waterloo, which ten years ago had a population of about 8,000 people, has increased to over 20,000 people by reason of manufacturing developments. During the last

year 1,000 acres of stone, suitable for making Portland cement, has been discovered at Mason City, and one cement mill with a capacity of 3,500 barrels a day is now under construction, which is immediately to be increased to 7,000 barrels per day and two other mills of equal capacity are in contemplation. The practically inexhaustible gypsum mines at Fort Dodge are assuming increased importance through the use of their product in the manufacture of plaster board, a fire proofing material, as well as for plastering, fertilizer, etc. A large beet sugar factory is building at Waverly, Ia. Two large terminal elevators have been built on our tracks at Omaha; large flour, malt and linseed mills are under contract to be built on our tracks at Minneapolis. *And the traffic of the smaller industries always exceeds the larger.*[20]

Two technological indicators also illustrate the Maple Leaf's commitment to networking and economies of scope: the extent of side track and the use of switch engines. Virtually every Great Western annual report from the midnineties to 1907 shows a growing investment in side track, whose main purpose was to provide specialized service to on-line shippers or switching facilities necessary to transfer cars and remix freight destined for diverse markets. By 1905 "side or passing track" on the 818 miles of the Great Western proper (excluding the Omaha division and the Mankato Loop) accounted for 26 percent of total mileage. On the Omaha division, side and passing track represented 18 percent. Of the total mileage run by all Great Western locomotives in 1905, 13 percent was devoted to switch engines, whose sole purpose was to add and remove cars at Oelwein, Hayfield, and the many other nodal points along the line. By 1906 this number had grown to 14 percent.[21]

By carefully mixing instead of segregating freight, the Maple Leaf achieved the highest level of freight density among a sample of prominent railroads west of Chicago[22] (see Table 7). Although a similar account of the organization of passenger service is unavailable, Table 7 shows that the Great Western was successful in realizing high density in this category as well.

In sum, the Chicago Great Western achieved economies of scope by carefully combining the carload and the less-than-carload, the long and the short haul, and by networking long-haul traffic through its hub in Oelwein. Note just how different is this application of economies of scope than the one we find in the new business history. According to that school, scale and scope are compatible because both increase the minimum efficient scale of the industrial enterprise and necessitate extensive managerial hierarchies. This case, however, shows that scale and scope are just as likely to conflict because joint production tends to place a lower limit upon size and hierarchy than does

Table 7. Number of Ton- and Passenger Miles per Mile of Road: Chicago Great Western v. Selected National Systems, 1905

Railroad	Ton-miles	Passenger Miles
Chicago Great W	885,028	100,607
Omaha	520,459	78,646
St. Paul	590,826	65,357
N Pac.	820,256	91,914
Soo Line	497,455	44,464

Source: A. B. Stickney, "Argument on Behalf of the Chicago Great Western Railway Company," before the Minnesota Railroad and Warehouse Commissioners, March 1906, 48.

uniform production. The extensive use of switching nodes to recombine freight, for example, resulted in a traffic ceiling beyond which they would become saturated. Consequently, maximum efficient scale was likely to be lower on regional than national railroads; while the efficient number of spokes was likely to be smaller on the former than feeders on the latter.

In addition, as recent studies of flexible manufacturing have shown, although the features of bureaucracy—bigness, hierarchy, formal rules, and a high division of labor—are functional in mass production, they also make it difficult for the firm to respond to change. Such characteristics were likely to be dysfunctional for regional railroads, where the task of integrating and networking heterogeneous freight by class and destination was rife with uncertainty. Great Western traffic managers learned that joint production necessitated high levels of discretion among station agents and roving engineers, as well as direct communication between chief dispatchers and train supervisors in Oelwein and agents in the field: in short, a flatter hierarchy, narrower division of labor, and fewer formal rules.[23] Scale and scope also conflicted on the railroads for reasons of politics. With the contest for regionalism all but lost in regulation by the turn of the century, the ICC's early champion among railroad men, A. B. Stickney, now found himself in conflict with the state. As in the case of morphology and traffic management, the Great Western pursued an increasingly unorthodox strategy in ratemaking as well.

Competitive Ratemaking for Regionalism

The Chicago Great Western's form and location were a mixed blessing. Though it succeeded in realizing high-density traffic through economies of scope, virtually all of this railroad was in competitive territory. Financial columnist E. S. Meade summarized the Maple Leaf's situation well.

With the exception of the [Mankato loop], the Great Western controls only a small amount of non-competitive traffic. Connecting four large centers of traffic, it is intersected at many points by the lines of some other company. The Illinois Central, the Milwaukee and St. Paul, the North-Western, the Rock Island, the Atchison, the Alton, the Burlington and the Iowa Central are all competitors of the Chicago Great Western. Its position is even more exposed to attack than that of the Wabash, because the Wabash is connected by the ties of mutual ownership with the Gould line at St. Louis, and is greatly favored by traffic agreement with the Lackawanna and Lehigh Valley at Buffalo. The Great Western, however, stands almost entirely alone. Its competitors at the terminal points from which it derives the largest share of its traffic, either bring in a large amount of this traffic themselves to these cities or receive it from the roads with which they stand in close alliance . . . Thus the Burlington receives lumber traffic from the Great Northern and the Northern Pacific; the Atchison operates its own line from Kansas City to Chicago, and the Alton receives the freight furnished by the Union Pacific at Omaha and Kansas City. The Great Western, however, occupies a peculiarly isolated and independent position, and it has always been conspicuous in insisting upon its rights to share in the traffic of its territory by cutting rates where this course seemed necessary.[24]

Consequently, the "Stickney road" earned the reputation of a "pirate" and a "ratecutter" among Plains states and midwestern railroads. When the managers of conservative interregionals tried to stabilize rates through pools, Stickney not only fought them at law, he often slashed rates, throwing negotiated market shares into disarray. Once the Maple Leaf began service to Kansas City and Omaha, it was only natural that he would favor a federal law equalizing long- and short-haul rates so that traffic might stop at his western terminals. From this perspective, Stickney's moral claims to regionalism appear to be no more than a mask for self interest.[25]

Throughout this study, however, I have argued that such material interests were, at best, ambiguous during the era of rapid industrialization. The putative determinants of such interests—technology and market geography—were malleable, and so open to influence by economic agents. At constitutive moments like these, the behavior of the business firm is better understood as a strategic effort to influence its economic and political environment, than optimization under exogenous constraints.

Since railroads were large, infrastructural, and novel projects, both national and regional strategies necessitated collaboration from agents whose economic interests were also ambiguous. Thus, railroad entrepreneurship was an inescapably social—a charismatic—activity: at critical moments of opportunity and conflict, the architects of both national and regional systems were compelled to articulate a model of industrial order general enough for potential allies to locate a place for themselves. Gould's national system, for example, survived an otherwise devastating setback, because he convinced judges and investors of the economic necessity for system integrity. This was equally true for Stickney, who found it necessary to voice a relatively universal model of regionalism to promising market allies and the agents of a state increasingly convinced national railroad systems were inevitable.

Consider the ambiguity of the Great Western's relationship with midwestern and Plains states farmers. Did they have a *natural* affinity with this regional carrier or with the long-haul interterritorial trunklines, who were likely to provide cheaper access to seaboard and overseas markets? There was no simple answer to this question on extant material grounds alone. Stickney understood this quite well. Following the international wheat glut of the 1870s and 1880s, for example, instead of advocating protectionism, he encouraged midwestern monocrop farmers to diversify and their merchants to invest in high-value-added processing.[26] Livestock, dairy farming, flax, rye, oats, corn and barley, milling and packing, he argued, might find regional, as well as national specialty markets.[27] Like Iowa Senator James Wilson, Stickney did not take the sectional division of agrarian labor for granted.

Similarly, where only latent economic interests were present at the Great Western's Missouri River terminals, Stickney labored to construct them. In Omaha and Kansas City, he attempted to persuade would-be entrepreneurs to establish a grain market where none existed, and in St. Paul he envisioned a stock yard and meatpacking industry. Moreover, just as system builders were compelled to articulate a general account of their project, so too did Stickney develop a relatively universal model of the "regional market town," from which merchants, manufacturers, farmers, and consumers might share advantages.

Upon opening the Maple Leaf's western division in 1903, Stickney brought his case to the Commercial Club of Omaha and the Nebraska Bankers Association. Why, he asked, should Missouri River entrepreneurs commit scarce resources to an Omaha grain, livestock, or dressed beef market when Chicago appeared to have such outstanding advantages?[28] In general, Stickney argued, agricultural market towns ought to be located as close to their source of supply as possible. To be sure, there were centripetal forces, such as the need to aggregate merchant capital and commodities, causing centralization in Chicago. Nevertheless, beyond a much smaller area than conventionally thought, national markets result in high levels of redundant transportation. Like the regional carrier that served them, regional market towns coped much more efficiently with the uncertainty and instability of demand for grain, grain products, livestock, and dressed beef.[29] Given the unpredictable seasonal location and extent of demand for these goods, regional markets reduced the costs of unnecessary transportation. Consider the advantages of a grain market in Omaha over those of Chicago. Suppose, Stickney told Nebraska bankers, a part of the year's demand for grain required shipment east, through Chicago: there would be no loss in transportation cost, because carriage from Omaha to Chicago would be the same, whether shipped at harvest time or at the time of demand. Suppose, however, demand arose from points north and south or west of Omaha during the year following harvest. In the former case, the whole cost from Omaha to Chicago at harvest would be saved. In the latter—demand from the west—at least twice the transportation cost of shipping east to Chicago and then west again would be saved. Such economies, Stickney concluded, justified Omaha grain merchants paying farmers more than Chicago market prices.[30]

These advantages were reinforced by other uncertainties in the size and location of demand. Quoting a well-known regional merchant, Stickney explained, "The place to carry grain is at the market-town *nearest* the place of production, because at that point it contains the smallest amount of transportation charges and is in a position to be sent *to the best markets as they develop, which no one can foresee,* at the least cost for transportation." Who would have guessed, for instance, that the largest market for Kansas City corn in 1904 would have been for livestock feed in the "great corn producing state of Iowa?"[31]

Like uncertainty, economic instability also provided an advantage to regional markets, which better balanced supply and demand and thereby more effectively regulated prices and quantities. Consider once again the regional market for grain. Since it "matures and is harvested once each year," and cannot be consumed immediately, "the relation of supply and demand and the consequent prices cannot be regulated, as in the case of live stock, by delaying the harvest a few days . . . ; the relation between supply and demand, which determines prices, must be regulated by storing and holding."[32] However, "the aggregate crop of a year is so vast that if accumulated and stored in any one market town, though as rich as Liverpool, or New York or Chicago, it would make so large a 'visible supply' and, for the moment, so great a surplus that it would break down the price far below its real value, and far below the cost of production." "It is easy to see," Stickney concluded, "the importance of having these [jobbing merchants and] great magazines of grain located in different and widely separated market towns."[33]

Regional markets also regulated quantities in the face of market instability better than their larger more centralized competitors. "The elevator of the nearby carrying grain market, in the transportation of grain, performs a function similar to the reservoir in a system of waterworks," Stickney said. "It equalizes the outgoing flow. When incoming streams are larger the grain in the elevators, and the water in the reservoirs, accumulates, thus providing for a steady outflow during the full year. Thus such elevators would tend to prevent 'car famines' as well as blockades at eastern terminals during the heavy grain shipping months."[34]

A grain market in Omaha, Stickney told Nebraska entrepreneurs, would produce cost efficiencies that could easily be shared by regional merchants, farmers, and the railroad. By reducing the costs of redundant transportation, Omaha jobbers could split the difference with tributary farmers, thereby offering higher grain prices than Chicago, and still earn a profit for themselves. The Great Western, through better regulation of supply and demand, could use its rolling stock more efficiently and reduce the investment necessary to handle the higher peak loads associated with seasonal shipping to centralized markets. "The transportion companies, which have lines extending through Omaha," Stickney told the bankers, were mistaken when "in the interest of the long haul," they looked "upon the establishment of an Omaha grain market with [disfavor] because they reason that the grain once loaded can be carried through to Chicago cheaper without unloading at" the Missouri River. Since the interregionals typically loaded their cars at country stations, where they were "practically never" filled to "maximum capacity, . . . in the through haul these light loaded cars must be carried the whole distance light loaded." With an intermediate market at Omaha, they would be under-utilized for shorter distances, "unloaded into elevators," then "loaded again to their maximum capacity, this greatly economizing in the cost of transportation."[35]

"Putting theories aside," Stickney added, "experience has proven that the market nearest the point of production can and does pay the farmer more for his grain products than a distant market. Experience has proven that if Nebraska grain, instead of being sent to Chicago for storage, could be stored in a market town in Nebraska it would add several cents per bushel to its value in the hands of the farmer, which in the aggregate, would add millions per year to the income of farmers."[36] This had been true for Chicago's earlier advantage over its eastern counterparts; now it was so for Kansas City, where tributary farmers received several cents more a bushel for grain than Nebraska farmers, and in Minneapolis, which paid "about seven cents a bushel more for wheat than the Nebraska farmers get for their wheat."[37]

Thus farmers, merchants, and railroads would prosper from the development of regional market towns. Even the processing industries—meatpacking and milling—were likely to thrive once jobbing merchants had established storage and marketing facilities. Although the establishment of a regional market was not a sufficient condition for processing, it was necessary. Whether everyone took advantage of Omaha's potential—especially the long-haul carriers—remained an open question. Nevertheless, once the Great Western completed its division to the Missouri River, the trunklines' stranglehold over Omaha had been broken; "the old adjustment of rates, which imposed a penalty of about five cents per bushel on grain which stopped in Omaha for market purposes, had been abolished." It was, Stickney implored, "Nebraska's hour of fate . . . the magnificent opportunity awaits!" "If sleeping, [Omaha,] wake; if feasting, rise and grasp the opportunity before it turns away."[38]

Stickney's entrepreneurial charisma involved the commitment of financial, as well as social, capital. Well before the Great Western entered Omaha, he joined with St. Paul jobbers and James J. Hill of the Great Northern Railway to establish the St. Paul Union Stockyards. By the turn of the century, the Twin Cities had become not only a livestock market, but an important regional center for meatpacking. In St. Paul, Omaha, and Kansas City, the Great Western abandoned the custom of charging more for finished goods (dressed beef and packing-house products) than raw materials (livestock). In Kansas City, the Maple Leaf built a grain elevator and devised an ingenious scheme for stopping western produce at the Missouri River. And in Omaha Stickney joined with merchants and bankers to establish the Omaha Grain Exchange. The Great Western also initiated competitive ratemaking in order to cultivate regional market development. This strategy, however, ran afoul of the long-haul trunklines, vested interests in Chicago, and, ironically, the ICC. Twice more, then, Stickney had to make public the principles of regionalism and cost-based ratemaking, as he defended the Maple Leaf before the state.

The first Great Western ratemaking practice to arouse the ire of its competitors occurred in the early 1890s. Upon opening service on the southern division, Stickney attempted to negotiate market share peacefully from Kansas City by joining the Western Trunkline Committee of the Chicago Union League Club. In 1896 members of this pool agreed to divide grain traffic from Kansas City to Chicago according to fixed shares of the total market.

No sooner had an accord been reached than the Burlington and the Rock Island cut their long-haul rates from Missouri and Iowa markets. Great Western traffic from Kansas City collapsed and Stickney turned to the Trunkline Committee for relief. Though the pool found in his favor, reparations were stingy, covering only half of the Maple Leaf's $90,000 claim.[39]

Experience had taught Stickney to mistrust railway pools. As he wrote in *The Railway Problem*, most pooling agreements reproduced standing cost distortions and inequities. Regardless of their word, it appeared that the trunklines were determined to favor through traffic and thus bypass the regional markets on the Missouri River the Great Western had labored to cultivate. Stickney protested; and as he withdrew from the Trunkline Committee, he reportedly told his colleagues: "Your integrity, honor and fine character as individuals is well known and unquestioned and as individuals I would trust you with my entire personal fortune. But gentlemen, as railroad presidents, I would not trust any one of you with my watch."[40]

Thus blocked on its western flank, the Great Western outmaneuvered its rivals in Kansas City. In 1894 Stickney quietly incorporated the Iowa Development Company to erect a million-bushel-capacity grain elevator in Kansas City. Once complete, he contracted with a Chicago merchant, the Anglo-American Provision Company, to purchase grain directly from the Kansas City corporation. In lieu of shipping charges to the Windy City, the Great Western would take its only profit from a share of the Iowa company's revenues. In this way, Kansas City would overcome the handicap imposed by the long-haul carriers and achieve its calling as a regional grain market. Nearby growers in Nebraska, Missouri, and Iowa would receive top dollar for their crops, the Maple Leaf would generate hefty freight loadings, and the Anglo-American Company would split the difference between the elevator company's higher grain price and its free transportation. The plan worked. All parties, save the interregionals, benefited, and in the peak grain season following the 1896 harvest, the Great Western hauled nearly 70 percent of the corn shipped from Kansas City to Chicago.[41]

The Chicago, Burlington and Quincy and the Rock Island protested. This time they turned to their old adversary, the ICC, for redress. By hauling its own grain, in effect at no cost, they argued, the Great Western had committed unfair discrimination. This charge contradicted the intent of the law, responded Maple Leaf counsel C. A. Severance. The Iowa Development Company was best seen in a context in which the complainants had refused to live up to their pledge to share traffic from Kansas City and so provide the Great Western a fair chance to compete. In fact, the prior rate structure, not Stickney's scheme, was discriminatory. The Great Western violated no law.

The ICC listened to Severance unsympathetically. By now it considered discrimination cases in their most prosaic form. Although the Iowa Development Company was not technically a special rate or rebate, the commission charged, "it was clearly a 'device' by which it [the Great Western] transported merchandise for a greater or less compensation than it exacted from all other persons for a like and contemporaneous service under similar circumstances and conditions."[42]

A second competitive tactic intended to nurture regional development also raised protest from national markets and interregional carriers. Early in the new century, the Maple Leaf slashed rates on dressed beef and packing-house products from its western terminals well below the equivalent rates on livestock. By doing so, Stickney hoped to build up the meatpacking industry in St. Paul, Kansas City, and Omaha—each of which had been stalled by the trunklines' low through rates on livestock to Chicago. In this way, regional market manufacturers, nearby ranchers, and the Great Western would share the cost efficiencies of regional development.

In 1902 Stickney announced a seven-year contract with Missouri River packers: in return for a guaranteed percentage of their entire output, the Great Western promised competitive rates from river markets to Chicago.[43] Though the long-haul carriers objected, they met Stickney's rate cuts, and dressed beef rates from the Missouri River and St. Paul to Chicago fell substantially below those on livestock. Angered by the diversion of business from Chicago to western market towns, the Chicago Livestock Exchange complained to the ICC: this was blatant discrimination against a commodity (livestock) and a location (Chicago). Though the Great Western was identified as the principal culprit, its long-haul competitors were also charged. The latter, however, were ambivalent about mounting a defense. If Stickney were forced to raise dressed beef rates, long-haul livestock traffic would become privileged once again. Only one other carrier, the Milwaukee and St. Paul, showed interest in joining the defense.[44]

The 1904 hearings found Stickney in his element. Marshalling reams of data, he lectured the commissioners on cost, discrimination, and the advantages of regionalism. Departing from conventional wisdom, he showed that it was not the case, as the Chicago packers claimed, that manufactured goods (dressed beef and packing-house products) were more expensive to carry than raw materials (livestock). Payload (the ratio of revenues to weight) was higher on the former than the latter as were ancillary costs, such as loading, watering, and stockyard maintenance. Because packers were also better able to respond to the uncertainties of market location and the instabilities of demand, they administered their own fleet of refrigerator cars more efficiently than the railroads. Consequently, the fixed costs of rolling stock were lower for finished goods as well. The Chicago packers' complaint that the Great Western charged less for dressed beef than livestock, despite its higher cost, responded Stickney, was not supported by the facts.[45]

In addition, even though Great Western rates were slightly higher on livestock, the result was nondiscriminatory. If Chicago were considered a regional market town, then the data showed that Missouri River and St. Paul dressed beef rates had absolutely no effect on the flow of western livestock from within a 150-mile radius. If meatpacking moved more and more to western market towns, this was because the location of animal husbandry had migrated west. The Great Western, Stickney concluded, had only redressed a previous pattern of discrimination against the Missouri River markets.

Once again the ICC was unreceptive. It declared Stickney's cost data inconclusive and defined Chicago's tributary market to include the region west of the Missouri River. There was no compelling reason, the commission said, for the Great Western to discriminate against Chicago. Systematically lower rates in packing-house products exposed "the live-stock market of Chicago . . . to undue and unreasonable prejudice and disadvantage, and [gave] to the traffic in the products of live stock and shippers and localities interested in such traffic undue and unreasonable preference and advantage."[46]

"The large interests affected, the immense amount of money invested, the many live-stock markets and packing centers that have been built up and maintained under the former relation of rates, and the injury that will result if the change in that relation is permitted to continue, amply warrant the conclusion that the discrimination in question is not justified by the desire of the Chicago Great Western Company to benefit its stockholders by increasing its business."[47] Instead the ICC called for a level playing field: "The relations of rates on these highly competitive kinds of traffic should not be adjusted with reference to the interests of any particular market or markets." It urged that the law be applied without reference to substantive consequences: "Rates relatively just and reasonable should be established, regardless of results that may ensue, and the live stock should be allowed to go wherever it will under such circumstances."[48]

Having abandoned the task of distinguishing fair from unfair competition, the ICC applied antidiscrimination rules to precisely the opposite intent of the law. Instead of granting regional markets substantive parity, ignoring past practice the commission ruled in favor of vested rights. However, as Severance told the court on appeal, his client's ratemaking practices did not violate the regionalist intent of the law. "There is no reason," he said, "why the products of the farms of Montana, North Dakota, Minnesota, Nebraska, Wyoming and the South West, or the states of Iowa and Wisconsin, should pass through packing house centers and towns where packing houses are located in those states and be brought on to be slaughtered in the city of Chicago. It is not in the interest of the public . . . that this monopoly, or quasimonopoly, should be encouraged and strengthened."[49]

Echoing Stickney's message to regional merchants, farmers, and bankers, Severance added, "It is a matter of sound public policy that . . . all kinds of raw material should be manufactured into their finished product as near the place they are produced as possible."[50] Since livestock production had moved west, excessively low long-haul rates to Chicago discriminated against western market towns and placed "a double cost upon the consumer" in the Plains states, by assuring that western stock would be shipped twice.[51] Moreover, "the farmer," like the consumer, "is entitled to his near-by market," where he "can get his cattle into market sooner" and realize part of the lower cost of transportation. Should the court uphold the commission's ruling, it would stifle these advantages and maintain "a practical monopoly of this business here in Chicago."[52]

The Great Western did not protest alone. Western millers and packers filed as interested intervenors before the court. Regional market development and domestic manufacturing, they complained, were being sacrificed to national markets and raw materials export. Given the international glut in grain, such policies hardly served American interests. "Does it not seem . . . the worst kind of bad policy that raw material, wheat, is permitted to go out of the country at the lowest possible rate of freight, and flour, the manufactured article, is checked thereby?" asked one Minneapolis miller. While the federal government supported low rates on grain destined for Liverpool by spending millions to encourage shipping on the Great Lakes, he added, "any railroad that attempts to meet the competition of the Lakes and carry the manufactured product at a comparable rate is enjoined" by the ICC.[53]

Chicago "ought to have its rights," added the Cedar Rapids packer, T. M. Sinclair, "but it is not entitled to all the rights there are." "Iowa and Iowa cities have some rights in their own products and manufactures thereof." In fact, when the Chicago Livestock Exchange complained to the ICC, they commanded 65 to 70 percent of the Iowa hog crop; by any standard of fairness, this was "more than enough." Chicago commission merchants were not "entitled to overturn existing conditions of prosperity for all and exterminate Iowa industries [for] *it is the settled policy of this country to build up local industries.*" The Interstate Commerce Act was enacted "to prevent the building up of some great cities and some great manufactures at the expense of the country at large and to give local industries a fair chance." The ICC, however, had wrongly conceived the case in reverse. Iowa's "industries," implored Sinclair, "are not asking to be built up by discriminations in their favor, but they have a very robust belief that there ought not to be further discrimination against them."[54]

Twice the federal courts heard ICC appeals to force the Maple Leaf into compliance. Each time they refused. Not discrimination, but "an honest and fair motive on the part of the Great Western in its effort to secure more business . . . was the cause of the change in rates." Ironically, citing the very case that had blocked the ICC's initial attempts to implement regionalist principles, *Alabama Midland*, the court concluded that "competition [between the Great Western and its rivals] eliminates from the case an intent to do an unlawful act."[55] If competitive packing houses had emerged along the Missouri River and in St. Paul, Chicago packers had no legitimate reason to complain. Since the Great Western was merely responding to competition, the ICC had no cause to protect vested interests.

The federal courts were now in a bind. If they held to corporate liberal doctrine and granted competition priority over discrimination, the law might appear arbitrary. After all, why outlaw discrimination if competition assured that railroad-shipper contracts were just? On the other hand, given the history of systematic advantages secured by some shippers over others, antidiscrimination law could be applied to protect vested interests. The ICC had done so, but this outcome hardly seemed consistent with the statute's intent. Only by squarely facing the ambiguities of application through the lens of the substantive intent of the law, could the courts have resolved this apparent contradiction. This being so, both sides complained of discrimination. The outcome of *ICC v. The Chicago Great Western Railway*, then, appears compatible with the regionalist intent of the Interstate Commerce Act, but it was achieved through serendipity, not by the rule of law.

Such experiences strengthened Stickney's commitment to regulatory reform. He continued to argue that fair rates should reflect cost. If the ratio of terminal to hauling costs advantaged the long haul over the short or through traffic over local, such proportional differences ought to be considered in publicly constructed and enforced rate schedules. Nevertheless, if "each city, each village, each merchant, each producer" was not provided with a "fair chance," others might gain cost advantages that were rooted in systematic forms of past discrimination. Only once the ICC was fully empowered to make rate schedules would the relative cost differences between classes of freight and types of traffic be fairly codified. This was not, as critics claimed, impossible. In 1909 Stickney constructed a sample rate schedule, showing how the ICC could simplify the task. Once rates were fixed by law, he urged, railroads would be compelled to compete on efficiency and service.[56]

Stickney coped, however, with regulatory conditions as he found them. The Great Western maintained its low rates on dressed beef, flour, and grain from the Missouri River and the Twin Cities. This strategy was viable only when coupled with intensive development and cost reduction. Substantial investments in new rolling stock, roadbed, and improved facilities at Oelwein and intermediate terminals became imperative. If the Maple Leaf was to manage local and less-than-carload freight effectively and improve its competitive position, it would have to find a secure source of new capital. In finance, as in size, shape, operations, and ratemaking, the Chicago Great Western broke from the emerging orthodoxy in the industry.

Finance: The Condominium of Ownership and Management

Pioneered in railroad receivership and reorganization, the separation of ownership from managerial control became a defining feature of the modern corporation. Like Gilded Age corporate jurists, historians and lawyers looking back have deemed this structure the natural result of high fixed-cost technology. Large-scale capital mobilization, they argue, necessitated passive owners, while complex technology required salaried professional managers.[57] At the turn of the century, however, the managerial corporation continued to vie with both a public and a more cooperative private model. The Chicago Great Western, for example, rejected the legal and financial structure introduced by its national competitors for a *condominium* of ownership and management.

In principle, A. B. Stickney conceived the railroad corporation as a public entity: its rights granted by the state, its obligations circumscribed by regulatory law. In practice, however, he worked with corporate capital markets as he found them. Neither state government, under a public theory, nor regional investors, under a propertied theory, were well situated to provide the Great Western with the capital necessary for intensive development. Nor, as the Chicago, St. Paul and Kansas City was reorganized into the Great Western in 1893, was the New York money market readily open to this unconventional carrier. Consequently, Stickney turned to London, where he established a permanent financial committee to share decision-making authority over all major capital expenditures.

Stickney's links to the London money market had begun in the 1880s. Searching for local sources of finance, he had enlisted the services of Iowa banker Robert Benson. With family ties in London, Benson mobilized considerable British support for Stickney's early drive from St. Paul to Chicago and Kansas City. Until it was reorganized in 1893, the "Stickney road" (as contemporaries called it) was conventionally financed: mortgage bonds were the primary source of long-term investment. Like many of its competitors, the Chicago, St. Paul and Kansas City was unable to service its debt during the depression of the 1890s.

As early as 1890, however, it had become clear that the road was in financial trouble. Once again the business press predicted that Stickney would sell out to a larger system (such as the Great Northern or the Canadian Pacific). A small regional road in this era of system building was inviable. But with the southern division operational, connecting service to St. Louis, and lines to Omaha and Sioux City on the drawing board, Stickney was fully committed to constructing a regional carrier. In reorganizing the Great Western, then, it was imperative to protect it from a hostile takeover in the New York money market. London appeared a safe haven.

Under the influence of its British benefactors, the Maple Leaf adopted a financial structure quite different from the dominant one emerging in America. Instead of following in Gould's footsteps—namely, receivership, cutting off mortgage bondholders, then using judicial leverage to scale back fixed costs—Benson suggested that the Great Western grant owners substantial power and responsibility. In return Chicago, St. Paul and Kansas City bondholders would exchange current debt for a larger amount of British-style "debenture stock," which had many of the favorable features of both stocks and bonds. Like stock, debentures participated in management through their authority to elect the board of trustees and a finance committee located in London. Like bonds, debentures bore a fixed rate of interest to be paid semiannually. Also, they held a lien upon corporate income for their interest. Unlike mortgage bonds, which mature and must be retired, but like stock, debentures were perpetual securities. In theory, then, the new corporation would be financed with high-grade securities, which unlike debt, might avoid interest reduction by default, reorganization, or foreclosure. The reorganized Chicago Great Western would also issue a class of preferred stock, which, removed from managerial discretion, paid regular dividends when earned. Finally, even though the company was empowered, like its larger counterparts, to issue new securities with rights prior to old ones, the latter were provided with a number of procedural safeguards.[58]

The corollary to debentures in lieu of debt was ongoing shareholder participation in management. The London finance committee, for example, had absolute veto power over the actions of directors and officers on questions of borrowing money, issuing new securities, and all other expenditures save operating expenses. In practice, this meant that the board submitted all proposals for improvements and additions to the finance committee for approval. The London committee also was empowered to appoint an independent auditor and provisions were made for an independent trustee to appoint its own treasurer in the event of an impending default. Hoping to avoid the high cost of receivership litigation, Stickney also wanted to preserve cooperation between owners and managers in the event of a financial crisis.[59]

In theory, the condominium of ownership and management would achieve several goals. First, the Great Western could virtually bypass the New York money market, where the threat of a hostile takeover seemed imminent. Second, it provided a vehicle for cooperation between owners and managers and the sort of shareholder loyalty executives expected in a closely held corporation. Third, it would make a steady source of new capital available at favorable rates. This was essential if the Maple Leaf was to compete with its larger and more powerful rivals. Finally, like the Gould and Morgan reorganizations, the Great Western scaled back fixed costs that might threaten the firm's viability in recessionary times.

Fresh from "reorganization without receivership" (as the press called it), the Great Western proceeded to make modest improvements through the depression of the 1890s. Though funds remained too scarce to realize the Oelwein plans or to complete service to Omaha and Sioux City, annual reports show a steady decline in operating costs due to investment in grading, new and double track, terminals, switching yards, and side track. Stickney proudly proclaimed that these improvements were made in the midst of recession, when costs were lowest. The Great Western was also remarkably successful in sustaining the loyalty of British security holders. Periodic signs of a hostile takeover came to naught. "A prominent New York banking house," reported the British press, "has made an offer at a price considerably above the market for the control of the Chicago Great Western Railway . . . the natural connecting link between the Baltimore and Ohio and the Great Northern." It was likely that the New York bankers were acting for the Great Northern's James J. Hill, in his ambitious plan to construct a new transcontinental. Similar stories surfaced routinely over the next decade. Although it is unclear whether such plans collapsed of their own accord or due to shareholder intransigence, in one case Stickney told the editors of *Railway World* that "no negotiations are pending for a sale of the Great Western to any other railroad or combination of capitalists. A majority of Great Western stock cannot be purchased in the open market, as the controlling interest is in the hands of a few men."[60]

Despite shareholder loyalty, the Great Western failed to realize its financial goals. For one thing, unlike the Morgan reorganizations, Stickney failed to use the power of receivership to assess old security holders in return for participation in the new company. By 1894 the Maple Leaf had raised barely one-third of the capital it hoped to derive from debenture sales and voluntary assessments on Chicago, St. Paul and Kansas City securities. The next decade proved little better. Still, the regional carrier was in no position to scale back on investment: the Oelwein shops were under construction, old track needed regrading, and with a new line to Omaha, single track on the eastern division to Chicago was overtaxed. Thus pressed for cash, the London finance committee agreed repeatedly to short-term notes (or "floating debt").[61]

By 1905 thousands of dollars in authorized debentures remained to be sold, and the Maple Leaf had taken on a considerable floating debt. What had gone wrong? Does the Great Western's failure to raise sufficient capital for intensive development indicate the superiority of national over regional systems? If so, we might conclude that efficient capital markets read the evidence correctly: the Chicago Great Western remained a high-risk, low-payoff proposition. The evidence, though, is ambiguous.

Maple Leaf traffic density was substantially higher than other roads in the region. By a number of other measures of capacity utilization, its operations compared favorably with the interregionals. Through economies of scope, the Great Western achieved average car payload weights better than some, and worse than others. This is significant, when we consider its handicap, namely, that the Maple Leaf carried a relatively high proportion of less-than-carload and local freight. While dispatchers and station crews had increased payload in this category substantially, they never achieved the weight possible on long-haul carload freight. Moreover, on the most costly aspect of freight operations—returning empty cars from low- to high-volume terminals—the Great Western compared favorably with its larger scale competitors (see Table 8). This was especially problematic for carriers in the Midwest and Plains, since the density of markets to the east was higher than that in the west. The Maple Leaf was steadily improving also. In 1901, it reported a substantial increase in ton-miles (a joint measure of weight and distance) carried. At the same time, the total number of miles run by freight trains decreased substantially; hence, the average trainload had increased 20 percent from the previous year.

Despite relatively high measures of capacity utilization, the Great Western's revenues remained comparatively low. Though its operating ratio—a measure of the ratio of revenue to cost used by the financial community—was steadily improving, it remained below that of its competitors (see

Table 8. Capacity Utilization: Chicago Great Western v. Selected National Systems, 1905

Railroad	% of Cars Hauled Empty	Payload/ Loaded Car (tons)	Payload/ Empty and Loaded Car (tons)	Payload/ Freight train mile (tons)
Chicago Great W	28.17	14.36	10.27	296.01
Omaha	27.35	15.13	10.99	234.48
St. Paul	30.03	13.73	9.61	296.09
N Pac.	29.27	16.10	11.38	366.52
Soo Line	24.22	15.44	11.70	308.55

Source: A. B. Stickney, "Argument on Behalf of the Chicago Great Western Railway Company," before the Minnesota Railroad and Warehouse Commissioners, Mar. 1906, 49–51.

Table 9). This might have indicated, as E. S. Meade suggested, the road's relentless ratecutting. Stickney defended the Great Western on this point: its revenues were below those on the interregionals because the Maple Leaf could not skim monopoly rents from noncompetitive traffic. Also, extensive competition meant that all Great Western traffic was carried at accelerated speed, thereby increasing the cost of fuel and grading, while limiting the size of freight trains.

Thus even though the Great Western's gross revenues were smaller than its competitors', by a number of criteria this regional carrier seemed a good prospect. That is until it is seen in the context of turn-of-the-century money markets. Recall that most of the railroad industry was in the midst of reorganization at this time. Corporate capital markets and intermediaries were preoccupied with consolidation, debt reduction, and intercorporate shareholding to forge "communities of interest" from the midnineties through the first decade of the twentieth century. In this context, the Maple Leaf's trouble with marketing British-style debentures takes on a new light. First of all, the very idea of an independent regional carrier ran counter to the emerging orthodoxy, that is, interregional consolidation and communities of interest. In addition, Stickney had aroused hostility from his competitors, whose directors typically came from New York or Boston. "Certainly the elimination of the Great Western from the railway situation in the West would be most desirable from the point of the other railroads in that section," wrote Meade in 1905.[62] Maple Leaf debentures faced a number of other disadvantages in both New York and London. The corporation's British ownership was a liability in the domestic market and debentures were unfamiliar to American investors. Further, even though the Great Western had secured a loyal British following, American railroad securities of all sorts fell into disrepute after the reor-

Table 9. Operating Ratio: Chicago Great Western v. Selected National Systems, 1905

Railroad	Ratio of Expenses and Taxes to Earnings
Chicago Great W	72.36
Omaha	64.37
St. Paul	64.74
N Pac.	56.01
Soo Line	56.43

Source: A. B. Stickney, "Argument on Behalf of the Chicago Great Western Railway Company," before the Minnesota Railroad and Warehouse Commissioners, Mar. 1906, 51.

ganizations of the 1890s. English bondholders had borne the brunt of railroad receiverships; consequently, the decade following 1896 saw massive repatriation of American railroad debt.

This is not to say that there was a conspiracy to starve the Great Western out of international capital markets, rather that capital markets do not merely respond to price and risk. Investors, like receivership courts, adopt norms or conventions to evaluate the prospects of an uncertain future. Admittedly, those who committed savings to railroads read measures of past performance. Such facts were open to interpretation, because the very criterion for economic efficiency—scale versus scope—was contested. Not only were Maple Leaf securities unorthodox, its size, shape, and operational strategies ran counter to the emerging consensus among managers and financial intermediaries. A relatively small number of leading figures had attained inordinate influence over corporate financial conventions during the industry's reorganization. Many roads emerged from receivership under the temporary control of prestigious investment bankers, whose stamp of approval assured success in raising long-term capital. The lessons Morgan and others learned from reorganization—setting debt to the trough of the business cycle, full-scale consolidation, communities of interest, and national system integrity—became market orthodoxy during the first decade of the twentieth century.

Seen in this light, Great Western debentures languished not for reasons of inefficiency, but rather because this regional carrier ran counter to prevailing norms at the turn of the century. Its defining features—corporate independence, regionalism, economies of scope, ratemaking for intensive development, and the condominium of ownership and management—fell beyond the bounds of railroad orthodoxy. By 1905 the Maple Leaf had a backlog of unsold debentures and more than nine million dollars in notes which would come due over the next five years. Still, British loyalties allowed Stickney to stave off default by refinancing short-term notes; that is, until 1907, when a series of events overloaded the carrier.

First of all, once the Omaha line had opened in 1903, traffic swelled on the established divisions. By 1906 station agents complained that freight had to be turned away due to car shortages and the limits of single track. The eastern line to Chicago desperately needed double track, new motive power, and rolling stock. Modest work to this end had begun as early as 1904. Unable to finance these projects with debentures, two years later the finance committee agreed to break with custom and issue a mortgage on the road's properties. Stickney estimated that twenty to twenty-five million dollars in first mortgage bonds would be necessary to raise enough money to retire short-term debt and provide an additional ten million dollars needed for improvements.[63]

No sooner had owners and managers agreed to change course than conditions turned for the worse. On September 14, 1907, Oelwein machinists and boilermakers walked off the job in a dispute over wages. Though management offered a compromise, both sides quickly hardened and fell into a protracted stalemate. Given its reliance upon repairs at the hub city, the Maple Leaf was particularly vulnerable to a strike. On top of car shortages, it now had costly repair inventories.[64] Stickney estimated that "during four months of the strike the average decrease [in gross earnings on the Great Western] was 15.5 percent" below the corresponding months of the preceding year.[65] If this were not enough, on October 26, following a stock-market panic, American banks were suspended. The prospects of completing the mortgage plan appeared more and more remote and nearly five million dollars in notes fell due in monthly increments over the next year.

In December Stickney traveled to London, where he sought guidance from the finance committee. Despite tensions, cooperation appeared secure. Several plans were discussed to alleviate the crisis, but rejected as too temporary, risky, or unfair. Owners and managers agreed to pursue the conventional option: receivership. Nevertheless, Stickney assured shareholders that he would not abuse the power of receiver. "I hope you will understand," he said, "that this is not a receivership as is required in the foreclosure of a railroad mortgage, where, in order to accomplish the purpose, it is necessary to sell the property and reorganize its securities. The securities of this company do not need reorganizing as there is ample power reserved for the issue of a first mortgage upon the property, which is the best security which could be issued, even if the property were sold."[66]

Stickney hoped to buy sufficient time through receivership to market new mortgage bonds. But not all creditors were so patient. Late in 1908 a small group of noteholders formed an autonomous protective committee and sought help from the House of Morgan. The slippery path to foreclose now became imminent. Morgan was not a newcomer to the Great Western: he had considered financing its takeover by larger carriers in the past. Also in December of 1907, just before Stickney left for London, Great Western representatives had met with Morgan and his partners, Gary and Perkins, to discuss the road's precarious state. Friendly, but noncommittal, they urged the Maple Leaf to roll over its notes and await better days. They indicated a willingness to help at some point in the future, but reiterated the conventional wisdom that the Great Western's greatest asset was its natural connection with the Canadian Pacific, the Soo, or another national carrier.[67]

Morgan did enter the picture, but not on terms favorable to the Stickney regime. As a representative for dissenting noteholders, he agreed to push the road to foreclosure, where an outside syndicate would take the bulk of its new first mortgage bonds. It seems, however, that the banker's participation was premised on Stickney's departure. After all, he had spent much of the previous decade consolidating large systems, reorganizing failed ones and engineering intercorporate communities of interest to stabilize rates. The Maple Leaf was precisely the sort of road Morgan had tried to bring to heel. As the *Railway World* wrote on the eve of foreclosure, "The Great Western has always been the thorn in the flesh of conservative managers . . . [T]here will be few tears if it passes into the control of some strong and respectable corporation."[68]

Stickney's Maple Leaf line was sold at auction in June of 1909, but it did not fall into the hands of a national carrier. Reincorporated as the Chicago Great Western *Railroad*, it remained independent under Morgan's temporary control and for a half century thereafter.

The Limits of Economic Dualism

Even though Stickney lost control of the Chicago Great Western in 1909, in retrospect, he constructed a viable regional carrier. Not until 1968, when the Chicago and North Western acquired it, did the Maple Leaf lose its independence. Admittedly, railroad regionalism in the twentieth century was not as Stickney had envisioned it. The Great Western, for instance, became famous for its exceptionally long freight trains, which near the end of its independence, ran less and less often. Nevertheless, under four successive regimes, this regional carrier carried on much of Stickney's hardheaded competitive strategy and continued to serve regional markets.[69] Like the Oelwein shops,

the Iowa Development Company, competitive ratemaking, and the early attention to intensive development, the Chicago Great Western continued to
meet competition from more powerful rivals through innovative service and
cost reduction. In 1910 the "Corn Belt Route" (it had been renamed) introduced the first gas-electric-powered passenger-mail express to serve local
and branch-line runs. Several years later, it acquired a fleet of small gasoline
motor cars for section crews. The Great Western was also one of the first
major carriers to adopt diesel motive power, and in January of 1929, it introduced the first "streamlined" gas-electric train to the Upper Midwest.
Likely the most famous of its innovations occurred in 1936, when, in response to competition from interstate trucking, the Corn Belt Route was the
first carrier to load truck trailers onto flatbed cars, introducing contemporary railroads to piggyback service. Even though the interregionals followed
suit, by the mid-1950s it still ranked fourth behind the Southern Pacific,
Pennsylvania, and New Haven among companies providing this service.
Once again, the Great Western found allies where others found enemies. By
pursuing an alternative path to cost reduction and market formation, it was
able to survive the onslaught of powerful competitors.[70]

This account of the Chicago Great Western from 1883 to 1908 does not
constitute decisive proof that regionalism was a viable alternative to national
system building and market centralization. Furthermore, the Great Western's survival in the twentieth century could be interpreted as an example of
"economic dualism." Like other sectors of modern industrial economies,
railroads settled into an equilibrium between two segments, each with its
own internal organization and style of efficiency. From this perspective, the
Chicago Great Western only qualifies, it does not disprove, the new business
history's account of industrialization.

However, seen against the backdrop of conflicts over regulation and finance, Stickney's enterprise looks much more ambitious than an effort to locate a protected market niche within an industrial structure dominated by
national systems. He shared with the architects of regulated competition a
relatively universal defense for making regional railroads more than an anti-
quarian curiosity. Like his counterparts among national system builders,
Stickney's Maple Leaf line would succeed or fail not merely for reasons economic. Regionalism and nationalism alike necessitated support from public
and private institutions.

If the architects of regional republicanism in state and economy lost the
battle for dominion, it was not because their plans were inherently inferior
on technical grounds. By carefully integrating and networking heterogeneous freight, the Chicago Great Western Railway realized economies of

joint production unavailable to national systems. As a result, it achieved levels of capacity utilization comparable to many of its larger scale competitors. If regionalism fell to the margins of an industrial order dominated by national systems, this was for reasons of politics, not economic efficiency. Holding Great Western size, shape, organization, operations, and corporate structure in mind, we can imagine a dual industrial structure in which national trunklines found a marginal niche in a chiefly regional industrial order. Either way, the outcome was determined in the political arena.

Part III   THE
              CORPORATE
              LIBERAL BASIS
              OF GROUP
              POLITICS

CHAPTER SIX

The Predicament of
Regulated Monopoly

Left a hollow shell at the turn of the century, the ICC nonetheless survived. By 1910 Congress had reinstated its formal powers and then some. The Supreme Court's victory, though, remained intact: both Congress and the commission reconceived regulation in corporate liberal terms. Field, not Cooley, loomed over the politics of Progressive Era regulation. Gone was regulated competition to the end of reconciling regionalism and railroad solvency. In its stead, the ICC was reborn with a warrant to balance the adverse distributive interests of corporations and consumers, that is, to *regulate monopoly*.

Pace the new institutionalism, the regulatory state was not born into a constitutional stalemate between old order and new; Progressive Era regulation was a decisive victory for the advocates of corporate liberalism. Moreover, the defining political features of that order share much with the picture of the modern state drawn by an earlier generation of society-centered scholars. Like the pluralist interpretation of American political development in the Progressive Era, we find regulatory politics restricted to conflict over the distribution of wealth within an industrial structure and market landscape presumed beyond the will of democracy (what we have called "the politics of power").[1] Like Marxist, or putatively "corporate liberal," interpretations of the modern state, we also find a twentieth-century ICC systematically subordinate to corporate enterprise and the market (the result of *Alabama Midland* and associated cases).[2] Nevertheless, as state-centered scholars have pointed out, neither pluralists nor Marxists can explain the many dysfunctional outcomes in twentieth-century governance. Judged by their own criteria, the case of Progressive Era railroad regulation falls far short. Against pluralist theory, even though regulation was limited to distributive conflict, it did not result in "partisan mutual adjustment," where groups agree to self-restraint in order to preserve the regime that benefits them. Despite the ICC's constitutional subordination to corporation and market, regulation did not achieve the twin goals "corporate liberal" theorists attribute to the capitalist state: legitimation and accumulation.

In practice, America's first experiment in twentieth-century business regulation failed on both counts. Once the ICC was licensed to regulate monopoly in 1910, it locked horns with the carriers in a bitter stalemate over the distribution of wealth. So paralyzed did regulation become that it stalled the transition from extensive to intensive railroad development.

This outcome, I contend, was not the result of constitutional stalemate or contradictions in the ICC's mission. Rather, it was due to the practical limits of corporate liberalism itself. Though coherent in theory, Field's liberal positivism turned out to be systematically flawed in practice. So mistrustful of one another had railroads and regulators become after years of conflict, they each internalized Field's dictum that the proximate interests of the corporation and the state were antagonistic. Consequently, the ICC took literally the positivist axiom that there was a discoverable empirical boundary between regulation and property confiscation, and its corollary that it was the task of regulators to find it.

But the promise of a factual solution to an inescapably political problem— namely, the trade-off between current consumption and future investment— turned out to be elusive; and without a minimum of trust between state and corporation, regulation became paralyzed. In mutual efforts to bind one another's discretion, commission and carriers appealed to necessity and fact beyond the range of collective will. Tragically, unable to form a consensus or to negotiate a compromise, railroads and regulators set the seeds for the industry's decline.

From Regulated Competition to Regulated Monopoly

Under pressure from the Supreme Court and the railroads after *Alabama Midland,* the ICC abandoned Cooley's mission to distinguish legitimate competition from destructive competition. In so doing its members reconceived railroad economics. No longer did they understand the industry as a complex hybrid, distinguished by features of competition and monopoly. The ICC declared in 1898, the "railroad is essentially a monopoly."[3] For too long "the benefits supposed to result from railroad competition [have been] greatly exaggerated," wrote Chief Commissioner Knapp.[4] Nevertheless, monopolization remained incomplete; therefore the remnants of competition caused rate wars *and* discrimination. Regulatory reform, therefore, ought to "exclude the idea of competition" altogether. The state should grant railroads monopoly status, encourage and enforce the organization of pools, and regulate maximum rates. That is to say, "if [the railroad] is essentially a monopoly, then it must be [price] regulated. The two things," the ICC concluded, "of necessity go hand in hand."[5]

Nothing so fortified this view on and off the commission more than the railroad merger wave at the turn of the century. Study after study showed that formerly competitive lines had come under control by six working groups: the Vanderbilts; the Pennsylvania Railroad; the Morgan-Hill alliance; the Gould-Rockefeller group; the Moore-Leeds group; and Harriman, Kuhn and Loeb. John Moody's *Truth about the Trusts* and the work of Harvard political-economist William Z. Ripley showed how, through holding companies, intercorporate shareholding, and outright ownership, six "communities of interest" had gained control over 90 percent of all railroad mileage in the United States. In 1908 the ICC corroborated this conclusion with a study of its own.[6]

Whether one drew from Moody, Ripley, or others, the ICC's assessment seemed to be borne out by events: "The tendency to combine continues" apace, the commission wrote at the turn of the century, competition is waning and railroads rates are steadily advancing.[7] Indeed, "five years ago," Commissioner Prouty told the American Economic Association in 1902, "the crying evil . . . was discrimination." Events since then have "largely eliminated competition" and the discrimination it caused. "In its place," however, "comes that other danger which always attends monopoly, the exaction of an unreasonable charge." It is no longer merely shippers who foot the bill of the abuse of market power, but the public—American consumers—at large.[8]

Impotent since judicial review in the 1890s, railroad concentration, the ICC complained, only exacerbated the flaws in its enabling law. "In view of the rapid disappearance of . . . competition, . . . attended as [it is] by substantial advance in charges on many items of household necessity," the commission wrote, adequate "safeguards required for the protection of the public will not be provided until the regulatory statute is thoroughly revised . . . So great a change in conditions calls for corresponding change in regulation."[9]

The Triumph of Liberal Positivism

By early in the new century the ICC had capitulated to the terms of debate laid down by the railroads and the Supreme Court. Ever since their attack on the Granger Laws, prominent railroad men and their allies among America's new intellectuals had attempted to shift the public discussion from market landscape to the distribution of wealth within an industrial organization presumed beyond the ken of democratic politics. Not until the Progressive Era, however, was the constitutional grammar of distributive conflict secure. Where the Granger roads found no relief from "confiscation" in nineteenth-century corporate theory, twentieth-century railroads enjoyed the wall between public and private that Justice Field had labored so hard to identify. Recall that, positivist as he was, Field thought it necessary to discover the empirical line between the rights of the corporation and those of the state, between confiscation and regulation. It was a matter of *fact* whether the railroad corporation (a private entity with public duties) had fulfilled its public function or, conversely, whether the public had invaded the private sphere. In the twenty-five years since *Munn*, Field's liberal positivism had moved from dissent to doctrine. In *Alabama Midland*, the Supreme Court had labeled competitive ratemaking a private affair, beyond the reach of democratic majorities. A year later (in 1898), when the high court took up the distributive question, Field's dissent had become orthodoxy.

Smyth v. *Ames* drew together two powerful strands of Gilded Age jurisprudence into a corporate liberal theory of distribution which would shape public debate over regulation for some time to come. From corporate theory, it appropriated the notion that the corporation was a natural entity, a person with rights under the Fifth and the Fourteenth amendments to the Constitution. From the law of eminent domain, the Court reasoned that although the state had the right to regulate, even to take, corporate property for public purposes, it could do so only once due process and just compensation had been accomplished. "If the state were to . . . acquire title to these roads under its power of eminent domain," wrote Justice Brewer in an earlier opinion, "is there any doubt that constitutional provision would require the payment . . . of just compensation, that compensation being the [market] value of property[, not that] prescribed by . . . the legislature? . . . Is it any less a departure from the obligations of justice to seek to take not the title but the *use* for the public benefit at less than its market value?"[10]

Despite his vigorous dissent in *Alabama Midland*, Justice Harlan followed Brewer in *Smyth* v. *Ames*. Writing for a unanimous Court, he declared, "The railroad corporation is a person under the Constitution, and a statute or regulation which does not allow just compensation for railroad service deprives it of property without due process of law." Thus, "the basis of all calculations as to the reasonableness of rates . . . must be the fair value of property being used . . . for the convenience of the public."[11] Moreover, fair value was to be empirically determined, Harlan said, by, among other criteria, the cost of construction and improvement, the market value of stocks and bonds, present costs, probable earning capacity, and operating costs.[12]

If the judicial attack on regulated competition caused the ICC to reconceive its mission in distributive terms, *Smyth v. Ames* furnished a rudimentary technology to accomplish Field's goals. Distributive justice, the ICC reasoned, would never be served until an objective basis was discovered upon which to calculate a fair rate of return on railroad investment. In a sharp departure from earlier practice, in 1903 the ICC called upon Congress for sufficient resources to complete a full physical valuation of the American railroad net. Although the Interstate Commerce Act had directed the commission to measure the value of railway property, for fifteen years ICC Chief Statistician Henry Carter Adams had rejected the task as impossible: the corporate history of American railroads, he wrote, was simply too checkered and complex.

Adams has been portrayed as the archetype of America's cosmopolitan intellectuals, an "economic mugwump," whose efforts to build a new American state were stymied by the residual privileges of nineteenth-century judges and politicians.[13] However, Adams's solution to the railway problem —state supervised pools—evaded the constitutive politics of market landscape and corporate form. Like Albert Fink and Charles Francis Adams, Henry Carter Adams failed to gain widespread political support for his prescriptions. Perhaps more telling for our claim that railroad economics were politically constituted was the extent to which Adams, the practitioner, hesitatingly capitulated to the victory of corporate liberalism.

Until *Smyth v. Ames*, Adams not only believed valuation technically impossible, he argued that the "commercial value" of railway property—that is, the market price of stocks and bonds—was the only reliable measure available. For all relevant purposes, he said, the statistics department adopted it.[14] Only after the turn of the century did he begin to doubt "that the par value of securities measures in any way the real value of railway property."[15] In 1901 Adams informed the Industrial Commission on Transportation that he no longer trusted the long-standing practice of evaluating reasonable rates according to whether they provided sufficient revenue to pay interest on bonds. Debt, he said, did not represent the true value of property. If, instead of bonds, the *physical* value of railroad property was determined, then the courts and the commission might have something solid to work on.[16]

Under Adams's guidance, the ICC officially requested authority and resources to complete a full valuation of American railroads from Congress. Citing *Smyth v. Ames* and subsequent decisions, the commission wrote, "No tribunal upon which the duty may be imposed, whether legislative, administrative or judicial, can pass a satisfactory judgement upon the reasonableness of railway rates without taking into account the value of railway property."[17] Only by carefully ascertaining the facts was it possible to establish "fair value" as the Supreme Court defined it.

Upon internalizing the natural entity theory of the railroad corporation, the ICC reconceptualized its mission. Like new business historians looking back, the commission reified a historically contingent outcome: it now perceived the decline of competition as the inevitable consequence of the high fixed costs of railroad technology. However, if fixed costs determined railway form, the commission reasoned, they also provided an objective foundation upon which to leverage the distinction between regulation and confiscation. Without it, regulated monopoly would be arbitrary, and the ICC's purpose would go unfulfilled. By 1903 the commission had abandoned Cooley for Field; nevertheless, it would be another decade before Prouty and Knapp convinced Congress that railroad ratemaking fell on the public side of the liberal boundary. Over and again, they petitioned lawmakers to grant the commission the full range of powers necessary to regulate monopoly—from physical valuation to maximum rates—only to be ignored. That is until a progressive president reconsidered the facts and an insurgent Congress took up the cause of American consumers. By 1913 the ICC had secured a license to regulate monopoly from the ground up.

Regulated Monopoly Enacted

The Hepburn Act

Not until Theodore Roosevelt personally embraced the cause of reform in 1905 did the ICC begin to regain its license to regulate. Of course, Congress had augmented the commission's authority earlier in the new century. The 1903 Elkins Antirebating Act empowered the ICC to act against the still widespread practice of granting secret rebates. Even though heartily endorsed by neoregionalists still actively opposed to discrimination in favor of large shippers, the Elkins Act was generally perceived as a railroad law. Written in consultation with Alexander Cassatt of the Pennsylvania Railroad, who hoped an antirebating act would further the cause of railroad "communities of interest," contemporaries agreed that the statute would augment railroad revenues—one observer estimated by as much as 15 percent.[18] As such, the Elkins Act added one more bit of evidence to the case for regulated monopoly. The ICC, for one, thought the statute did little to address the most pressing problem since the turn of the century, namely the decline of price competition.[19]

Only with Roosevelt's prodding did the legislature begin to hear the commission's pleas. The result of the president's able party leadership, in 1905 Congress overturned the Maximum Rate Case. The Hepburn-Dolliver Act empowered the ICC to rectify an unreasonable rate or practice by prescribing a maximum charge allowable by law.[20] The statute, however, met with the political limits of reform in 1905. Roosevelt identified them well. He shared the widespread opposition to granting "the commission . . . *general authority* to fix railroad rates." It was, he said, unnecessary and very likely unconstitutional. Still, the president applauded the Hepburn Act for the power it granted the ICC to rectify particular rate injustices.[21]

The ICC's broader message, however, did not go unheard in Congress. Progressive Wisconsin Senator Robert M. LaFollette began a decade-long campaign for regulated monopoly in 1905. Although LaFollette has been portrayed as radical on the railroad question, he took his cue from the Interstate Commerce Commission. As debate over the Hepburn Act waned, "Fighting Bob" delivered a three-day speech on regulatory reform. The Hepburn Act, he conceded, "is not bad for its provisions, but weak because of its omissions."[22] Congress, he charged, had failed to implement its own statutory injunction. Recognizing the experimental nature of regulation, LaFollette reminded his colleagues that the 1887 law directed the ICC to recommend corrective legislation. Each year for a decade, when the commission enumerated "the fatal weaknesses of the law . . . and [proposed] amendment[s] to cure the defects," no one listened.[23] Congress, he charged, "must have forgotten that the law required the Commission to make recommendations. *It must have forgotten the existence of the Commission*" altogether.[24]

Meanwhile, "the situation was growing more serious." Repeatedly, the ICC explained how railroad concentration had resulted in rate inflation passed on to consumers in higher prices on a variety of "necessary and household commodities."[25] LaFollette had not forgotten the aspirations of Gilded Age regionalists. This was, after all, the same speech in which he recounted their bitter disappointments and in which he demanded the power to structure markets be taken out of the hands of the railroads.[26] Nevertheless, market centralization and railroad concentration had become fact. Even though he was the rightful heir to McCrary and Wilson in the Senate, LaFollette actively redirected the debate from market landscape to the distribution of wealth, from production to consumption. Prophet of later twentieth-century liberalism, he found his protagonists no longer among shippers—

manufacturers and farmers—but among American consumers. The Hepburn Act, he charged, was

> not a bill for the great body of American people who constitute the consumers of the country . . . Consumers do not deal directly with the carrier, and yet they pay practically all of the fifteen hundred millions collected by the railway companies annually for carrying the freight of the country . . . The consumer does not know how much of the cost is a freight charge. He does not know that prices are steadily advancing. He feels the increasing burden. He is certain that someone is wronging him. He believes that the railroads are directly responsible for a part of it and indirectly responsible for all of it. He wants relief. What does this bill do for him? He cannot make complaint on his own behalf. He has not the detailed knowledge upon which to base such a complaint. The items of overcharge, if he could specify them, are small, but in the aggregate they are important to him. He could not afford to institute proceedings for reduction if he were able to formulate the specific allegations of a complaint.[27]

Although it reinstated the ICC's authority to rectify rate inequalities once detected, LaFollette went on, the Hepburn Act did nothing to check excessive charges. By leaving initiative to shippers, the consumer was left out in the cold. If the public was to be served "the commission should be authorized to act on its own motion."

Regulated monopoly also required an objective rate base. Following the Supreme Court through the commission, LaFollette told the Senate, "If this bill is to protect the *consumer* as well as the shipper—then the foundation must be laid for ascertaining the reasonable rate; that is, the rate which in and of itself *is reasonable*." Without authority to measure "the value of property of the corporation in question [the ICC] is inevitably driven [to] comparisons with other rates fixed by the railroads." While this might be a fair standard in discrimination cases, it did nothing to redress excess pricing. Consumers, LaFollette concluded, were entitled to "*real* justice, not merely *relative* justice."[28]

If Fighting Bob seemed on the radical fringe in 1906, his demand for regulated monopoly became increasingly mainstream as the Progressive Era wore on. By the final year of his presidency, Roosevelt asked Congress to enact much of LaFollette's program: ICC initiative powers, physical valuation, commission supervision of railroad securities, and federal, rather than state, incorporation. Like the ICC and the "economic mugwumps," the president added lawful pools to the list, but the idea of legitimate cartels had taken on a new meaning in the Progressive Era. A public recognition of *nat-*

ural monopoly, rate agreements would be sanctioned and enforced *only* when accompanied by ICC authority over maximum charges. "The articles under which such associations operate, . . . all their operations"—ratemaking and otherwise—must be authorized by the commission, said President Roosevelt. Only once the ICC had attained full powers over pooling practices, he concluded, would corporation and public alike be assured that rates generated a "fair return on fair value"—no more, no less.[29] But Roosevelt left for Africa in 1908, and despite growing support for regulated monopoly in Congress, LaFollette would have to wait another four years for action.

The Mann-Elkins Act of 1910

The election of 1908 placed regulated monopoly atop of the political agenda. Even though it left a president, Taft, less committed to commission-regulated monopoly than his predecessor, it transformed Congress. Insurgent Republicans swept through the West: Joseph Bristow in Kansas, Albert Cummins in Iowa, William Borah in Nebraska, and Joseph Dixon in Montana joined LaFollette in the Senate. The election also vitalized incumbent senators whose support for regulated monopoly had been steadily growing: Albert Beveridge of Indiana, Jonathan Dolliver of Iowa, and Moses Clapp of Minnesota. In the House, fellow travelers took all of Wisconsin's seats: John Nelson, Clarence Miller, and Irvine Lenroot; while a delegation of insurgents from Iowa won office on Albert Cummins's coattails. Progressives Miles Poindexter of Washington and Victor Murdock of Kansas also got their start in the Sixty-first Congress. Moreover, weakened by the widening fissure between old guard and Progressives, Republicans took less than half the popular vote garnered four years before. In the election of 1910, they would lose control over the Lower House altogether.[30]

Despite the muscle behind the ICC and LaFollette in the Sixty-first Congress, policy initiative came from the president. The centerpiece of Taft's reform was a specialized commerce court. In lieu of the federal circuit courts, this body was to hear all appeals to ICC decisions "on both [questions of] law and fact." The Supreme Court would only become active when explicitly constitutional questions were raised. Taft reasoned that a commerce court, staffed by experts in railroad law, would expedite the ICC caseload and return legitimacy to a judiciary harmed by years of toppling legislative initiatives.[31] Introduced in the Senate by Stephen Elkins (R. W. Va.), the president's bill also legalized traffic agreements; outlawed intercorporate shareholding (but made mergers easier); empowered the ICC to make specific, not just maximum, rates; and granted shippers authority to choose routes. Though Taft perceived it a moderate bill, intended to mediate the increasingly antagonistic wings of his party, Republican insurgents denounced it in no uncertain terms. "In a stinging minority report," Clapp and Cummins called the administration's bill "a long step backward." This was a railroad bill, they charged: the president had consulted exclusively with management before submitting it to Congress. Procedurally biased and stingy on substance, Taft's proposal betrayed the public interest.[32]

The Commerce Court met the sharpest attack. In the first place, said the insurgents, only the carriers had standing before the tribunal. The Department of Justice would plead the government's case, while shippers and the ICC were shut out. Second, in practice the Commerce Court was likely to become the forum of last resort, since Taft's bill severely restricted access to the Supreme Court. Finally, even though the Supreme Court had recently restricted its own powers of review over the ICC, a long and checkered history of court oversight gave the insurgents little reason to trust another judicial body.

The attack on procedure only served to open a first line of offense. When Taft's attorney general returned to the upper house with a compromise bill, the radicals were intransigent. Not only did the Commerce Court procedure come under their knife, with Albert Cummins's able floor management, the insurgents succeeded in augmenting ICC powers considerably. In particular, Cummins added an amendment to the clause legalizing pools, which empowered the ICC to supervise and adjust all collectively determined rates.[33] It would be impossible, he told the administration, to "persuade his colleagues to consent to any provision that did not compel the railroads to get *advance approval* from the Commission for both the rates and the nature of traffic agreements concluded."[34] Lastly, the insurgents added an amendment to reinstate the long-haul–short-haul clause, by striking the phrase "under similar conditions" from Section Four of the 1887 statute.

While Cummins led the floor fight for regulated monopoly, LaFollette remained its most articulate spokesperson. Once again he took to the Senate floor to reiterate his earlier message. Like the Hepburn Act, Taft's bill ignored the ICC's recommendations and the interests of ninety million consumers "who pay all the freight charges of the entire country."[35] Rates on critical commodities, from coal to grain products, had risen steadily since the 1905 law. Yet the ICC still remained powerless. Until it was fully authorized to set all maximum rates and complete a valuation of railway property, LaFollette charged, the commission would remain unable to accomplish its mission, namely to discover and enforce "reasonable rates."[36]

LaFollette and the ICC were no longer ignored after 1908. "I can recall," noted the chair of the Senate Interstate Commerce Committee, Francis

Newlands (D. Nev.), "the contemptuous disregard expressed by Congress . . . and the committee of the actions and recommendations of the Interstate Commerce Commission. I have seen them . . . treated with disrespect; I have heard their recommendations challenged in terms of abuse; . . . and I recall how hard a struggle they had to have their recommendations fairly considered in the Interstate Commerce Committee . . . I am glad to say that the entire attitude of Congress toward the Commission has changed since and . . . it is not one of contemptuous indifference."[37]

ICC documents and reports suddenly attained an air of authority in the Sixty-first Congress. Its 1908 study of intercorporate relations was widely read and cited. As Representatives Cole (R. Ohio) and Safford (R. Wis.) told the House, it documented in bold detail the rapid decline of railroad competition since the turn of the century. One could only conclude with the commission that "railroads are natural monopolies" which perform a necessary public service, Safford said, and therefore ought to be regulated as such.[38] If there was any doubt left, it was put to rest in 1909 when twenty-four carriers west of the Mississippi jointly filed for rate increases from 13 to 50 percent. Within months they were joined by an equally large group of midwestern and northeastern carriers.

This was well more than a tactical mistake, as a number of historians have noted, which stoked the flames of self-interest among the nation's shippers.[39] More important, it clinched the ICC's diagnosis in Congress: railroad rates were set monopolistically, not in response to open market competition. "By common understanding," charged Representative Hitchcock (R. Neb.), railroads in the west "simultaneously" and "arbitrarily" announced an average rate increase of 16 percent. If such monopolistic practices went uninvestigated, added Representative Borland of Missouri, they will become the "basis upon which the railroads intend to crystallize an agreement between the competitive carriers," unassailable by shippers, consumers, or the state.[40]

Taking their lead from the ICC through LaFollette, more and more politicians identified the public interest with consumers by 1910. Virtually gone from the debate was the regionalist appeal to "bring consumers and producers closer together and thereby lessen the cost of transportation altogether." As Progressives saw it, consumers and shippers not only had different interests, in many instances they were at odds. While statutory law had "resulted in benefit to shippers and merchants," said Robert Turnbull (D. Va.), "very little benefit has resulted to the consumers who really pay the freight . . . It does not matter with the shipper what the freight amounts to, so that he is not discriminated against, in favor of other shippers. It does not matter to the merchant what freight he pays, so that he is not discriminated against in favor of other merchants, because he adds the freight to the bill of goods and it is paid by the consumer. There is no question about the fact that the time is coming . . . when the rates have got to be fixed by the commission, in order to protect the consumer," Turnbull concluded.[41] Even though rates continue to rise, added Georgia Representative William Adamson, shippers remain more or less protected. More often than not they "can transfer that charge to their customers and not suffer themselves at all . . . Now that is a beautiful theory for *them*, but the *people* are interested in the amount of rates. They want as low rates as are reasonable and just."[42] It is the "men of small means, who constitute the large majority of consumers of this country, who have at last to pay the charges of the railroad," complained Adamson's Georgia colleague, Charles Bartlett. "There is complaint all over the country . . . that railroads are permitted to fix excessive rates without being controlled. The people in this country will never be satisfied until common carriers shall be controlled to a greater degree than they are to-day," echoed Republican Frank Dickinson of Illinois.[43]

But consumers, unlike shippers, who "deal in large amounts," were helpless before the railroads.[44] "It is very easy for great and wealthy merchants and shippers; . . . for boards of trade; . . . [and] for municipal organizations . . . to institute complaints against unreasonable and unjust rates at the hands of the railroads of the country; but . . . consumers . . . are not able ordinarily to come to the commission and incur the expense, labor and the time, as well as the delay, in having charges investigated," added Bartlett.[45] Only when Congress consigns the ICC with "the duties of investigating" and fixing rates on its own accord will we have served the general "interest of the people of the country" in relief from "unjust and unreasonable rates."[46]

For many in the lower house, consumers would only be served by "continuous [ICC] control over rates."[47] Texas's Rufus Hardy, for example, thought his own state's railroad commission provided a good model. Under the sure guidance of the former champion of regulation in the House, John Reagan, the Texas tribunal had gained "the right to fix and establish permanent rates . . . [which] remain in force until changed by authority of the commission." Following his state's lead, Hardy concluded that federal law ought to assure that "no new rate shall go into effect until approved by the commission."[48] Whether the partisans of regulated monopoly advocated initiative powers or full ICC supervision over railroad ratemaking, they all agreed that monopoly was the problem and consumers were the injured party.

The same politicians disagreed over the causes of railroad monopoly. Some, like Newlands and Dolliver in the Senate, saw railroads as natural monopolies and therefore heartily supported rate agreements and consolidation coupled with public supervision. Others accepted the railroads' monopoly status more reluctantly. For example, although LaFollette and Cummins in the Senate, Lenroot, and not a few Democrats in the House agreed that consolidation was the order of the day, they remained unwilling to give railroads complete immunity from antitrust laws. Concentrated as the industry was, individual carriers, they thought, might still abuse their powers in the marketplace. Interlocking directorates between railroads and industrial monopolists was just such a case. Besides, many recent mergers had resulted in overly generous capitalization. Especially under a regime of regulated monopoly, where the value of securities was one among several criteria used to estimate the fair value of property, mergers left unchecked by antitrust might add one more burden to the rate base.

However divided they were about the causes of monopoly, congressional Progressives gave no indication they hoped to turn the clock back to an era of competition through aggressive antitrust action. Senate insurgents, for example, agreed to sanction collective ratemaking "as long as the sovereign hand of the United States should control" and continually "inspect" such practices.[49] This was a long way from the administration's initial proposal on rate agreements—unequivocal legalization and immunity from antitrust. Nevertheless, the Republican old guard rejected Cummins's compromise proposal. Rather than accept explicit ICC supervision or confront the insurgents in an open floor fight, they struck the rate agreement clause from the Elkins Act altogether. Legalized pools failed to see the light of day not because they were opposed on principle or because Congress represented the parochial interests of farmers; rather, they were struck from the Mann-Elkins Act for reasons of legislative maneuver. As long as it fell within the principled embrace of regulated monopoly, congressional insurgents accepted railroad cooperation.[50]

More and more members of Congress had also come to agree with LaFollette and the ICC that regulated monopoly necessitated supervision from the bottom up. Invoking the authority of *Smyth* v. *Ames*, they advocated physical valuation, at a minimum, and securities regulation, at the extreme. The idea that "real, not merely relative justice" required a true rate base was sufficiently convincing for the House to attach both a valuation amendment and ICC supervision over railroad securities to its bill (the Mann Act). By contrast, LaFollette was unable to muster sufficient support in the Senate to add either provision to Elkins's bill. Even so, the upper house successfully amended Taft's legislation in ways that can only be understood as an effort to regulate monopoly. In addition to assigning initiative powers to the commission, the Senate bill shifted the burden of proof on contested rate increases from shippers to the railroads. Also, it extended the period of time during which the ICC could lawfully suspend rate *increases*, pending an investigation, from 120 days to ten months.[51]

Worried the progressive provisions of both bills would be expunged in conference committee by the Senate old guard, LaFollette's Wisconsin colleague in the House, Irvine Lenroot, introduced a motion to vote the Senate bill into law. The House would lose its valuation amendment, but that was better than squandering every advance toward regulated monopoly. Short by only six votes, the Mann Act went to conference committee, where, contrary to Lenroot's fears, it emerged with nearly every progressive amendment intact. The Mann-Elkins Act of 1910 empowered the ICC to set maximum rates on its own initiative or upon complaint by shippers. It licensed the commission to suspend rate increases for up to ten months, while hearings were held and while it collected data. The burden of proof was shifted to the carriers, and the long-haul–short-haul clause was reinstated without its qualifying language, but subject to ICC-sanctioned exceptions. To LaFollette's chagrin, the valuation amendment was omitted from the House bill, and the securities regulation was left to investigation.[52]

Neither the president nor the Senate regulars lost all in conference committee. The Mann-Elkins Act also created a five-member Commerce Court, which would review all contested ICC cases. The insurgents, however, had succeeded in granting shippers the right to intervene in judicial proceedings and restricting the Court's jurisdiction to that possessed by the circuit courts. The power of the federal courts had apparently been restricted to questions of law, not fact, by the Supreme Court in a recent landmark case (*ICC v. Illinois Central Railway*).[53] But true to Progressive fears, the Commerce Court proceeded to overturn nearly every ICC decision it heard. Of the thirty cases it ruled on during its first year, only three were decided in favor of the commission.[54]

The partisans of regulated monopoly were quick to regroup. In the next Congress, House and Senate voted to abolish the Commerce Court, only to be vetoed by Taft. A year later, after a prominent member of the new court was indicted on several counts of conflict of interest, Congress voted once again to abolish it. This time President Wilson willingly signed the constitutional experiment into oblivion. The Sixty-third Congress also easily enacted LaFollette's Valuation Act in 1913. Once it became clear that the carriers would continue to act in concert, seeking rate advances over extensive traffic areas, support for valuation broadened. In addition to the insurgents, LaFollette now found unlikely support from railroad partisans, who believed valuation would prove the ICC had unjustly denied the Trans-Missouri Rate

Association's request for a rate increase during the Mann-Elkins debate.[55]

Once supplemented by the Railway Valuation Act of 1913, Mann-Elkins was the high-water mark for the mandate to regulate monopoly. Short of explicitly legalizing railway rate agreements, Congress had finally enacted the ICC's ten-year old program. But once the commission acquired dominion over advance rates, it became clear that neither Taft nor Wilson would initiate antitrust proceedings against collective ratemaking. Though it had failed in Congress, Progressive Era pooling would be accepted under the regime of regulated monopoly.

Congress caught up with the commission by 1913, and the commission had finally caught up with the Supreme Court. Licensed to discover an empirical base upon which to exercise its dominion over peak rates, the ICC promised to fulfill its constitutional warranty, namely, to distinguish confiscation from regulation. If the Court took a less active role after it restricted its powers of review to procedure in *ICC v. Illinois Central,* its tacit dominion over regulatory theory and practice was secure: both Congress and the commission had fully internalized the principles of corporate liberal constitutionalism. Indeed, students of Progressive Era railroad regulation have systematically underestimated the high court's influence after *Illinois Central.* Skowronek, for example, has argued that this case was a clear victory for shippers and Congress. True, his point is carefully nuanced: judicial powers over ICC procedure remained substantial.

Nevertheless, this interpretation has distorted our understanding of the relationship between Court and commission because it underestimates the authority corporate liberal doctrine had attained throughout the state. The Court declared it would no longer review ICC determinations of fact, "except in cases of confiscation." But this amounted to all cases of regulated monopoly, in which confiscation was after all the only issue at stake. Also, despite the resurrection of Section Four in 1910, time had been on the Supreme Court's side. *Alabama Midland* had shaped ratemaking practice for well over a decade, and the commission was hard put to find a mandate to overturn the status quo after the Mann-Elkins Act. Most important, the ICC itself did not perceive *Illinois Central* as a grand victory, a great "act of abnegation" by a court under democratic attack. Tempered by years of mistrust for both carriers and courts, the commission read the ruling quite cautiously. After all, Commissioner Prouty wrote to Representative Bartlett during the Mann-Elkins debate, *Illinois Central* will not stop the Court from "attack[ing] our order[s]" if "we ha[ve] no power to make" them, or if the "effect upon the rates of the carrier [is] confiscatory." Indeed, "notwithstanding the decision in the Illinois Central case," he added, "the carrier can take *every case* to court upon the ground that the order of the commission is confiscatory." Therefore, the constitutional question was always one of fact, regardless of the Supreme Court's agreement to limit itself to procedure. Under *Smyth v. Ames,* this was virtually the only ground upon which carriers would appeal. Had the new rule been in effect, Prouty concluded, the proportion of cases going to judicial review would have been unchanged.[56]

The ICC, in short, continued to perceive its mission through the corporate liberal lens of *Alabama Midland* and *Smyth v. Ames.* Congress, in the commission's eyes, was no more than a conduit necessary to fulfill its court-appointed constitutional mandate. Thus licensed to regulate monopoly in 1910, the ICC turned its attention to the railroads' demand for collective rate increases. But no sooner had the commission attained the technology to carry out a task the Court had laid before it, than did the fatal flaws of Field's liberal-positivism become apparent.

The Predicament of Regulated Monopoly

Once the ICC was empowered to rule on "advance rates," it became clear that the state would tolerate collective pricing. Taft had signaled as much when he directed Attorney General Wickersham to cancel an injunction against the Western Freight Association by aborting a justice department antitrust initiative.[57] Consequently, once the Mann-Elkins Act was signed into law, the Eastern and Western Freight Associations returned to the ICC to request an across-the-board rate increase. In its first ruling under regulated monopoly, the ICC refused. Within three years, the railroads had regrouped and returned with a proposal to advance rates 5 cents on every dollar. After a month of hearings, the commission split the request, denying a general increase, but allowing a 5 percent raise in the Central Classification Territory with the exception of some bulk low-grade commodities. The carriers, however, would not be put off; this was a paltry sum for an industry straitened by cost inflation. Only ten months passed this time before they pressed their case again. This time the railroads proposed that the ICC accept rates advances on a wide variety of commodities and relax regulations on charges for specialized services. As in 1914, some requests were approved, others denied, and the railroads were left thoroughly disappointed.

By 1917 the commission and the carriers had locked horns in what many have come to see as a single tragedy in three acts. Bitter from years of fighting, they accused one another of bad faith: instead of resting the case on its merits, their adversary turned regulation into a public relations spectacle. If public acrimony was not enough, railway services were strained beyond capacity by the enormous demand to supply the war effort overseas. Into a void riddled with conflict and mistrust stepped President Wilson. Invoking emergency administrative authority, he nationalized the railroads for the duration of the war.

In its first public act, the Railway War Board granted the carriers a sizable 28 percent across-the-board rate increase. The carriers, it seems, had been vindicated: the crisis in railway service proved they had been starved of resources. So too, it seems, have those looking back, who have condemned the Progressive Era ICC as "vengeful," "punitive," "archaic," "childish," "shortsighted," "one-sided," and "irrational." Turning Kolko's capture thesis on its head, scholars have come to see late–Progressive Era railroad regulation as a victory for shippers (particularly small merchants and farmers) over the railroads and Congress over the Court. Captured by provincial shippers, Congress enacted one-sided regulations; and the ICC, having escaped the oppression of judicial review, heeled narrowly to its new mandate. In the account most generous to the regulators, caught in the conflict between Congress and the Court, the ICC never achieved sufficient autonomy from either to suppress the particularistic claims that threatened the long-run health of the industry. After more than a decade of dormancy the ICC became a ward of its new patron, Congress. In a less-generous account, the advance rate hearings have been labeled "Reagan's revenge"—an archaic, neopopulist attack on phantasmic robber barons. Either way, shippers and Congress were ascendant, railroads were at bay and mature, professional public policy suffered at the hands of vestigial institutions and parochial interests.[58]

This account of the advance rate cases is theoretically flawed and empirically incorrect. Neither shippers nor Congress fashioned the ICC's mission after 1910. Mann-Elkins and the Valuation Act realized no more than the powers to regulate monopoly requested by the ICC for well over a decade. Congress was bereft of imagination on the question of regulatory reform. Although some politicians remained ambivalent about whether to accord the distribution of wealth priority over market landscape, by 1913 they followed the ICC through LaFollette and others down the path to regulated monopoly. If Congress drew its program self-consciously from the commission, the commission drew its program from the Supreme Court.

As for shippers, it might be the case that the ICC perceived itself redressing railroad power over them after 1910. But, as we have seen, the *content* of shipper interests was always problematic. After all, Thomas Cooley believed the commission was redressing shipper grievances under his guidance by allowing long-haul rates to rise. As the century wore on, the ICC convinced Congress that it was not mainly shippers whose ox had been gored by railroad monopoly. It was the great mass of American consumers—that voiceless public, who had neither sufficient stake nor resources to force their claims in a regulatory tribunal. Monopoly, Congress agreed in anticipation of New Deal or "interest group" liberalism, necessitated countervailing power in the state.[59]

Our understanding of Progressive Era railroad regulation, in particular, and business-government relations in modern America, more generally, has been eviscerated by the compulsive search for whose private interests were served by ICC policy. The evidence shows that economic interests were at best ambiguous, fixed only dialogically through the process of forging alliances and identifying adversaries in economy and politics. The politics of Gilded Age regulation involved interest *formation* as much as, if not more than, *representation*. Nevertheless, by 1900 the boundaries of dialogue had been circumscribed, the interests of actors hardened. Less receptive to Cooley's compromises, shippers and railroads pressed their full weight in regulation.

The ICC also narrowed its horizons. Thrust reluctantly into a moral universe not of its own making, the commission tightened the very rules that marked the limits of its authority. Its behavior in the advanced rate cases has remained unintelligible, because students have systematically confused the power to press public entitlements within a hierarchical industrial order for authority over that order itself. The victory of corporate liberalism left the ICC systematically subordinate to the corporate person and market competition. Within these moral constraints, the commission lobbied for reform and, once it had achieved its license, carried out that mission.

Paradoxically, the same doctrine that marked ICC subordination to the corporation and the market was also the source of its power. Cast as corporate liberalism was in general terms, it provided the opportunity for challenge from below.[60] And eviscerated as its conception of politics was, Field's political economy provided regulators with the moral authority and method to check corporate caprice. If the ICC acted rigidly like a litigant before the bench, this was because it had finally internalized Field's dictum that the proximate interests of state and corporation were adverse. In practice, it tested all rate disputes against a putatively observable line between regulation and confiscation. If, in retrospect, regulated monopoly failed to achieve its formal promises, this was not because the ICC was irrational, vengeful or captured. It was due to a deeper flaw in the liberal positivist project itself.

Liberal Positivism in Practice

Imagine a fourth advance-rate hearing on the eve of war-time nationalization. Try as they will, commission and carriers cannot reach a policy compromise or locate grounds for consensus. The promise of "partisan mutual adjustment" pluralists predict when politics becomes bargaining over tangible wealth, rather than ideology, has not been achieved. Instead, rivals hurl bitter recriminations. Looking back on a seven-year fight, commission and carriers harden their positions. Rather than recounting all three rate cases in detail, I will relate the fight as it might have transpired in a single encounter. Though stylized, the following account is accurate: I will draw verbatim from ICC rulings and management testimony, adding citations where appropriate. My object is twofold: first, to show the extent to which Field's liberal positivism shaped this fight; and second, to show how, as long as it remained on this turf, the conflict was irresoluble. The positivist ratemaking project outlined by Harlan in *Smyth v. Ames* was indeterminate. Neither the Supreme Court nor Congress had provided a clue as to how to weigh the many factors identified as legitimate parts of the rate base. Besides, the commission would wait nearly eight years before valuation was complete. As it turned out, though, this was a minor problem. More vexing, the effort to locate an empirical division between regulation and confiscation resulted in intractably circular reasoning. Commission and carriers, nonetheless, pressed on. Tragically, a dispute resolvable only by consensus or compromise was left in interminable conflict. While both parties found ample evidence to support their own logic concerning *historical* trends in the distribution of wealth, the uncertain question of what to do with the industry in the future was left unresolved.

The ICC opened the 1917 session by recounting the previous seven years. In 1910 the railroads from official classification territory and the West proposed across-the-board increases in class and commodity rates, the commission said. "After investigation it was held . . . that the carriers had not substantiated their contentions, and the proposed increased rates were required to be cancelled." "In 1914 a general increase was again attempted by the carriers in official classification territory." Some rate increases were found reasonable, others were not. Once again, in 1915 and 1916 roads from the Official and Western territories, respectively, requested rate advances. As in 1914, some were deemed reasonable; those that were not were cancelled.[61] We believe, the ICC concluded, that we have carried out both our statutory and constitutional mandate. Thirty years of regulation has taught us that the public owes the railroads "a fair return on investment," while the railroads owe the public "efficient service at reasonable rates." As regulators our task has been to find the actual rate level that best achieves a "just balancing of the mutual rights of the public and of the carriers."[62]

But, responded the railroads in their first sign of discontent, your calculations have consistently fallen short. As a result, you have tipped the distributive balance unfairly to labor and shippers. Over and over we have explained why "we need money," only to have the evidence ignored. Costs have risen, but railroad rates and revenues have fallen substantially behind. We have not begrudged labor and suppliers their fair share. "Higher charges for just about everything," explained the president of the Pennsylvania Railroad, James McCrea, in 1910, "were justified to a certain extent by the general rise in the cost of living." Nevertheless, "net profits retained by the railroads were becoming less and less adequate to meet [our] needs. Since 1887, in fact, the Pennsylvania alone had plowed back a quarter of a billion dollars of profits that the stockholders, it was becoming painfully clear, would probably never see."[63] President McCrea's message has been echoed by, among others, officials from the New York Central, the Burlington, the Chicago Great Western, and the Baltimore and Ohio.

This might be true, the ICC responded. Surely, though, the railroads have also gained as much by their monopoly status since the turn of the century, as they have lost in advancing costs. For one thing, since 1905 "rates [have] not been made under the influence of competition." Vast systems of intercorporate shareholding have been organized "for the purpose of acquiring . . . influence in the management of [other] companies as would enable [the railroads] to compel an observance of the published tariff."[64] Legislation also furthered monopoly. "In 1896 the payment of rebates upon competitive traffic was almost universal." As a result of the Elkins and Hepburn Acts, however, "rebates [have been] gradually disappearing . . . It is impossible to say how much has been added to . . . net receipts . . . from this cause, but the amount is great . . . A great many concessions which competition had forced in the way of special privilege have been withdrawn or are now charged for."[65] In addition to the decline of competition, the railroads have gained enormously from scale economies. The "commonly accepted theory that unit costs decrease with increase in the units produced" has meant that you have steadily profited from the growth in traffic during the twentieth century. Surely, the cost increases you complain of have been more than offset by decreases in other areas.[66]

Admittedly, gross revenues have grown substantially over the past decade or so—the result of growing traffic, improved service, and even a decline in rebates, responded the railroads. Still, railroad rates have failed to keep pace with price inflation throughout the economy. In addition to rising wages, we have also seen the price of fuel, construction, land, and steel advance at a much faster pace. When compared to costs, net revenues have persistently lagged behind. One need only look at the most widely accepted measure of financial health, namely the ratio of a single year's operating expenses to operating revenues, or the "operating ratio," to see how much revenues have fallen behind expenses. The operating ratio on western trunklines and carriers in the Trans-Missouri territory has gone from approximately 69 percent in 1901 to 79 percent in 1914; on southwestern roads it has become worse, jumping from 66 percent to 78 percent during the same period.[67] Even a cursory look at these trends indicates that the railroads have been falling steadily behind since the turn of the century. As economist Charles Conant testified on our behalf, " 'What would have been said if it had been proposed by law in 1896 to require the railways to reduce their rates 35 percent to 50 percent within fifteen years?' . . . Yet that was just what had happened. 'We have substituted statute law for economic law,' he scolded. Index numbers of purchasing power . . . revealed that a shipper was paying, on the average, 37 percent less to have a ton hauled a mile than at the end of the nineteenth century. The shippers, who were free to raise *their* prices, in fact 'have transferred an unearned increment to their own coffers at the expense of the railways.' "[68]

The commission paused. What, precisely, does the operating ratio tell us anyway, it asked? "It is almost a commonplace to say that [it] can be used as an index of the relative prosperity of carriers *only after* due allowance is made for other factors which might qualify the showing which the operating ratio indicates upon its face . . . An increased operating ratio is compatible with increased net return on investment where, without corresponding increase in the carriers' investment, the gross revenues rise and still afford a larger net revenue over the contemporaneously increased expenses of operation."[69]

"The exact problem to be solved must be kept in mind," added the ICC. "[You] have attempted to show that the cost of operation has increased and will increase in proportion to gross operating revenue. *This is not the question.*" Remember, "the courts have often said that a public-service corporation is entitled to a fair return upon the value of its property being devoted to the public use." Therefore, "even though the percentage of net to gross is less, still the total net may be more and the percentage of net to *value* [the lawful measure of 'reasonable rates'] may also be more." We cannot mechanically accept the operating ratio as a measure of reasonableness. For seven years, we have labored "to determine whether [your] net return . . . upon the value of . . . property devoted to the public service [was] sufficient without an advance in rates." Of course, "these statements are truisms; the real inquiry [remaining has been] How much?"[70]

Admittedly, the commissioners went on, we have worked under a handicap. Although we first asked Congress for authority and resources to undertake the physical valuation of railway property in 1903, we waited until 1913 to get it. It will be some time before this project is complete and before we will be able to calculate reasonable rates with greater accuracy.[71] We understand ratemaking will never attain "mathematical exactness," but we can come close and to stop short would be to capitulate to the arbitrary. Given this impediment, we have done our best. Without an independent and objective foundation, we reluctantly accepted your own estimation of the "book value" of property, as mandated by Hepburn Act accounting procedures. From this we estimated the trend in the rate of return on property value over the past decade. Although imperfect, the results have been discriminating and, we believe, fair.

Also, we have not been so intransigent as you suggest, the ICC said. In 1913, for example, we found rates in the Official Classification Territory too low. In 1914 we allowed advances on a wide variety of classes and commodities, because rates had fallen and the return on "book value" of investment had declined with them. In order to assess whether this trend was secular or cyclical, we looked at the data over a seven-year period. Our calculations showed the "ratio of net operating income to property investment" peaked in 1906 and 1907, after which "there was a sudden drop in the net operating income and the tendency since that time has been downward." In fact, the ratio had fallen to 5.36 percent in 1913—nearly as low as it had been in 1900, and well below the average for the entire period.[72] Thus we granted a rate increase. When we have found confiscation in *fact*, your constitutional rights have been protected.

Your calculations might be accurate, responded the carriers. We will even grant you the benefit of the doubt on your historical data, but this gives us little comfort in the present. Since the turn of the century, we have completed vast capital improvements, made necessary by extensive overbuilding during the nineteenth century and the enormous growth in traffic since. As Baltimore and Ohio President Daniel Willard showed the commission, the roads east of Buffalo and Pittsburgh have made $660 million in net additions to property since 1911. However, "in the fiscal year ending in mid-1913 [they] showed a gain in gross revenues of $187 million, a rise in operating costs of $203 million, and a net profit . . . that was $16 million less than in 1910." Frederic Delano, president of the Wabash, described similar conditions in his region. Even though midwestern railroads had invested $175 million since 1910, and gross traffic revenues increased from $239 million in 1910 to $275 million in 1913, net profits had slumped by $16 million. "These results," he said, "were due to a number of factors, including the need for even greater efficiency all along the line, but the main reason was that rates had now fallen far behind costs and would do so even more rapidly in the foreseeable future unless rates were raised. If investment in the railroads continue[s] to produce such negative results, who could be expected to invest in [our] business in the future?"[73]

Although the ICC might have the luxury to calculate revenue trends over a decade or more, our investors do not, snapped the railroads impatiently. They read current returns. Consequently, the more we invest, the worse our profitability becomes, and the harder it is to borrow money for intensive development made necessary by the growth in traffic. This only serves to expose a deeper flaw in your logic, the railroads charged. "Need," you tell us, does not in and of itself justify a rate increase. If so, you have come dangerously close to telling us that *all* improvements must be funded from private capital. We are not allowed to accumulate a surplus from which to fund improvements and assure steady dividends necessary to raise new money at favorable rates. Surely *this* is not your theory of regulation. If so, then ratepayers enjoy all the benefits of improvements and investors have no reason to invest. The logic is painfully circular.

Not at all, responded the commission. This is not our intent. All we said was, "so long as the improvement is for the future the present must not be entirely taxed to provide [for] it." In 1911, for example, we considered a case where "the elevation of . . . tracks ha[d] added to the cost of [a] railroad; the value of the property which that company [was] using for the public benefit ha[d] been enhanced." Therefore, it was justified "in demanding from the public a greater return than formerly, *but not in demanding the price of the improvement itself.*" In short, we said that any addition to fair value should be realized in additional return—no more, no less.[74]

Besides, added the commission, did the railways expect that every time there was an increase in labor costs there would be a commensurate increase in rates?[75] To advance rates with each increase in cost would result in an absurd theory of regulation, one in which railroads gain and the shipping public always loses. Worse still, you are coming dangerously close to saying that the state ought to guarantee railroad profits. How could this be so? The result would be to reward theft and inefficiency on the same basis as honesty and good management. Should "the general public . . . stand responsible for . . . mistakes" in financing? "Rates can not be increased with each new demand of labor, or because of wasteful, corrupt, or indifferent management."[76] Had we acted on this logic in 1915, the St. Louis and San Francisco, which was in receivership as a result of shady financial practices, would have been rewarded on a par with well-managed roads like the Burlington or the Chicago and Northwestern. Is the public to bear all the risk and every cost incurred by honest management mistakes, and the corporation none? To be sure, "the public owes to the private owners of these properties, when well located and managed, the full opportunity to earn a fair return on the investment." The carriers also "owe to the public an efficient service at reasonable rates."[77] The theory that costs—labor or otherwise—should automatically be compensated by advanced rates achieves neither goal. In practice, such a theory removes all incentives to improvement, concluded the commission; "we may ruin our railroads by permitting them to impose each new burden of obligation upon the shipper."[78]

The search for an empirical foundation upon which to draw the distinction between public and private was elusive. Short of a complete physical valuation of railroad property, the ICC used available data to estimate "fair value" and the rate of return railroads had earned since the turn of the century. Although it was possible to contest such estimates on how well they weighed the criteria outlined in *Smyth v. Ames,* a more intractable predicament riddled the advance-rate hearings. The promise of a factual solution to an inescapably political problem (namely, the trade-off between current consumption and future investment) resulted in circular logic. Any way commission and carriers looked at it, the value of railroad property depended upon net earnings and net earnings, in turn, depended upon rates. "But," as legal realist Gerard Henderson wrote, "it [was] precisely the level of rates which the regulating commission [was] trying to fix. Whenever it reduces rates it reduces earnings and whenever it reduces earnings it reduces value. We cannot tell what rates the company is to charge until we know what its value is, and we cannot tell what its value is till we know what rates it may charge."[79]

The carriers acknowledged as much when they complained that low rates depressed the value of property and thereby dashed their right to a rate increase just when they needed it most. They were not immune from the perverse results of *Smyth v. Ames* either. As the ICC charged, the notion that railroads should be allowed to pass on cost increases in higher rates led to equally circular reasoning. If new investment from savings *depressed* short-run net profits, and thereby justified higher rates, then every time railroads made improvements rates would increase. New investment from savings would justify higher rates, from which improvements might be made, thereby warranting yet another rate increase. The result would be a never-ending inflationary spiral.

Either way the vicious circle was inescapable. Both commission and carriers tried to determine rates by ascertaining value, and neither was able to do so until they knew what rates would be.[80] Nor, as Henderson showed, did the more subtle attempts to specify reproduction or original costs resolve the predicament of regulated monopoly. "The relation between the public utility and the community," he concluded,

> cannot be expressed in terms of a simple, quantitatively ascertainable fact, for the relation involves numerous and complex factors *which depend on compromise and practical adjustment rather than deductive logic*. The whole doctrine of *Smyth* v. *Ames* rests upon a gigantic illusion. The fact, which for twenty years the court has been vainly trying to find does not exist. "Fair value" must be shelved among the great juristic myths of history, with the Law of Nature and the Social Contract. As a practical concept, from which practical conclusions can be drawn, it is valueless.[81]

The Triumph of Adversarialism

Wedded as it had become to an adversarial theory of regulation, mistrustful of managment, the ICC was unable to locate a compromise acceptable to consumers and carriers. The promise of twentieth-century pluralism to "partisan mutual adjustment," as Henderson anticipated it, was well beyond reach in 1917. Counter to liberal-pluralist claims, the historical eclipse of ideological (or constitutive) politics by instrumental bargaining (the politics of power) did not result in moderation and compromise.[82] In practice, a minimum of trust between state and corporation proved necessary to ward off paralysis and industrial decline. Paradoxically, it appears as though Cooley's republican and *substantive*, not Field's liberal and putatively *neutral*, theory of regulation was a precondition for the pluralist outcome. "The end of ideology," in other words, proved to be an insufficient condition for an effective moderate bargaining regime.

Nonetheless, the regional and mutualist aspirations realized by the early ICC in regulated competition fell prey to the corporate liberal alliance of Supreme Court and national carriers. As a result, the moral economy of regional republicanism lost its claim to political legitimacy. Instead, regionalism appeared to many in the Progressive Era as merely the particular desires of some shippers, no more or less legitimate than the claims of any other interest group bargaining for wealth and advantage. It is little wonder, then, that the few who recalled the ICC's genesis, like LaFollette, mistrusted carriers and courts; while those, like Commissioner Prouty, who forgot it, heeled so closely to judicial instructions. Either way—by the experience and mistrust or by juridical design—the adversarial outcome was not destined, as new institutionalists argue, by the historical sequence of democratization, industrialization, and statebuilding in the United States.[83] Despite the fact that it came first, a democratic legislature proved capable of drawing a blueprint for a cooperative alternative. By a number of measures, the ICC's early experiment in regulated competition was successful.

The corporate liberal alliance of federal courts and national carriers, however, proved more powerful than the alliance of regionalists in society, Congress, and the early ICC. Consequently, cooperation was eclipsed by adversarialism, regulated competition by regulated monopoly, and compromise by the promise of a factual solution to the boundary between regulation and confiscation. Though politically victorious, corporate liberalism turned out to be flawed in practice. Thrust into an atmosphere of mistrust engendered by years of ICC incapacity, Field's adversarialism achieved only stalemate and paralysis, as the ICC heeled closely to its judicial mandate. Thus, counter to Marxist interpretations of statebuilding in the Progressive Era, corporate liberalism turned out to be dysfunctional: it served neither capitalist accumulation nor legitimation.[84] For as historically particular as the corporate liberal industrial order was, it was also cast in relatively universal terms. Ironically, though, regulators found in its promise to generality a mandate to press the very rules that marked their subordination to the corporate person and the market. Tragically, the industry bore the cost.

CHAPTER SEVEN

Beyond Corporate Liberalism

The modern railroad corporation was politically constituted. Its victory was won not on the field of Darwinian market competition. Rather its defining features were deeply contested in the states, in the federal and Supreme Courts, in Congress and the Interstate Commerce Commission. Fighting was hardly limited in scope to questions of corporate form, however. Socialized to varying degrees, this became a public conflict over the institutional norms by which twentieth-century Americans would define the nature of democratic citizenship, market landscape, state structure, and the relationship between public and private. Railroad politics constituted a modern American industrial order I have labeled corporate liberalism.

An ideal-type, corporate liberalism is discernable by its features in the railroad corporation, industrial landscape, and regulation. On the first, the capitalist enterprise became huge, vertically integrated, and internally hierarchical, that is, distinguished by the separation of ownership from control and plan from execution. On the second, a relatively steep "urban pyramid," in which the distribution of city size falls off rapidly from large to small, came to characterize modern market landscape. Finally, business regulation became an adversarial enterprise in which the state acts to broker distributive claims between the corporation, no longer disciplined by competition, and noncorporate classes.

Although contested in isolation and in partial combination, these features formed a coherent whole. Corporate liberalism became a model of industrial order intelligible not only to social scientists in retrospect, but to natives at the time as well. For, unable to act on inescapably ambiguous interests in an uncertain world, economic and political agents were obliged to devise criteria for choice. With models partially formed, railroad entrepreneurs enlisted allies to experiment in the market, interest groups identified their adversaries, and statebuilders constructed policy coalitions. At some moments, however, the architects of corporate liberalism were compelled to articulate their assumptions and the relations between the economic and political features of industrial order with remarkable clarity and detail. Field's dissenting opinion in *Munn*, Brewer's decision in the *Wabash* receivership, the Supreme Court in *Alabama Midland*, and the Interstate Commerce Commission's efforts to redesign regulation after the turn of the century were four such moments.

In this study I identify corporate liberalism not merely by its features but also by its principles of analysis and moral conduct. I call it corporate because its practitioners made explicit the notion that the corporation was a natural entity, an organic body, with rights and status prior to the state and the individual. I call it liberal because they also articulated the principle that property and markets were presocial in nature, hence the wellspring of primary rights which necessitated protection from democratic politics. In synthesis, corporate liberalism held that economy was separate from politics and that the "laws of trade were stronger than the laws of men." Like much of the social science by which we in the late twentieth century still apprehend economic and political development, the architects of corporate liberalism conceived industrialization as a technical process, largely exogenous to politics, and statebuilding as an adaptive enterprise, an adjustment in large part to novel economic circumstances.

Corporate liberalism was advantaged, but hardly assured, by the Civil War. By realigning the American economy from king cotton and Atlantic trade to western development and by restructuring domestic capital markets and federal fiscal policy, the war accorded railroad system building a dominant status in industrialization. This turned out to be an ambiguous legacy for corporate liberalism: it made enormous resources available for national railroad system building, but postbellum capital markets fueled such extensive overbuilding that they threatened to sabotage the very experiment they made possible. Unable to meet mounting debt, well over half of all railroad mileage in the United States collapsed in the late nineteenth century and fell into court-ordered receivership. Here the prevailing rules of corporate jurisprudence threatened to dismember national systems and strip their architects of authority. Nevertheless, a federal judiciary, appointed by the same administrations that had successfully fended off third-party challenges to federal money and banking policy, systematically reallocated intracorporate entitlements. The result was to shield huge systems, to institutionalize the separation of ownership from control, and to reduce railroad debt (fixed costs) on average by one-third. Railroad cost structure was thus politically contingent, not technologically necessary.

The advantages accorded to corporate liberalism by the Civil War were ambiguous in a second sense. In economy, the war opened railroad development to a much wider array of experiments than typically thought. In politics, the more the state subsidized corporate development, directly and indirectly, the more those who envisioned an alternative track to industrialization became willing to use government to achieve their ends. In time the elements of another industrial order, regional republicanism, emerged in state and economy to vie for hegemony with corporate liberalism. Like its counterpart, regional republicanism is an ideal type, distinguished by its features in the railroad corporation, market landscape, and regulation. Within the railroad corporation, it was characterized by an emphasis upon economies of scope or networking, moderate size, regional service, hub-and-spoke form, a condominium of ownership and management, and a flatter internal hierarchy. In market landscape, regional republicanism was distinguished by a relatively decentralized pattern of modest-sized urban markets (an "urban pyramid" of moderate slope). Finally, railroad competition was to be regulated, not superseded by a state empowered to set maximum rates.

Like corporate liberalism, regional republicanism is also identifiable by its principles of moral economy as well as by its measurable features. For it, too, was a native model, its language of cultural authority articulated most clearly by its architects at moments of crisis and conflict. I label this model regional because its architects and practitioners envisioned, to recall the language of Henry Carey, a "social economy . . . of the multiplication of convenient centers of trade and industry, of . . . many small cities well distributed over the country." I call it republican for two reasons. First, the regionalist vision itself was rooted in the republican notion that the state was responsible for the material conditions necessary to individual autonomy. Extreme market centralization, regional republicans thought, resulted in equally extreme disparities in wealth and widespread economic dependence—neither of which were hospitable to the self-sufficiency necessary for individuals to shoulder the burdens of democratic citizenship. Second, I call this model republican because its practitioners—from James Wilson to A. B. Stickney to Thomas Cooley—could not imagine an economy separate from politics. For these men the content of property rights, contract, and the corporate charter were social conventions, necessarily embedded in history and politics. Nor did they conceive government regulation as a substitute for a self-regulating market; rather they saw it as a set of democratically defined moral boundaries placed upon state and corporate behavior. Once in place, the mission of regulatory administration was not merely to exercise police powers over business; it was to cultivate self-limiting behavior—a sense of republican moral personality—among corporate managers and noncorporate groups.

Though regional republicanism and corporate liberalism traveled separate tracks throughout the late nineteenth century, their practitioners clashed in the states, in Congress, in the federal and Supreme Courts, and in the Interstate Commerce Commission. Initiatives from society to enlist state power to consolidate one or another economic strategy typically generated political opposition. Initiatives from within the state to build administrative capacity invariably generated conflict over the *ends* of industrial society. Rarely, however, was the clash between alternative principles of industrial order so comprehensive and poignant than in the denouement between the Supreme Court and the ICC in the 1890s. Coupled with the outcome of many neighboring skirmishes in receivership courts, Granger states and Congress, only one model of industrial order emerged dominant: corporate liberalism. Although its victory has been judged the result of *technical* superiority by later generations, I have attempted to show that this was not the case. Judged on economic grounds, the history of the Chicago Great Western Railroad indicates that high levels of productive efficiency were attainable by a railroad of modest size and hierarchy, which served decentralized or regional market development. Through economies of scope or networking, the Great Western achieved productive efficiencies equivalent to or better than a number of its national competitors.

Regional republicanism was also successful by the criterion of effective public administration, defined here as state capacity to broker competing claims and to ensure conditions favorable for reinvestment and sectoral prosperity. Guided by Thomas Cooley's sympathy for regionalism and his administrative imagination, the early ICC devised a regulatory architecture capable of serving regional development *and* railroad efforts to check rate wars. By regulating, rather than superseding, competition through strictly enforced rules against discrimination, the ICC provided the railroads with an effective prophylactic against rate demoralization. Short-lived as it was, regulated competition showed signs of achieving more than this minimum criterion for administrative success. It also began to cultivate cooperation between state and corporation and to make substantial progress toward reconciling the American creed of equality, individual autonomy, and decentralization with the necessities of modern industry.

Though successful on both economic and political criteria, the architects of regional republicanism lost their war of position over capital markets and regulation. Just when corporate reorganizers had secured the judicial machinery to hedge national railroad systems against dismemberment and insolvency, A. B. Stickney found the New York money market closed to his experiment in railroad regionalism. Though efficient by a number of measures, Great Western organization, traffic management, and rate-setting practices fell beyond the bounds of an emerging corporate orthodoxy shared by investment bankers and reorganization managers. Similarly, although regulated competition was successful on a number of criteria, it lost its war with a judiciary increasingly committed to a corporate liberal orthodoxy. Stickney eventually lost control of the Great Western, and Cooley's heirs on the ICC capitulated to a corporate liberal theory of regulation.

Regionalism persisted at the margins of political consciousness and economic practice: the Chicago Great Western remained a regional carrier, and even though the ICC could no longer justify regional ratemaking on universal principles, it did not become unlawful. Still, railroad "communities of interest" were consolidated and the ICC was reborn corporate liberal in the Progressive Era. The commission abandoned regulated competition for regulated monopoly, production for consumption, and the republican idea that economic form was politically determined for the liberal notion that the modern state would countervail the corporation's natural market power.

Evaluated in isolation, the modern railroad corporation was extremely successful. As Chandler has so appreciatively shown, the hierarchical national railroad system achieved remarkable scale economies and made similar advances possible in other industries by unifying a huge domestic market. However, evaluated as an *industrial order*—that is, a complex of institutions designed to govern the relationship between economy and society—America's first experiment in corporate liberalism was less successful. For, despite the ICC's promise to find a *factual* solution to the corporate liberal problem of balancing regulation with confiscation, it remained an inescapably *political* problem. Tragically, the result was a regulatory paralysis that so stalled the transition from extensive to intensive railroad development that it set the seeds for the industry's long-term decline.

The Politics of Memory

If the Progressive Era ICC recalled enough of its past to mistrust railroad estimates of the facts, it surely forgot its genesis in regional republicanism. By the time the commission had regained the authority to regulate railway rate discrimination, the difference between one general principle of market landscape and another seemed arbitrary, no more than a logic of justification for one or another private group interest. Unable to choose, the ICC endorsed the status quo: national market ratemaking.

Together, the advance-rate cases and Arlington Fruit signaled the cultural authority of corporate liberalism in twentieth-century American political economy. Corporate form and market landscape, from this perspective, were determined outside the realm of collective action or democratic choice. Claims upon either were deemed private matters; only redistributive questions remained public. Thus the role of the administrative state was to locate the empirical balance between public and private or legitimate regulation and property confiscation.

By mid-twentieth century much in institutional practice had been reified in political theory. A political science that hoped to explain things as they were, not merely as they were meant to be, posited politics as a clash of private interests. In America, pluralists wrote, bargaining over means—"partisan mutual adjustment"—was successful precisely because of consensus over ends: everyone agreed over the goals of industrial society and the rules of procedural democracy. Hence, interest groups learned to moderate their claims upon the state and the redistribution of corporate income in order not to kill the goose that laid the golden egg. Grand questions of ideology—in political economy, *what* to produce and *how* to produce it—were thought to be resolved. The defining characteristics of the modern corporation and the administrative state taken for granted, politics had become a matter of group competition and generating countervailing powers for underrepresented interests. Coupled with ideological consensus, then, such fluid group bargaining, pluralist scholars argued, ensured political stability and representation.[1]

Economic stagflation and public fiscal crisis in the 1970s, however, appeared to undermine this picture of American politics. Where political scientists once found moderation and stability in group bargaining, they now find rent seeking, hyperpluralism, distributive coalitions, and a governability crisis.[2] Where consensus over the organization of production had once relegated politics to bargaining over income, now the consumptionist emphasis upon self-gratification undermines the qualities of abstention and self-discipline necessary for capitalist development and democratic politics.[3] And where the distributive trade-off between inflation and unemployment once seemed a permanent fixture of macroeconomic management, slow growth reigns.

As a result, students of American politics have rediscovered political economy. Capitalism, pluralists have pointed out, places an iron cage around polyarchy. The market, Lindblom writes, imprisons democracy, because all majoritarian efforts to redistribute wealth are "self-punishing." By decreasing investment and increasing unemployment, redistributive majorities ultimately bear the cost of their own program. Beyond a certain point, others write, labor militancy undermines economic growth and so the material conditions necessary for subordinate classes to consent to capitalist democracy. There is, many scholars agree, an inevitable trade-off between equity and efficiency, or as Stephen J. Field wrote a century before, between regulation and confiscation.[4]

Seen from the perspective of *Alternative Tracks*, however, the perverse effects of distributive politics in the late twentieth century is not an empirical verification of the laws of capitalist democracy. Rather, it more likely signals the limits of an industrial order established during the Progressive Era. If the experience of the advance-rate cases is generalizable, the current era is better understood as an example of the "predicament of regulated monopoly" than a systemic law. Indeed, this case suggests that in a society, like the United States, where the aspirations to substantive equality, individual autonomy, and self-government are never far below the surface of cultural authority, narrowing the scope of politics to redistributive questions tends to generate mistrust for business among noncorporate groups and the public administrators licensed to redress, not fashion, corporate power. Students of modern labor relations have long noted the danger of paralysis in such adversarial bargaining regimes: too weak to shape the principles that govern working life, workers vulnerable to management caprice often act to protect themselves by holding narrowly to bureaucratic job descriptions, or "working to rule"[5] Paradoxically, such weakness results in an inordinate negative power, namely, the ability to immobilize assembly line production. ICC behavior in the late Progressive Era indicates a similar dynamic in regulation. Its mandate to shape corporate form and industrial landscape dashed, the ICC was left with the relatively narrow mission of protecting vulnerable consumers from the exercise of capricious monopoly power. Like the worker who obstructs by invoking bureaucratic rule, an ICC deeply mistrustful of railroad power paralyzed regulation by taking its liberal positivist mission literally.

Note just how different is this understanding of the perverse effects of distributive bargaining (regulated monopoly) than structural theories which posit a necessary trade-off between equality and efficiency. Where the latter argue that the rational pursuit of self-interest in a capitalist democracy results in a fundamental conflict between representation and accumulation, the former suggests that no bargaining regime can function without a minimum level of trust and compromise. Put in terms of the conflict explored in this study, despite the political victory of Field's corporate liberal theory of regulation, in practice Cooley's republican or mutualist theory turns out to be empirically superior. For it is not merely the case that the ICC's experiment in regulated competition was more successful than regulated monopoly. It is also true that Cooley's mutualist theory of the corporation anticipated the conclusion that Gerard Henderson drew from observing over two decades of American experience with public utility and railroad regulation, namely, that the promise of a technical solution to an inescapably political question—where to draw the line between regulation and confiscation—was a chimera. Absent accommodation and compromise, Henderson wrote echoing Cooley, regulation faced the imminent dangers of stalemate and paralysis.

Moreover, from the perspective of this study, the corporate liberal regime that was judged so successful at mid-twentieth century and structurally contradictory in the 1970s and 1980s was no more than what Robert Dahl has called a "historic commitment," the result of an overt and protracted conflict with an institutional and conceptual alternative. In short, three insights of this study—the success of regulated competition from 1887 to 1895, the superiority of Cooley's mutualist theory of the corporation in explaining the perverse effects of regulated monopoly, and the fact that corporate liberalism was politically constituted—indicate that neither pluralist nor structural theories can fully explain the dangers of paralysis in a distributive bargaining regime. Seen historically, then, it is likely that the contemporary crisis is better understood as the limits of a corporate liberal industrial order first experienced in railroad regulation three-quarters of a century ago.

As in the late nineteenth century, today we can reopen American political economy to constitutive questions. For the first time in nearly a century, the defining features of corporate capitalism and efficiency principles of mass production have been called into question. Long considered the ingredients of economic success, the modern corporation's huge size, vertical integration and separation of ownership from control and plan from execution now look like liabilities in an age of constantly changing technology and markets.[6] Yet in America, corporate liberal principles remain extraordinarily tenacious in public policy. Having mistaken a historical commitment for scientific law, scholars and practitioners alike have advocated shifting the balance from redistribution to accumulation.[7] Thus, Reagan-era deregulation endeavored to reinvigorate economic growth and solve a governability crisis by systematically dismantling the rights of noncorporate classes and the state's licence to discipline corporate discretion.

A cursory look at the results of this policy indicates that a distributive theory of capitalist democracy was no better in the 1980s than it was in 1915.[8] For just as the Railway War Board's rate increase failed to overcome the deeper handicaps of regulated monopoly, the dramatic redistribution of wealth from bottom to top in the 1980s failed to achieve its sanguine promises to national prosperity. Moreover, although deregulation has altered the composition of interest groups and their points of access to the state, it did not achieve its promise to depoliticize allocative decisions in American political economy. More groups than ever attempted to enlist state power in their efforts to reap the rewards of economic change and foist its costs onto others.[9]

In the 1980s, as in the Progressive Era, the promise to remove politics from allocative decisions inevitably fell short. Thus, if the ideas of Cooley and Henderson are as cogent in the 1990s as they were in their own time, we should expect the redistributive (corporate liberal) policies of the past decade to produce perverse results. We have seen how the Supreme Court's effort to privatize the *ends* of the corporation in the 1890s resulted in rigid and narrow claims upon the railroad income after the century's turn. While such an adversarial regime need not result in paralysis, it is unlikely to cope well with economic uncertainty and change. For, fearful that they alone will bear the cost of experimentation, noncorporate groups and their self-styled guardians in the state hold fast to hard-won privileges.[10] Just as this was the case in late Progressive Era railroad regulation, it will likely be so in the next generation. As American politics takes its routine swing back to the left and nonbusiness groups seize new rights, it is likely that the predicament of a low-trust bargaining regime will replay itself all over again.

There is, however, another possibility. Like Cooley, Wilson, Stickney, and LaFollette, we can seize the current constitutive moment to reassess America's historic commitment to corporate liberalism. As economic routine once held immutable now appears fragile, it has become possible once again to pose the question critics of corporate power from William Leggett to Robert Dahl have asked: is there a form of commercial enterprise more compatible with the American commitment to pluralist democracy than the hierarchal private corporation? This study has shown that it is neither utopian nor parochial to do so. Only by taking more seriously the American creed of equality, individual autonomy, and self-government can we come closer to achieving the realist's promise to distinguish economic necessity from political choice. To accept less, when neither the facts of history nor the current era indicate that corporate liberalism was the best of all possible worlds, is not "wisdom, but self-inflicted blindness."[11]

NOTES

Chapter 1. Toward a Constitutive Political Economy

1. On the principles of Fordism or the virtuous circle of mass production and consumption, see Michael J. Piore and Charles F. Sabel, *The Second Industrial Divide: Possibilities for Prosperity* (New York: Basic Books, 1984), 49–132; Robert B. Reich, *The Next American Frontier* (New York: Time Books, 1983), 47–114; Michel Aglietta, *A Theory of Capitalist Regulation* (London: New Left Books, 1979); George E. Garvey and Gerald J. Garvey, *Economic Law and Economic Growth: Antitrust, Regulation, and the American Growth System* (New York: Praeger, 1990), 33–39; Paul Hirst and Jonathan Zeitlin, "Flexible Specialization versus Post-Fordism: Theory, Evidence, and Policy Implications," *Economy and Society* 20 (Feb. 1991), 1–56.

2. For classical criticisms of regulation as a form of "capture," see Theodore Lowi, *The End of Liberalism: The Second Republic of the United States*, 2d ed. (New York: Norton, 1979), 67–126; Grant McConnell, *Private Power and American Democracy* (New York: Alfred A. Knopf, 1966), 246–97. On labor's inability to secure full employment in this redistributive industrial order, see Mike Davis, *Prisoners of the American Dream: Politics and Economy in the History of the U.S. Working Class* (London: Verso, 1986), 246–97. On the plight of the structurally dispossessed, see Michael Harrington, *The Other America* (New York: Macmillan, 1962); Frances Fox Piven and Richard Cloward, *Regulating the Poor: The Functions of Public Welfare* (New York: Pantheon, 1971).

3. There is an enormous mid-twentieth century literature that identified the modern corporation as the inevitable byproduct of industrialization and countervailing or redistributive institutions as the best cause for modern democracy. The classic statements are Adolf Berle and Gardiner Means, *The Modern Corporation and Private Property* (New York: Harcourt, Brace & World, 1968); John Kenneth Galbraith, *American Capitalism: The Concept of Countervailing Power* (Boston: Houghton Mifflin Company, 1952); John Kenneth Galbraith, *The New Industrial State* (Boston: Houghton Mifflin, 1967); James Burnham, *The Managerial Revolution: What Is Happening in the World* (New York: John Day, 1941); Thurman Arnold, *The Folklore of Capitalism* (New Haven: Yale University Press, 1937).

4. Charles Lindblom, *Politics and Markets: The World's Political-Economic Systems* (New

York: Basic Books, 1977), 170–233; Charles Lindblom, "The Market as Prison," in Thomas Ferguson and Joel Rogers, eds., *The Political Economy* (Armonk, N.Y.: M. E. Sharpe, 1984), 3–11; Robert Dahl, "On Removing Certain Impediments to Democracy in the United States," in Robert H. Horowitz, ed., *The Moral Foundations of the American Republic*, 3d ed. (Charlottesville: University Press of Virginia, 1986), 230–52.

5. See Samuel P. Huntington, *American Politics: The Promise of Disharmony* (Cambridge: Harvard University Press, 1981); Walter Lippmann, *Drift and Mastery: An Attempt to Diagnose the Current Unrest* (1914; reprint, Englewood Cliffs, N.J.: Prentice-Hall, 1961); James W. Ceaser, "In Defense of Republican Constitutionalism: A Reply to Dahl," in Horowitz, ed., *The Moral Foundations of the American Republic*, 253–81; Richard Hofstadter, *The Age of Reform: From Bryan to F.D.R.* (New York: Vintage Books, 1955); Louis Hartz, *The Liberal Tradition in America: An Interpretation of American Political Thought since the Revolution* (New York: Harcourt, 1955); Walter Dean Burnham, *The Current Crisis in American Politics* (New York: Oxford University Press, 1982); James Morone, *The Democratic Wish: Popular Participation and the Limits of American Government* (New York: Basic Books, 1990).

6. On the growing doubts about the effectiveness of the modern corporation, see William Abernathy, *The Productivity Dilemma: Roadblock to Innovation in the Automobile Industry* (Baltimore: Johns Hopkins University Press, 1978); Thomas J. Peters and Robert H. Waterman, *In Search of Excellence: Lessons from America's Best-Run Companies* (New York: Harper & Row, 1982); Piore and Sabel, *The Second Industrial Divide*, 194–220, 240–50; Reich, *The Next American Frontier*, 117–224; James P. Womack, *The Machine That Changed the World* (New York: Rawson Associates, 1990).

7. On economic deregulation, see Martha Derthick and Paul Quirk, *The Politics of Deregulation* (Washington: Brookings Institution, 1985); Richard A. Harris and Sidney Milkis, *The Politics of Regulatory Change: A Tale of Two Agencies* (New York: Oxford University Press, 1989). On doubts about the welfare state, see Bruce Scott, "Can We Survive the Welfare State?" *Harvard Business Review* 60 (Sept.–Oct. 1982): 70–84; Charles Murray, *Losing Ground: American Social Policy, 1950–1980* (New York: Basic Books, 1984); David T. Elwood, *Poor Support: Poverty in the American Family* (New York: Basic Books, 1988). On the changing role of trade unions, see Thomas Kochan, Robert McKersie, and Harry Katz, *The Transformation of American Industrial Relations* (New York: Basic Books, 1986).

8. Bruce Ackerman, *We the People 1: Foundations* (Cambridge: Harvard University Press, 1991); Dahl, "On Removing Certain Impediments to Democracy." See also Robert Dahl, *Dilemmas of Pluralist Democracy: Autonomy vs. Control* (New Haven: Yale University Press, 1982), 108–37, 197–202.

9. Alfred D. Chandler, Jr., *The Visible Hand: The Managerial Revolution in American Business* (Cambridge: Harvard University Press, 1977). Chandler's work has since influenced well more than business historians. For his influence on the historiography of other large-scale, bureaucratic institutions that characterize modern American life, see Louis Galambos, "The Emerging Organizational Synthesis in Modern American History," *Business History Review* 44 (Autumn 1970): 279–90; Louis Galambos, "Technology, Political Economy, and Professionalization: Central Themes of the Organizational Synthesis," *Business History Review* 57 (Winter 1983): 471–93; Thomas K. McCraw, "Introduction: The Intellectual Odyssey of Alfred D. Chandler, Jr.," in Thomas K. McCraw, ed., *The Essential Alfred Chandler: Essays toward a Historical Theory of Big Business* (Boston: Harvard Business School Press, 1991), 1–21, where the author also explores Chandler's influence on economics, sociology, and management science. For a useful discussion of Chandler's

theoretical relevance to political science, see Peter Hall, *Governing the Economy: The Politics of State Intervention in Britain and France* (New York: Oxford University Press, 1986), 36–37, 42.

10. Chandler, *The Visible Hand*, 79–187; Alfred D. Chandler, Jr., *Scale and Scope: The Dynamics of Industrial Capitalism* (Cambridge: Harvard University Press, 1990), 26, 53–58; Alfred D. Chandler, Jr., *The Railroads: The Nation's First Big Business; Sources and Readings* (New York: Harcourt, 1965), 3–12, 21–24.

11. On the "three investments" necessary for success more generally, see Chandler, *Scale and Scope*, 21–34; Chandler, *The Visible Hand*, 6–12.

12. Chandler, *Scale and Scope*, 235–392.

13. Charles F. Sabel, *Work and Politics: The Division of Labor in Industry* (Cambridge: Cambridge University Press, 1982), 4–10; Charles F. Sabel and Jonathan Zeitlin, "Historical Alternatives to Mass Production: Politics, Markets, and Technology in Nineteenth-Century Industrialization," *Past and Present* 108 (Aug. 1985): 133–76; Philip Scranton, *Proprietary Capitalism: The Textile Manufacture at Philadelphia, 1800–1885* (Cambridge: Cambridge University Press, 1983), 1–71; James Livingston, *Origins of the Federal Reserve System: Money, Class, and Corporate Capitalism, 1890–1913* (Ithaca, N.Y.: Cornell University Press, 1986), 33–67; Roberto M. Unger, *Social Theory: Its Situation and Its Task* (Cambridge: Cambridge University Press, 1987).

14. Chandler, *Scale and Scope*, 21–29. Although Chandler argues that economies of scope necessarily leads to larger size, the logic and evidence are ambiguous on this point. As chapter 5 will show, economies of scope in railroads placed an upper limit on size and the extent of managerial hierarchy.

15. For a new business history view of regulation as economically constrained rather than economically constitutive, see Thomas K. McCraw, "Regulation in America: A Review Article," *Business History Review* 49 (Summer 1975): 181, where the author concludes, "If, as seems likely, the inherent nature of an industry [its high ratio of fixed to variable costs in the case of railroads] is the most important single context in which regulators must operate, then the range of policies open to them has been narrower than many observers have hitherto believed."

16. For a similar critique of the role attributed to market size (commercial expansion) in the transition from feudalism to capitalism, see Robert Brenner, "The Origins of Capitalism: A Critique of Neo-Smithian Marxism," *New Left Review* 104 (1977); and Robert Brenner, "Economic Backwardness in Eastern Europe in Light of Developments in the West," in Daniel Chirot, ed., *The Origins of Backwardness in Eastern Europe* (Berkeley: University of California Press, 1989), 15–52.

17. For an excellent summary of these propositions, see Theda Skocpol, "Bringing the State Back In: Strategies of Analysis in Current Research," in Peter B. Evans, Dietrich Rueschemeyer, and Theda Skocpol, eds., *Bringing the State Back In* (Cambridge: Cambridge University Press, 1985), 3–37. On the role of the state and politics in economic development, see Dietrich Rueschemeyer and Peter B. Evans, "The State and Economic Transformation: Toward an Analysis of the Conditions Underlying Effective Intervention," in Evans et al., eds., *Bringing the State Back In*, 44–77.

18. See especially Stephen Skowronek, *Building a New American State: The Expansion of National Administrative Capacities, 1877–1920* (Cambridge: Cambridge University Press, 1982). See also Margaret Weir, Ann Shola Orloff, and Theda Skocpol, *The Politics of Social Policy in the United States* (Princeton: Princeton University Press, 1988); Martin Shefter,

"Trade Unions and Political Machines: The Organization and Disorganization of the American Working Class in the Late Nineteenth Century," in Ira Katznelson and Aristedes Zolberg, eds., *Working Class Formation: Nineteenth-Century Patterns in Western Europe and the United States* (Princeton: Princeton University Press, 1986), 197–276; David Vogel, "Why Businessmen Distrust Their State: The Political Consciousness of American Corporate Executives," *British Journal of Political Science* (Jan. 1978): 45–78; Edwin Amenta and Theda Skocpol, "Taking Exception: Explaining the Distinctiveness of American Public Policies in the Last Century," in Francis G. Castles, ed., *The Comparative History of Public Policy* (New York: Oxford University Press, 1989), 292–333.

19. Ackerman, *We the People*, 34–57; Dahl, "On Removing Certain Impediments to Democracy in the United States"; Walter Dean Burnham, *Critical Elections and the Mainsprings of American Politics* (New York: W. W. Norton, 1970). On the theme of "fluid" and "rigid" moments in history more generally, see Unger, *Social Theory*; Max Weber's discussion of charisma in *Economy and Society: An Outline of Interpretive Sociology* (Berkeley: University of California Press, 1978), 2: 1111–57; Pierre Bourdieu, *Outline of a Theory of Practice*, trans. Richard Nice (Cambridge: Cambridge University Press, 1977), 168–71; and Antonio Gramsci, *Selections from the Prison Notebooks*, trans. Quintin Hoare and Geoffrey Nowell Smith (New York: International Publishers, 1980), 325–43.

20. Piore and Sabel, *The Second Industrial Divide*, 38–43; Roberto M. Unger, *False Necessity: Anti-Necessitarian Social Theory in the Service of Radical Democracy* (Cambridge: Cambridge University Press, 1987), 169–71, 246–355.

21. Clifford Geertz, "Ideology as a Cultural System," in Clifford Geertz, *The Interpretations of Cultures* (New York: Basic Books, 1973), 220, 193–233.

22. Unger, *False Necessity*, 28–29; Max Weber, *The Methodology of the Social Sciences*, trans. and ed. Edward A. Shils and Henry A. Finch (New York: Free Press, 1949), 164–88; Suzanne Berger and Michael J. Piore, *Dualism and Discontinuity in Industrial Societies* (Cambridge: Cambridge University Press, 1980); Sara M. Evans and Harry C. Boyte, *Free Spaces: The Sources of Democratic Change in America* (New York: Harper & Row, 1986).

Chapter 2. Corporate Capital Markets Transformed

1. There is a long-standing debate over the economic effects of the Civil War. For representative examples, see Thomas C. Cochran, "Did the Civil War Retard Industrialization," in Ralph Andreano, ed., *The Economic Impact of the American Civil War* (Cambridge, Mass.: Schenkman, 1967), 167–79; Douglass C. North, *Economic Growth of the United States, 1790–1860* (New Jersey: Prentice-Hall, 1961); Stanley L. Engerman, "The Economic Impact of the Civil War," *Explorations in Economic History*, 2d ser. 3 (1966), 176–99; Stanley Lebergott, *The Americans: An Economic Record* (New York: W. W. Norton, 1984), 233–48. For a general criticism of the view that the war had little durable effect on American economic development, see Harry S. Scheiber, "Economic Change in the Civil War: An Analysis of Recent Studies," *Civil War History* 11 (Dec. 1965): 396–411.

2. See especially Chandler, *The Visible Hand*, 79–187; Alfred D. Chandler, Jr., and Richard S. Tedlow, *The Coming of Managerial Capitalism: A Casebook on the History of American Economic Institutions* (Homewood, Ill.: Richard D. Irwin, 1985), 173–309; Maury Klein, "The Strategy of Southern Railroads," *American Historical Review* 73 (Apr. 1968): 1052–68; and Thomas K. McCraw, *Prophets of Regulation: Charles Francis Adams, Jr., Louis D. Brandeis, James M. Landis, Alfred E. Kahn* (Cambridge: Harvard University Press, 1984), 1–56.

3. Chandler, *The Visible Hand*, 89–93; Alfred D. Chandler, Jr., *The Railroads: The Nation's First Big Business* (New York: Harcourt, Brace & World, 1965), 43–47; and Alfred D. Chandler, Jr., *Henry Varnum Poor, Business Editor, Analyst, and Reformer* (Cambridge: Harvard University Press, 1956), 73–103, 158–80.

4. *Historical Statistics of the United States*, 200–204.

5. James Livingston, "The Political Economy of Consumer Culture: The United States, 1850–1970," paper prepared for Conference on Global Americanization, Nov. 15–17, 1989, 48.

6. Ibid., 48–49.

7. Fritz Redlich, *The Molding of American Banking: Men and Ideas* (1947; reprint, New York: Johnson Reprint Co., 1968), 2: 357–65.

8. Livingston, "The Political Economy of Consumer Culture," 48; Leonard Curry, *Blueprint for Modern America: Non-Military Legislation of the First Civil War Congress* (Nashville: Vanderbilt University Press, 1968), 182–93, 199, 206.

9. Henrietta M. Larson, *Jay Cooke, Private Banker* (Cambridge: Harvard University Press, 1936), 98–118.

10. Redlich, *The Molding of American Banking*, 2: 360–61; Vincent Carosso, *Investment Banking in America: A History* (Cambridge: Harvard University Press, 1970), 15–17.

11. Redlich, *The Molding of American Banking*, 2: 362–63; Carosso, *Investment Banking in America*, 17–20; Barry Supple, "A Business Elite: German-Jewish Financiers in Nineteenth-Century New York," *Business History Review* 31 (Summer 1957): 143–51.

12. Carosso, *Investment Banking in America*, 20.

13. Redlich, *The Molding of American Banking*, 2: 364–65; Carosso, *Investment Banking in America*, 20–22; Vincent Carosso, *The Morgans, Private International Bankers, 1854–1913* (Cambridge: Harvard University Press, 1987), 105–19, 133–39.

14. Redlich, *The Molding of American Banking*, 2: 363–65; Carosso, *Investment Banking in America*, 22–23; Dolores Breitman Greenberg, *Financiers and Railroads, 1869–1889, A Case Study of Morton, Bliss and Company* (Newark: University of Delaware Press, 1980).

15. Robert P. Sharkey, *Money, Class, and Party: An Economic Study of Civil War and Reconstruction* (Baltimore: Johns Hopkins Press, 1959), 146–58.

16. Livingston, "The Political Economy of Consumer Culture," 54–55; Irwin Unger, *The Greenback Era: A Social and Political History of American Finance, 1865–1879* (Princeton: Princeton University Press, 1964), 151–67, 273–74; Irwin Unger, "Businessmen and Species Resumption," *Political Science Quarterly* 74 (Mar. 1959): 46–70. Although Unger insists that the Board's shift of opinion represented no more than temporary opportunism, as Livingston points out, when seen among other changes in the New York mercantile community, it is more plausible to conclude it represented a genuine and durable change in opinion.

17. Quoted in Unger, *The Greenback Era*, 166–67.

18. Paul Trescott, *Financing American Enterprise: The Story of Commercial Banking* (New York: Harper & Row, 1963), 41–63; Margaret G. Myers, *A Financial History of the United States* (New York: Columbia University Press, 1970), 162–65; Redlich, *The Molding of American Banking*, 2: 99–105; Andrew McFarland Davis, *The Origin of the National Banking System*, National Monetary Commission, Senate, 61st Cong., 2d sess., Document #582 (Washington: Government Printing Office, 1910), 13–26, 104–12.

19. Myers, *A Financial History of the United States*, 164; Myers, *The New York Money Market: Origins and Development* (New York: Columbia University Press, 1931), 218–33;

Richard Eugene Sylla, *The American Capital Market, 1846–1914: A Study of the Effects of Public Policy on Economic Development* (New York: Arno Press, 1975), 90–93.

20. On the New York call loan market see Myers, *New York Money Market*, 265–87; Sylla, *The American Capital Market*, 85–134; and Edward Chase Kirkland, *Industry Comes of Age: Business, Labor, and Public Policy, 1860–1897* (New York: Holt, Rinehart & Winston, 1961), 30–32. On the growth of the stock exchange, see Comptroller of the Currency, *Annual Report*, 1873 in 43d Cong., 1st sess., House Exec. Doc. 3; and Robert Sobel, *The Big Board: A History of the New York Stock Market* (New York: Free Press, 1965), 65–79. On the importance of rails in the New York stock market, see Thomas R. Navins and Marian V. Sears, "The Rise of a Market for Industrial Securities, 1887–1902," *Business History Review* 29 (June 1955): 105–38.

21. John James, *Money and Capital Markets in Postbellum America* (Princeton: Princeton University Press, 1978), 264.

22. Comptroller of the Currency, *Annual Report*, 1873, xxviii.

23. Sylla, *The American Capital Market*, 52–53.

24. Ibid.; Lance Davis, "The Capital Markets and Industrial Concentration: The U.S. and U.K., A Comparative Study," *Economic History Review* 19 (1966): 255–72.

25. On fiscal policy generally, see Myers, *A Financial History of the United States*, 149–63; Lawrence Goodwyn, *Democratic Promise: The Populist Moment in America* (New York: Oxford University Press, 1976), 10–21. On railroad securities held abroad and the predominance of debt in railroad finance, see Myers, *The New York Money Market*, 290–91; A. M. Sakolski, *American Railroad Economics* (New York: Macmillan, 1913), 31–42: H. Parker Willis and Jules I. Bogen, *Investment Banking* (New York: Harper & Brothers, 1929), 176–78; and Dorothy R. Adler, *British Investment in American Railways, 1834–1898* (Charlottesville: University Press of Virginia, 1970), 165–68.

26. Sylla, *The American Capital Market*, 163–203.

27. *Historical Statistics of the United States*, 200–204.

28. Robert P. Sharkey, "Commercial Banking," in David T. Gilchrist and W. David Lewis, eds., *Economic Change in the Civil War Era* (Greenville, Del.: Eleutherian Mills-Hagley Foundation, 1965), 30.

29. Henry H. Swain, "Economic Aspects of Receiverships," *Economic Studies of the American Economic Association* 3 (1889): 66–69.

30. Comptroller of the Currency, *Annual Report*, 1873, xxii.

31. U.S. Congress, House, *Report of the Committee on Banking and Currency on Bills HR 3834 and 4377*, 43d Cong., 2d sess., Report No. 328, 1874–1875, 119–21.

32. Ibid.

33. Unger, *The Greenback Era*, 218–20; Unger, "Businessmen and Species Resumption," 50, 58, 65.

34. Washington Townsend (R. Pa.), *Congressional Record*, 43d Cong., 1st sess., 2, pt. 1, 1873–1874, 736.

35. Ibid., pt. 2, 1874, 1503. For a more complete account of western attitudes toward national banking after the panic of 1873, see George L. Anderson, "Western Attitudes toward National Banks, 1873–74," *Mississippi Valley Historical Review* 23 (Sept. 1936): 205–16. See also William Carleton, "The Money Question in Indiana Politics, 1865–1890," *Indiana Magazine of History* 42 (June 1946): 107–50; and R. C. McGrane, "Ohio and the Greenback Movement," *Mississippi Valley Historical Review* 11 (Mar. 1925): 526–42.

36. Unger, *The Greenback Era*, 221-22.

37. Ibid., 233-45; Myers, *Financial History of the United States*, 189-96; Morton Keller, *Affairs of State: Public Life in Late Nineteenth-Century America* (Cambridge: Harvard University Press, 1977), 193-95.

38. Unger, *The Greenback Era*, 237.

39. John R. Commons et al., *A Documentary History of American Industrial Society* (Cleveland: Arthur H. Clark, 1910), 9: 33-43; Fred E. Haynes, *Third Party Movements since the Civil War* (Iowa City: The State Historical Society of Iowa, 1916), 89-201; Nathan Fine, *Labor and Farmer Parties in the United States, 1828-1928* (New York: Russell & Russell, 1961); Walter Dean Burnham, "The System of 1896: An Analysis," Department of Political Science, Massachusetts Institute of Technology, 1982.

40. Though there are many subtle differences among these authors, many agree that greenback reformers were hopelessly out of step with the necessities of industrial society. See, for example, Unger, *The Greenback Era*; David Montgomery, *Beyond Equality: Labor and the Radical Republicans, 1862-1872* (New York: Alfred A. Knopf, 1967), 425-47; Walter T. K. Nugent, *Money and American Society, 1865-1880* (New York: Free Press, 1968), 37-43, 205-15; and Hofstadter, *The Age of Reform*, 1-30.

41. The ideology of "producer's republicanism" among workers and farmers in the late nineteenth century has been explored by Victoria Hattam, "Economic Visions and Political Strategies: American Labor and the State, 1865-1896," *Studies in American Political Development* 4 (1990), 82-129; Goodwyn, *Democratic Promise*; Leon Fink, *Workingmen's Democracy: The Knights of Labor and American Politics* (Urbana: University of Illinois Press, 1983); Eric Foner, *Free Soil, Free Labor, Free Men: The Ideology of the Republican Party before the Civil War* (London: Oxford University Press, 1970); Richard Oestreicher, "Terrence Powderly, the Knights of Labor, and Artisanal Republicanism," in Melvyn Dubofsky and Warren Van Tine, eds., *Labor Leaders in America* (Urbana: University of Illinois Press, 1987), 30-60; and Nick Salvatore, *Eugene V. Debs: Citizen and Socialist* (Urbana: University of Illinois Press, 1982).

42. Chester McArthur Destler, *American Radicalism, 1865-1901* (1946; reprint, Chicago: Quadrangle, 1966), 50-77; Hattam, "Economic Visions and Political Strategies," 90-98; Oestreicher, "Terrence Powderly"; Commons, *Documentary History of Industrial Society*, 9: 33-43; Montgomery, *Beyond Equality*, 427-32.

43. Edward Kellogg, *A New Monetary System: The Only Means of Securing the Respective Rights of Labor and Property, and of Protecting the Public from Financial Revulsions* (New York: Rudd & Carleton, 1861); Destler, *American Radicalism*, 54-55; Goodwyn, *Democratic Promise*, 135-39, 149-53, 565-81; Unger, *The Greenback Era*, 96-100; William A. Berkey, *The Money Question: The Wealth and Resources of the United States, and Why the People Do Not Enjoy General Prosperity* (Grand Rapids: W. W. Hart, 1878), 353-55; Alexander Campbell, *The True American System of Finance* (1864; reprint, New York: A. M. Kelley, 1971).

44. Quoted in Ellis P. Usher, *The Greenback Movement of 1875-1884 and Wisconsin's Part in It* (Milwaukee: Meisenheimer, 1911), 26.

45. On western agrarian support, see note 35; Solon Buck, *The Granger Movement: A Study of Agricultural Organization and Its Political, Economic, and Social Manifestations, 1870-1880* (Lincoln: University of Nebraska Press, 1965), 114-15. On support for greenbackism, or the "subtreasury plan" from within the Farmer's Alliance, especially in the South, see Goodwyn, *Democratic Promise*, 154-76.

46. Hattam, "Economic Visions and Political Strategies." For examples of cooperative

experiments associated with the Knights of Labor and the NLU, see Commons, *Documentary History of Industrial Society*, 9: 122, 148–52, 182.

47. This account is taken from Livingston, *Origins of the Federal Reserve System*.

Chapter 3. Reconstituting Fixed Costs

1. Chandler, *The Railroads*, 14.

2. Henry C. Swain, "Economic Aspects of Receiverships," *Economic Studies of the American Economic Association* 3 (1889): 68.

3. On the relationship between fixed cost and size, see especially Chandler, *The Visible Hand*, 79–187; Chandler and Tedlow, *The Coming of Managerial Capitalism*, 173–309; Klein, "The Strategy of Southern Railroads"; and McCraw, *Prophets of Regulation*, 1–56. On the relationship between fixed cost and the separation of ownership from managerial control in the modern corporation, see Chandler, *The Visible Hand*, 8–10; and Alfred D. Chandler, Jr., "The Separation of Ownership and Control," Harvard Business School Case No. 1-380-215. Like the new business historians, legal scholars have provided a similar explanation of the separation of ownership from managerial control. See, for example, Robert Charles Clark, "The Four Stages of Capitalism: Reflections on Investment Management Treatises," *Harvard Law Review* 94 (1981): 561–82; Richard Posner, *Economic Analysis of Law*, 2d ed. (Boston: Little, Brown & Co., 1977), 300–303; James Willard Hurst, *The Legitimacy of the Business Corporation in the Law of the United States, 1780–1970* (Charlottesville: University Press of Virginia, 1970), 39–57; and Berle and Means, *The Modern Corporation and Private Property*.

4. On the public theory of the corporation, see Morton J. Horwitz, *The Transformation of American Law, 1780–1860* (Cambridge: Harvard University Press, 1977), 109–22; Skowronek, *Building a New American State*, 24–31; Hurst, *The Legitimacy of the Business Corporation*, 13–41; Frederick A. Cleveland and Fred Wilbur Powell, *Railroad Promotion and Capitalization in the United States* (New York: Longmans, Green, 1909), 96–116; Morton Keller, "Public Policy and Large Enterprise: Comparative and Historical Perspectives," in Norbert Horn and Jurgen Kocka, eds., *Law and the Formation of the Big Enterprises in the Nineteenth and Early Twentieth Centuries* (Göttingen: Vandenhoek & Ruprecht, 1979), 519–23.

5. On early receivership practice, see Arthur Stone Dewing, "The Theory of Railroad Reorganization," *American Economic Review* 8 (Dec. 1918): 779–81.

6. On state investment in railroads, see Cleveland and Powell, *Railroad Promotion*, 212–32; and Carter Goodrich, *Government Promotion of American Canals and Railroads, 1800–1890* (New York: Columbia University Press, 1960), 51–65.

7. On the collapse of the grant theory, see Morton J. Horwitz, "Santa Clara Revisited: The Development of Corporate Theory," *West Virginia Law Review* 88 (1985): 173–224, at 181; Hurst, *Legitimacy of the Corporation*, 33–43; and Tony Alan Freyer, *Forums of Order: The Federal Courts and Business in American History* (Greenwich, Conn: JAI Press, 1979). On state disinvestment, see Cleveland and Powell, *Railroad Promotion*, 230–39; and Goodrich, *Government Promotion*, 71–75, 148–52.

8. On the trust-fund theory more generally, see Horwitz, "Santa Clara Revisited," 181–86; and Hurst, *Legitimacy of the Corporation*, 51–54. On the trust-fund theory as it applied to the obligations of corporate directors to act as fiduciaries for shareholders, see Harold Marsh, Jr., "Are Directors Trustees: Conflict of Interest and Corporate Morality," *The Business Lawyer* 22 (Nov. 1966): 35–39.

9. Dewing, "The Theory of Railroad Reorganization," 781n10.

10. On railroad securities held abroad and the predominance of debt in railroad finance, see *Historical Statistics of the United States, 1789–1945* (Washington, 1949), 204; Myers, *The New York Money Market*, 290–92; Sakolski, *American Railroad Economics*, 31–33; Willis and Bogen, *Investment Banking*, 176–78; Ripley, *Railroads: Finance and Organization*, 105–8; Swain, "Economic Aspects of Receiverships," 88; and Dewing, "Theory of Railroad Reorganization," 780–82. On mortgage finance, see Ray Morris, *Railroad Administration* (New York, 1910), chap. 7.

11. J. F. Crowell, "Railway Receiverships in the United States," *Yale Review* 7 (Nov. 1898): 326; Dewing, "Theory of Railroad Reorganization," 781–84.

12. Stuart Daggett, *Railroad Reorganization* (Cambridge: Harvard University Press, 1908), 38–49; Dewing, "Theory of Railroad Reorganization," 783–84. See also Charles Francis Adams, Jr., and Henry Adams, *Chapters of Erie* (1869; reprint, Cornell University Press, 1968).

13. Daggett, *Railroad Reorganization*, 75–117.

14. Dewing, "Theory," 797n7; *Poor's Manual of Railroads*, 1900, lxxviii–lxxxiii.

15. Unless otherwise indicated, the story of the Wabash Railway comes from Julius Grodinsky, *Jay Gould, His Business Career, 1867–1892* (Philadelphia: University of Pennsylvania Press, 1957).

16. On the corporate history of the road prior to Gould's acquisition, see Maury Klein, *The Life and Legend of Jay Gould* (Baltimore: Johns Hopkins University Press, 1986), 233–34.

17. On Gould's aggressive strategy more generally, see Alfred D. Chandler, Jr., "Jay Gould and the Coming of Railroad Consolidation," in Chandler and Tedlow, *The Coming of Managerial Capitalism*, 227–56; and Klein, *The Life and Legend of Jay Gould*, 235–38, 252–69, 298–300.

18. Albro Martin, "Railroads and the Equity Receivership: An Essay on Institutional Change," *Journal of Economic History* 34 (Sept. 1974): 685–709.

19. Central Trust Co. v. Wabash, St. L. & P. Ry. Co., 29 Fed. Rep. 623–24.

20. "A Chapter of Wabash," *North American Review* 146 (1888): 190.

21. Atkins v. Wabash, St. L. & P. Ry. Co., 29 Fed. Rep. 161; "A Chapter of Wabash," 184–90; "The Wabash Receivership Case," *American Law Review* 21 (Jan.–Feb. 1887): 141–45.

22. Atkins v. Wabash, St. L. & P. Ry. Co., 29 Fed. Rep. 168.

23. Exhibit D, "Report of the Committee of Bondholders of the Wabash, St. Louis and Pacific Ry Co." (Aug. 12, 1886), in *Wabash Railroad Company Annual Report*, 1891, Appendix.

24. Central Trust v. Wabash, St. L. & P. Ry. Co., 29 Fed. Rep. 618; Quincy, Missouri and Pacific Railroad Company v. Humphreys, 14 U.S. 182.

25. D. H. Chamberlain, "New Fashioned Receiverships," *Harvard Law Review* 10 (Oct. 26, 1896): 145.

26. "The Wabash Receivership Case," *American Law Review* 21 (Jan.–Feb. 1887): 144, emphasis added.

27. Henry Wollman, "The Bane of Friendly Receiverships," *North American Review* 158 (1894): 251; Chamberlain, "New Fashioned Receiverships," 145.

28. Charles Fisk Beach, Jr., *Commentaries on the Law of Receivers* (New York: L. K. Strouse, 1894), 265 (§ 326).

29. Wollman, "The Bane of Friendly Receiverships," 251.

30. Ibid., 250–51.

31. Charles W. Calhoun, *Gilded Age Cato: The Life of Walter Q. Gresham* (Lexington: University of Kentucky Press, 1988), 107-8.

32. See Securities and Exchange Commission, *Report on the Study and Investigation of the Work, Activities, Personnel and Functions of Protective and Reorganization Committees: Pursuant to Section 211 of the Securities and Exchange Commission Act of 1934* (May 10, 1937), Part I, Sec. 2, 243; Martin, "Railroads and the Equity Receivership," 687; Oscar Lasdon, "The Evolution of Railroad Reorganization," *Banking Law Journal* 88 (Jan. 1971): 3-9; and Swain, "Economic Aspects of Receiverships," 91-92.

33. In the Matter of Francis S. Reisenberg, 28 Sup. Ct. Rep. 220, 225.

34. On the general acceptance of Wabash, see Dewing, "The Theory of Railroad Reorganization," 784-88; Chamberlain, "New Fashioned Receiverships"; Martin, "Railroads and Equity Receiverships"; and A. A. Berle, "Receivership," *Encyclopedia of the Social Sciences* (1936), 50. On the natural entity theory of the corporation, see Horwitz, "Santa Clara Revisited."

35. Hurst, *Legitimacy of the Corporation*. For a similar approach, see Freyer, *Forums of Order*.

36. For a good discussion of management's worry that property in receivership would be sold profitably to competitors, see Arthur Stone Dewing, "The Purposes Achieved by Railroad Reorganization," *American Economic Review* 54 (June 1919): 283-87.

37. Daggett, *Railroad Reorganization*, 133.

38. For classic examples of interest group approaches to legal change, see Lawrence M. Friedman, *A History of American Law* (New York: Simon & Schuster, 1973); Lawrence M. Friedman and Jack Landinsky, "Social Change and the Law of Industrial Accidents," *Columbia Law Review* 67 (1967): 50-82; and Gabriel Kolko, *The Triumph of Conservatism: A Reinterpretation of American History, 1900-1916* (Chicago: Quadrangle Books, 1963).

39. Robert Gordon, "Legal Thought and Legal Practice in the Age of Enterprise," in G. L. Gieson, ed., *Professions and Professional Ideologies in America* (Chapel Hill: University of North Carolina Press, 1984), 70-139; Horwitz, "Santa Clara Revisted," 216-22.

40. John Lauritz Larson, *Bonds of Enterprise: John Murray Forbes and Western Development in America's Railway Age* (Cambridge: Harvard University Press, 1984), 164-69; Chandler, "Jay Gould and the Coming of Railroad Consolidation."

41. On the Reading's interregional expansion of the 1880s, see Daggett, *Railroad Reorganization*, 120-25. On the Baltimore and Ohio and the Rock Island, see ibid., 315-16.

42. Ibid., 194-96.

43. Ibid., 275-83.

44. On competitive interregional system building in the South, see Maury Klein, *The Great Richmond Terminal* (Charlottesville: University Press of Virginia, 1970); John Stover, *The Railroads of the South, 1865-1900* (Chapel Hill: University of North Carolina Press, 1955).

45. Swain, "Economic Aspects of Receiverships," 68.

46. On the Baltimore and Ohio, see Daggett, *Railroad Reorganization*, 11-13. On the AT&SF, see ibid., 200-203; and on the Northern Pacific, see ibid., 282.

47. On the federal court's procedure to secure consent from shareholders, see Paul D. Cravath, "The Reorganization of Corporations," "Bondholders' Protective Committees," "Reorganization Committees," and "The Voluntary Recapitalization of Corporations," in Association of the Bar of the City of New York, *Some Legal Phases of Corporate Financing,*

Reorganization, and Regulation (New York: Macmillan, 1917); and Gordon, "Legal Thought and Legal Practice," 101–5.

48. Greenberg, *Financiers and Railroads*; Carosso, *Investment Banking in America*; Redlich, *The Molding of American Banking*, 2: 304–423.

49. Carosso, *The Morgans*, 121–23, 146–59, 238–42, 245; Ron Chernow, *The House of Morgan: An American Banking Dynasty and the Rise of Modern Finance* (New York: Atlantic Monthly Press, 1990), 44.

50. Carosso, *The Morgans*, 246.

51. Ibid., 246–67.

52. Grodinsky, *Jay Gould*, 220; Chernow, *The House of Morgan*, 54–58.

53. On the competitive system building that led to this tripartite receivership, see Klein, *The Great Richmond Terminal*; and Stover, *The Railroads of the South*, 233–53.

54. Daggett, *Railroad Reorganization*, 146–91; Edward G. Campbell, *The Reorganization of the American Railroad System, 1893–1900* (New York: Columbia University Press, 1938), 149–62; Carosso, *The Morgans*, 369–73.

55. On the Morgan reorganizations more generally, see Carosso, *The Morgans*, 352–90; Campbell, *The Reorganization of the American Railroad System*, 145–89; and Redlich, *The Molding of American Banking*, 2: 384. On the role of other investment bankers in railroad reorganizations, see Redlich, *The Molding of American Banking*, 2: 384–88; and Carosso, *Investment Banking*, 33–42. For other brief examples of the "friendly receivership" in practice, see Swain, "Economic Aspects of Receivership," 93–97.

56. On the variety of institutional possibilities to solve the problem of economic flux and uncertainty in advanced industrial societies more generally, see Berger and Piore, *Dualism and Discontinuity*; and Piore and Sabel, *The Second Industrial Divide*, 49–132.

57. Cravath, "The Reorganization of Corporations"; Gordon, "Legal Thought and Legal Practice," 101–7.

58. On the use of the term "consent receivership" after *Wabash*, see Berle, "Receivership," 150.

59. *Report of the Industrial Commission on Transportation*, 9 (Washington, 1901), 456. For this sort of assessment of Morgan's reorganization of the Southern Railway and the Erie, see Campbell, *The Reorganization of the American Railroad System*, 160, 172.

60. For a good general discussion of the exchange of fixed for contingent securities, see Arthur Stone Dewing, "The Purposes Achieved by Railroad Reorganization," *American Economic Review* 10 (June 1919): 290–95.

61. Willis and Bogen, *Investment Banking*, 124–28; Campbell, *The Reorganization of the American Railroad System*; Daggett, *Railroad Reorganization*, 15, 22, 342–43. So important did "corporate surplus" become to the modern corporation that by the 1920s it was the single largest source of investment funds. See Willis and Bogen, *Investment Banking*, 124.

62. E. S. Meade, "The Reorganization of Railroads," *Annals of the American Academy of Political and Social Science* 17 (Mar. 1901): 236; Dewing, "The Purposes Achieved by Railroad Reorganization," 295.

63. On the repatriation of American capital, see Willis and Bogen, *Investment Banking*, 179.

64. Chandler, *The Visible Hand*, 173–75; John Moody, *The Truth about the Trusts* (New York: Moody, 1904), 431–50; Sakolski, *American Railroad Economics*, 44–84; Campbell, *The Reorganization of the American Railroad System*, 331–33.

Chapter 4. Regional Republication in Policy: Regulated Competition

1. Henry J. Fletcher, "The Doom of the Small Town," *Forum* 19 (Apr. 1895): 217. Between 1870 and the turn of the century, cities ranked from twenty-first to fiftieth in size grew by 158 percent compared to New York, Philadelphia, and Chicago, which grew by 245 percent. See David Gordon, "Capitalist Development and the History of American Cities," in William Tabb and Larry Sawers, eds., *Marxism and the Metropolis* (New York: Oxford University Press, 1978), 39.

2. See Brian J. L. Berry and W. C. Garrison, "Functional Bases of the Central Place Hierarchy," *Economic Geography* 34 (1958): 98–107; and Ray M. Northern, *Urban Geography* (New York: John Wiley & Sons, 1975), 98–107.

3. This literature is extensive, but for representative examples, see Lee Bensen, *Merchants, Farmers, and Railroads: Railroad Regulation and New York Politics, 1850–1887* (Cambridge: Harvard University Press, 1955); Gabriel Kolko, *Railroads and Regulation, 1887–1916* (Princeton: Princeton University Press, 1965); Edward A. Purcell, Jr., "Ideas and Interests: Businessmen and the Interstate Commerce Act," *Journal of American History* 55 (Dec. 1967): 561–78; Richard H. K. Vietor, "Businessmen and the Political Economy: The Railroad Rate Controversy of 1905," *Journal of American History* 64 (June 1977): 47–66; and Albro Martin, *Enterprise Denied: Origins of the Decline of American Railroads, 1897–1917* (New York: Columbia University Press, 1971).

4. The two most important studies of the Granger Laws are Solon Buck, *The Granger Movement: A Study of Agricultural Organization and Its Political, Economic, and Social Manifestations, 1870–1880* (Lincoln: University of Nebraska Press, 1965); and George H. Miller, *Railroads and the Granger Laws* (Madison: University of Wisconsin Press, 1971). The former attributes the Granger laws to farmers, the latter to merchants.

5. Miller, *Railroads and the Granger Laws*, 108.

6. Bensen, *Merchants, Farmers, and Railroads*.

7. On the importance of a farm-merchant alliance in passing the Granger laws, see Buck, *The Granger Movement*, 89–91, 161–64, 169–70; Miller, *Railroads and the Granger Laws*, 135, 151–60; and Mildred Throne, "The Repeal of the Iowa Granger Law," *Iowa Journal of History* 51 (Apr. 1953): 99.

8. Miller, *Railroads and the Granger Laws*, 163–64; William D. Barns, "Oliver Hudson Kelley and the Genesis of the Grange: A Reappraisal," *Agricultural History* 41 (July 1967): 239–42.

9. Horace Samuel Merrill, *Bourbon Democracy of the Middle West, 1865–1896* (Baton Rouge: Louisiana State University Press, 1953), 95.

10. Nathan Fine, *Labor and Farmer Parties in the United States, 1828–1928* (New York: Russell Sage, 1961), 58–61.

11. Elizabeth Sanders, "Farmers, Railroads, and the State: A Political Economy Perspective," paper delivered at the Annual Meeting of the American Political Science Association, Aug. 1990. For a similar argument applied to antitrust, see Elizabeth Sanders, "Industrial Concentration, Sectional Competition, and Antitrust," *Studies in American Political Development* 1 (1986): 142–214. See also Richard Bensel, *Sectionalism and American Political Development, 1880–1890* (Madison: University of Wisconsin Press, 1984).

12. For a powerful critique of the model from which the sectionalist approach is drawn, Emmanuel Wallerstein's world systems theory, see Robert Brenner, "The Origins of Capitalism: A Critique of Neo-Smithian Economics," *New Left Review* 104 (1977). Like

the approach here, Brenner stresses the political determinants of economic development.

13. Buck, *The Granger Movement*, 173–74.

14. Throne, "Repeal of the Iowa Granger Law," 100; Buck, *The Granger Movement*, 187; Miller, *Railroads and the Granger Laws*, 174.

15. A. B. Stickney, *The Railroad Problem* (St. Paul, Minn: D. D. Merrill, 1891), 102–8.

16. Buck, *The Granger Movement*, 150–52, 160–61, 174, 187–88; Miller, *Railroads and the Granger Laws*, 172–73.

17. Sinking Fund Cases, 99 U.S. 700 (1898) at 747.

18. Munn v. Illinois, 94 U.S. 113 (1877) at 132, 134. See the excellent discussion in Charles W. McCurdy, "Justice Field and the Jurisprudence of Government-Business Relations: Some Parameters of Laissez-Faire Constitutionalism, 1863–1897," *Journal of American History* 61 (Mar. 1975): 994–98.

19. Quoted in McCurdy, "Justice Field," 1002.

20. Ibid., 999, italics mine.

21. Stone v. Wisconsin, 94 U.S. 181 (1877), at 184–85, quoted in McCurdy, "Justice Field," 999–1000.

22. See Miller, *Railroads and the Granger Laws*; and Thomas C. Cochran, *Railroad Leaders, 1845–1890: The Business Mind in Action* (Cambridge: Harvard University Press, 1953), 191.

23. Quoted in Charles R. Detrick, "The Effects of the Granger Acts," *Journal of Political Economy* 11 (Mar. 1903): 238.

24. Charles Francis Adams, Jr., "The Railroads and the Granger Laws," *North American Review* 120 (Apr. 1875): 406–8.

25. Quoted in Detrick, "Effects of the Granger Acts," 240–41.

26. Arthur Twining Hadley, *Railroad Transportation: Its History and Its Laws* (New York: G. P. Putnam's Sons, 1885), 125–45.

27. Stickney, *The Railroad Problem*, 24, 89–113.

28. Ibid., 109–13; Buck, *The Granger Movement*, 185.

29. Detrick, "The Effects of the Granger Acts."

30. Ibid., 256.

31. McCraw, *Prophets of Regulation*, 57.

32. *Regulation of Railway Rates and Services. Relation of Government to Commerce and Transportation. Speeches of Hon. Robert M. LaFollette of Wisconsin in the Senate of the United States*, 20 April 1906 (Washington, 1906), 54.

33. Lewis H. Haney, *A Congressional History of Railroads in the United States, 1850–1887*, Bulletin of the University of Wisconsin, no. 342 (Madison, Wis., 1910), 2: 282–85; Buck, *The Granger Movement*, 214–16; Miller, *Railroads and the Granger Laws*, 102–4. On the conservative power of the Senate, see Matthew Josephson, *The Politicos* (New York: Harcourt, Brace & World, 1933), 33–140; Sanders, "Railroads, Farmers, and the State," 21; and Thomas W. Gilligan, William J. Marshall, and Barry R. Weingast, "Regulation and the Theory of Legislative Choice: The Interstate Commerce Act of 1887," *Journal of Law and Economics* 33 (Apr. 1989): 35–62.

34. Henry Demerest Lloyd, "Story of a Great Monopoly," *Atlantic* (Mar. 1881), 317–34; Chester MacArthur Destler, *Roger Sherman and the Independent Oil Men* (Ithaca, N.Y.: Cornell University Press, 1967); Chester MacArthur Destler, *Henry Demerest Lloyd and the Empire of Reform* (Philadelphia: University of Pennsylvania Press, 1963), 290–354; Henry Demerest Lloyd, *Wealth against Commonwealth* (New York: Harper & Brothers,

1894). For a recent version of this argument, see Richard B. DuBoff and Edward S. Herman, "Alfred Chandler's New Business History: A Review," *Politics and Society* 10 (1980): 100–102.

35. Alfred D. Chandler, Jr., "The Standard Oil Company: Combination, Consolidation, and Integration," in Chandler and Tedlow, *The Coming of Managerial Capitalism*, 343–71; Thomas K. McCraw, "Rethinking the Trust Question," in Thomas K. McCraw, *Regulation in Perspective: Historical Essays* (Boston: Harvard Business School Press, 1981), 1–55.

36. Gerald D. Nash, "Origins of the Interstate Commerce Act of 1887," *Pennsylvania History* 24 (July 1957): 181–90.

37. On the independents' claim to locational and other advantages, see Harold Williamson and Arnold R. Daum, *The American Petroleum Industry: The Age of Illumination, 1859–1899* (Evanston, Ill.: Northwestern University Press, 1959), 292; and Destler, *Roger Sherman*.

38. U.S. Bureau of Corporations, *Report of the Commissioner of Corporations on the Petroleum Industry* (Washington, 1907–1909), Part I, 22–26, and Part II, 52–58. See also New York State Assembly, *Report of the Special Committee on Railroads, Appointed under a Resolution of the Assembly, Feb. 28, 1878 to Investigate the Alleged Abuses in the Management of Railroads* (Albany: Weed, Parsons & Co., 1880), Summary, 40–46.

39. On relational contracting, see Ronald Dore, *Taking Japan Seriously: A Confucian Perspective on Leading Economic Issues* (Stanford: Stanford University Press, 1987), 173–92; Edward Lorenz, "Neither Friends nor Strangers: Informal Networks of Subcontracting in French Industry," in Diego Gambetta, ed., *Trust: Making and Breaking Cooperative Relations* (New York: Basil Blackwell, 1988), 194–210; and Charles F. Sabel, "Flexible Specialization and the Re-emergence of Regional Economies," in Paul Hirst and Jonathan Zeitlin, eds., *Reversing Industrial Decline? Industrial Structure and Policy in Britain and Her Competitors* (Oxford: Berg Publishers, 1989), 26–31.

40. *Congressional Record*, 44th Cong., 1st sess., Appendix, 111–14. See also comments by Iowa Senator James Wilson, *Congressional Record*, 44th Cong., 1st sess., 1876, 113.

41. Ben H. Proctor, *Not Without Honor: The Life of John H. Reagan* (Austin: University of Texas Press, 1962), 225–40; Haney, *Congressional History of Railways*, 288–90; Ari Hoogenboom and Olive Hoogenboom, *A History of the ICC: From Panacea to Palliative* (New York: W. W. Norton, 1976), 8–13.

42. *Who Was Who in America, 1607–1896* (Chicago: A. N. Marquis Co., 1963).

43. U.S. Congress, *Interstate Commerce Debate in 48th Cong., 2d sess. on the Bill (H.R. 5461) to Establish a Board of Commissioners of Interstate Commerce, and to Regulate Such Commerce [etc.]* (Washington, 1884), 30. (Hereafter cited as *ICC Debate, 48th.*) On the 1866 legislation, see also Haney, *Congressional History of Railways*, 2: 214–30.

44. Keller, *Affairs of State;* Samuel P. Hays, *The Response to Industrialism, 1885–1914* (Chicago: University of Chicago Press, 1957); Robert Wiebe, *The Search for Order, 1887–1920* (Chicago: Quadrangle Books, 1962); Samuel P. Hays, "Political Parties and the Community-Society Continuum," in William N. Chambers and Walter Dean Burnham, eds., *The American Party Systems: Stages of Political Development*, 2d ed. (London: Oxford University Press, 1979).

45. Foner, *Free Labor, Free Soil, Free Men*, 37.

46. *ICC Debate, 48th*, 97.

47. Ibid., 32.

48. Ibid., 209.

49. Stickney, *The Railway Problem*, 36–57.

50. *ICC Debate, 48th*, 31.

51. Ibid., 243.

52. Congress, *Interstate Commerce Debate in 49th Cong. on the Bill to Establish a Board of Commissioners on Interstate Commerce, and to Regulate Such Commerce, etc.*, Compiled by V. H. Painter (Washington, 1887), 27–28. (Hereafter cited as *ICC Debate, 49th*.)

53. Ibid., 453.

54. *ICC Debate, 48th,*, 30–32.

55. Ibid., 37–38.

56. Ibid., 30–32.

57. Ibid., 32.

58. Ibid., 103–5.

59. *ICC Debate, 49th*, 26–28; Wilson, *ICC Debate*, 48th, 32.

60. For others in Congress who expressed similar concerns, see *ICC Debate, 49th*, statements by Senators Gorman (D. Md.), 108; Sherman (R. Ohio), 112; Longer (R. Mich.), 126; and Coke (D. Tex.), 217; and *ICC Debate, 48th*, statements by Senator Long, 31; Congressman Anderson (R. Kan.), 53; Congressman Shively (D. Ind.), 72; and Senator Beck (D. Ken.), 243.

61. McCraw, *Prophets of Regulation*, 47–52; Testimony by Albert Fink before Congress in *ICC Debate, 48th*, 274–85; Albro Martin, "The Troubled Subject of Railroad Regulation in the Gilded Age—A Reappraisal," *Journal of American History* 61 (Sept. 1974): 339–71; Chandler, *The Visible Hand*, 137–43.

62. Kolko, *Railroads and Regulation*.

63. Chandler, *The Visible Hand*, 538–39n50.

64. Martin, "The Troubled Subject of Railroad Regulation," 370. See also Skowronek, *Building a New American State*, 127–30, 141–50; Gerald Nash, "The Reformer Reformed: John H. Reagan and Railroad Regulation," *Business History Review* 29 (June 1955): 189–96; Chandler, *The Visible Hand*, 144; and Sanders, "Farmers, Railroads, and the States," 15–20.

65. *ICC Debate, 49th*, 456–58. See also Wilson, ibid., 23. For a similar critique of pooling by Stickney, see H. Rodger Grant, *The Corn Belt Route: A History of the Chicago Great Western Railroad Company* (DeKalb: Northern Illinois University Press, 1984), 20.

66. William H. Joubert, *Southern Freight Rates in Transition* (Gainesville: University of Florida Press, 1949), 40–63.

67. William Z. Ripley, *Railroads: Rates and Regulation* (New York: Longmans, Green, 1913), 384–93.

68. Joubert, *Southern Freight Rates*, 73–82.

69. Thomas McIntyre Cooley, "Popular and Legal Views of Traffic Pooling," *Railway Review* 24 (Apr. 26, 1884): 211–14; Henry C. Adams, "A Decade of Federal Railway Regulation," *Atlantic Monthly* 81 (Apr. 1898): 433–43.

70. Quoted in *ICC Debate, 49th*, 463.

71. Stickney, *The Railway Problem*, 54.

72. *ICC Debate, 49th*, 23.

73. Quoted in Stickney, *The Railway Problem*, 124.

74. Ibid.

75. Ibid., 131.

76. Proctor, *Not Without Honor*, 258; Haney, *Congressional History of Railways*, 2: 293–98.

77. On this point, see Skowronek, *Building a New American State*, 150–60; Martin, "The Troubled Subject of Railroad Regulation in the Gilded Age"; and McCraw, *Prophets of Regulation*, 62.

78. Alan Jones, "Thomas M. Cooley and 'Laissez-Faire Constitutionalism': A Reconsideration," *Journal of American History* 53 (Mar. 1967): 751–71.

79. Ibid., 752–57.

80. Quoted in ibid., 756.

81. T. M. Cooley, "State Regulation of Corporate Profits," *North American Review* 137 (Sept. 1883): 206.

82. Ibid., 207, 210, emphasis added.

83. Ibid., 207–8.

84. Hon. D. J. Brewer, *Protection to Property from Public Attack* (New Haven, Conn: Hoggson & Robinson, 1891), 4.

85. Jones, "Thomas M. Cooley and 'Laissez-Faire Constitutionalism,'" 759, emphasis added.

86. Ibid., 763.

87. Cooley, "State Regulation," 210, emphasis added.

88. Ibid., 210. Cooley's effort to locate constitutional grounds for institutions intermediate between state and economy extended to his jurisprudence on the "municipal corporation" as well. Here, too, he articulated an alternative to the emerging liberal scientific synthesis, which subordinated cities to states in order to ensure the strict separation of public and private. (The latter doctrine is well known as "Dillon's Rule.") See Gerald Frug, "The City as a Legal Concept," *Harvard Law Review* 93 (Apr. 1980): 1113.

89. In the Matter of Louisville and Nashville R.R. Co., ICC 31 (1887), quoted in Ralph L. Dewey, *The Long and Short Haul Principle of Rate Regulation* (Columbus: Ohio State University Press, 1935), 70.

90. ICC, *Annual Report*, 1887 (Washington, 1887), 78.

91. Ibid., 79, emphasis added.

92. Ibid., 1893 (Washington, 1893), 13.

93. Quoted in Alan Jones, "Thomas M. Cooley and the Interstate Commerce Commission: Continuity and Change in the Doctrine of Equal Rights," *Political Science Quarterly* 81 (Dec. 1966): 619.

94. ICC, *Annual Report*, 1890 (Washington, 1890), 47.

95. Ibid., 1888 (Washington, 1888), 17.

96. Ibid., 35.

97. Paul W. MacAvoy, *The Economic Effects of Regulation: The Trunk-Line Railroad Cartels and the Interstate Commerce Commission before 1900* (Cambridge, Mass.: M.I.T. Press, 1965), 120–23.

98. James C. Clarke, president of the Illinois Central, as quoted in Cochran, *Railroad Leaders*, 198. See also Sidney L. Miller, *Inland Transportation: Principles and Policies* (New York: McGraw-Hill, 1933), 116.

99. ICC, *Annual Report*, 1890 (Washington, 1890), 39.

100. MacAvoy, *Economic Effects of Regulation*, 124.

101. See, for example, Robert M. Spann and Edward W. Erikson, "The Economics of Railroading: The Beginning of Cartelization and Regulation," *Bell Journal of Economics and Management Science* 1 (Autumn 1970): 227–44; Richard O. Zerbe, "The Costs and Benefits of Early Regulation of the Railroads," *Bell Journal of Economics and Management Science* 11

(Spring 1980): 343–50; and Thomas W. Gilligan, William Marshall, and Barry Weingast, "The Economic Incidence of the Interstate Commerce Act of 1887: A Theoretical and Empirical Analysis of the Shorthaul Pricing Constraint," Hoover Institution, Domestic Studies Program, Working Paper No.P-90-6, April 1990.

102. 1 ICC 158 (1887), quoted and discussed in Dewey, *Long and Short Haul Principle*, 74. See also Osbourne v. Chicago and Northwestern Railroad Company, 52 Fed. Rep. 915; and MacAvoy, *Economic Effects of Regulation*, 155–56.

103. ICC, *Annual Report*, 1893 (Washington, 1893), 33–36. See also Jones, "Thomas M. Cooley and the Interstate Commerce Commission," 616–21, on Cooley's disappointment over management's failure to cooperate.

104. Interstate Commerce Commission v. Alabama Midland Railway Co., 168 U.S. 172 (1897).

105. On the Court's contradictory posture toward substantive review—namely, granting commission findings prima facie status, but reviewing fact in practice—see Louisville and Nashville Railroad Company v. Behlmer, 175 U.S. 648 (1899), at 673–75.

106. See especially Texas & Pacific Railway Company v. Interstate Commerce Commission, 162 U.S. 184 (1896), at 218–20, where the Court says the rule forbidding "any undue or unreasonable preference or advantage in favor of any person, company, firm, corporation or locality . . . [is a] question not of law, but of fact."

107. ICC, *Annual Report*, 1897 (Washington, 1897), 42.

108. Ibid.

109. East Tennessee Virginia and Georgia Railway v. Interstate Commerce Commission, 181 U.S. 1 (1901), at 16.

110. Ibid., 18, 20. See also the Court's opinion in Interstate Commerce Commission v. Louisville and Nashville Railroad Company, 190 U.S. 273 (1902), at 282–84.

111. ICC v. Alabama Midland Railway Co., 168 U.S. 176–77 (1897). See also Harlan's dissent in Texas & Pacific Railway Company v. Interstate Commerce Commission, 162 U.S. 184 (1896), at 239.

112. ICC, *Annual Report*, 1898 (Washington, 1898), 16.

113. Ibid., 20.

114. MacAvoy, *Economic Effects of Regulation*, 187.

115. Dewey, *Long and Short Haul Principle*, 78.

116. MacAvoy, *Economic Effects of Regulation*, 188–91.

117. Interstate Commerce Commission v. Cincinnati, New Orleans and Texas and Pacific Railway Company, 167 U.S. 479 (1897); MacAvoy, *Economic Effects of Regulation*, 184–85.

118. McCraw, "Rethinking the Trust Question," 20–23.

119. Arlington Heights Fruit Exchange et al. v. Southern Pacific Company et al., 22 ICC 149, at 157–58.

120. *Regulation of Railway Rates and Services*, 54–55, emphasis added.

121. Ibid.

122. *Congressional Record*, 61st Cong., 2d sess., 5493, 5659–60.

123. Earl Latham, *The Group Basis of Politics: A Study in Basing-Point Legislation* (Ithaca, N.Y.: Cornell University Press, 1952); Bensen, *Merchants, Farmers, and Railroads*.

124. See, for example, Fink, *Workingmen's Democracy*; Alan Dawley, *Class and Community: The Industrial Revolution in Lynn* (Cambridge: Harvard University Press, 1976); Oestreicher, "Terrence Powderly, the Knights of Labor, and Artisanal Republicanism";

and Livingston, *Origins of the Federal Reserve*. For a more extensive account and critique of how social historians have handled the rise of corporate capitalism, see Gerald Berk, "Corporate Liberalism Reconsidered: A Review Essay," *Journal of Policy History* (Winter 1991): 70–84.

125. See Skowronek, *Building a New American State*; Keller, *Affairs of State*; McCraw, *Prophets of Regulation*; Theda Skocpol and John Ikenberry, "The Political Formation of the American Welfare State in Historical and Comparative Perspective," 25–27; and essays on the twentieth century in Weir, Orloff, and Skocpol, *The Politics of Social Policy in the United States*.

Chapter 5. Regionalism in Economic Practice: The Chicago Great Western Railway, 1883–1908

1. Grant, *The Cornbelt Route*, 29–30.

2. Ibid., 5.

3. *Oelwein Register*, Feb. 14, 1895, quoted in Grant, *The Cornbelt Route*, 6.

4. Ibid., 1–72.

5. Ibid.

6. For a detailed account of how Stickney enlisted the financial support of Oelwein entrepreneurs, see James Thomas Craig, "Oelwein Secures the Machine Shops of the Chicago Great Western Railway Company, 1894," *Annals of Iowa* 24 (Jan. 1943): 211–36; and Grant, *The Cornbelt Route*, 36–38.

7. James Thomas Craig, "Great Western Builds Oelwein Shops: Construction of the Chicago Great Western Railway Machine Shops in 1894–1899," *Annals of Iowa* 26 (July 1944): 106–7.

8. George A. Damon, "Power Equipment for Railroad Shops," *Railroad Gazette* (June 21, 1901): 430–31.

9. See, for example, Grant, *The Cornbelt Route*, 94–103; and H. Roger Grant, "Prairie Innovator: The Chicago Great Western Railway," *Railroad History* (Autumn 1983): 74–77.

10. Samuel Stickney, "Changes in Operation Divisions of the Great Western," *Railroad Gazette* 29 (Aug. 6, 1897): 549.

11. On the internal organization of the interregionals, see Chandler, *The Visible Hand*, 175–85.

12. See, for example, Arthur L. Stinchcombe, "Bureaucratic and Craft Administration of Production: A Comparative Study," *Administrative Science Quarterly* 4 (Sept. 1959): 168–87; Michel Crozier, *The Bureaucratic Phenomenon* (Chicago: University of Chicago Press, 1964); and Alan Fox, *Beyond Contract: Work, Power and Trust Relations* (London: Faber & Faber, 1974).

13. On economies of scope in today's hub-and-spoke airline operations, see Steven A. Morrison and Clifford Winston, *The Economic Effects of Airline Deregulation* (Washington: Brookings Institution, 1986), 5–10; and more generally in transportation, Steven A. Morrison and Clifford Winston, "Intercity Transportation Route Structures under Deregulation: Some Assessments Motivated by the Airline Experience," *American Economic Review* (Papers and Proceedings of the AEA, 1984) 75 (May 1985): 57–61; and Elizabeth Bailey and Ann F. Friedlander, "Multiproduct Industries," *Journal of Economic Literature* 20 (September 1982): 1025–28. On economies of joint production in nineteenth-century rail-

roads, see F. W. Taussig, "A Contribution to the Theory of Railway Rates," *Quarterly Journal of Economics* 5 (July 1891): 438–65.

14. A. B. Stickney, "Argument on Behalf of the Chicago Great Western Railway Company," before the Minnesota Railroad and Warehouse Commissioners, Mar. 1906, 4–6. (Hereafter cited as Stickney, "Argument on Behalf of the CGW.")

15. Ibid., 35–36.

16. See, for example, Frank P. Donovan, Jr., "The Amazing Great Western," *Railroad Magazine* 61 (Sept. 1953): 29–31; and Frank P. Donovan, Jr., "The Great Western in Iowa," *The Palimpsest* 34 (June 1953): 280.

17. Stickney, "Argument on Behalf of the CGW," 26, 40.

18. Ibid., 27.

19. *An Analysis of the Relation of the Rates on Live Stock and the Products of Live Stock, Based on the Cost of Carriage*, Testimony of A. B. Stickney in the trial in the United States Court, September 1905, of the case of: Interstate Commerce Commission v. The Chicago Great Western Railway Company, and other Companies, 35–36. (Hereafter cited as *Stickney Testimony, ICC v. CGW.*)

20. *Commercial and Financial Chronicle* 85 (Mar. 30, 1907): 745, emphasis added.

21. *Annual Reports, Chicago Great Western Railway Company.* 1893: 7, 9; 1894: 10, 23; 1896: 10–11; 1897: 29; 1898: 17; 1899: 6; 1901: 13, 31; 1902: 2, 10; 1903: 30; 1904: 17–18; 1905: 21, 37; 1906: 19, 35; 1907: 19–20.

22. The Maple Leaf Route boasted that "a study of [its] map will convince you that along this line are located a greater number of large cities and towns, with a greater aggregate population, than on any other western road of equal mileage." *Chicago Great Western Railway Company, The Great Steel-Rail Highway for Freight and Passenger Traffic,* Davis, Kellogg and Severance (DKS) Papers, 30.A.4.2F.

23. Recent literature on economies of scope has stressed precisely these sorts of advantages among today's batch manufacturers. See, for example, J. Goldhar and M. Jelinek, "Plan for Economies of Scope," *Harvard Business Review* (Nov.–Dec. 1983). See also Piore and Sabel, *The Second Industrial Divide,* 28–35, 258–77; and Hirst and Zeitlin, "Flexible Specialization versus Post-Fordism."

24. E. S. Meade, "The Chicago Great Western," *Railway World* (Aug. 25, 1905): 675.

25. As the Interstate Commerce Commission put the problem in livestock transportation: "Those whose lines reach Chicago and also run through live-stock districts in states west, northwest and southwest of the Missouri River desire the long haul they will obtain if the live stock is shipped to Chicago, while those whose lines terminate at the river wish the live stock to be slaughtered there, because this will give them an opportunity to participate in hauling the products." Chicago Livestock Exchange v. C.G.W Ry. Co., et al., 10 ICR 433.

26. The diversification and manufacturing option associated with economic regionalism has remained an unexplored option by those who see domestic interest formation, in response to the world wheat glut of the 1870s, in less ambiguous terms. See, for example, Peter Gourevich, "The Second Image Reversed: International Trade and Domestic Coalitions," *International Organization* 32 (Autumn 1978): 881–912; and Charles Kindleberger, *Economic Response* (Cambridge: Harvard University Press, 1978), 19–38.

27. "Railroads and Milling Business," *Fort Dodge Java Messenger* (Sept. 28, 1905); "Alpheus Beede Stickney," untitled newspaper clipping in ABS papers.

28. A. B. Stickney, *Omaha as a Market Town: The Distinguishing Characteristics of the*

Market-Town and the Economic Law upon Which It Is Founded (St. Paul: Pioneer Press Co., 1903); A. B. Stickney, *Nebraska's Opportunity to Increase the Prosperity of Her Farms* (St. Paul: Pioneer Press Mfg. Depts., 1904).

29. On the variety of institutions designed to cope with economic instability and uncertainty in advanced industrial societies more generally, see Berger and Piore, *Dualism and Discontinuity in Industrial Societies*.

30. Stickney, *Nebraska's Opportunity*, 7.

31. Stickney, *Omaha as a Market-Town*, 16.

32. Stickney, *Nebraska's Opportunity*, 6.

33. Ibid., 7. See also *Omaha as a Market-Town*, 15–16.

34. Stickney, *Omaha as a Market-Town*, 17.

35. Ibid.

36. Stickney, *Nebraska's Opportunity*, 7–8.

37. Ibid., 9.

38. Ibid., 15.

39. Interstate Commerce Commission, *Annual Report*, 1896 (Washington, 1896), 80.

40. Frank P. Donovan, Jr., and W. B. Davids, "A. B. Stickney," *Railway Progress* (Dec. 1952), 15.

41. Grant, *The Cornbelt Route*, 41–42; Interstate Commerce Commission, *Annual Report*, 1896 (Washington, 1896), 75–86; 71 ICR 33, 1896; *Railroad Gazette* 29 (Feb. 19, 1897).

42. 71 ICR 37, 1896. See also *Railroad Gazette* 29 (Feb. 19, 1897).

43. *Commercial and Financial Chronicle* 75 (Aug. 16, 1902): 341; Chicago Livestock Exchange v. C.G.W.R. Co. et al., 10 ICR 436.

44. Kellogg to J. M. Dickinson, General Counsel, Illinois Central Railroad, Mar. 17, 1904, DKS Letterpress Book.

45. *Stickney Testimony, ICC v. CGW*.

46. 10 ICR 447.

47. 10 ICR 453.

48. 10 ICR 452.

49. *Argument of C. A. Severance on Behalf of the Chicago Great Western Railway Company in Circuit Court of the United States for the Northern Division of the Northern District of Illinois,* ICC v. C.G.W. Ry. Co., et al., 1–3, DKS Papers, 30.A.3B.

50. Ibid., 3.

51. Ibid., 4.

52. Ibid., 9.

53. Charles Bovey, Washburn, Crosby Co., to Kellogg, Jan. 27, 1903, DKS Papers, 30.A.3B, Box 3.

54. *Brief for Intervenor, T. M. Sinclair & Co., Ltd, ICC v. CGW Ry Co.*, et al. (Chicago: Eastman Bros., Law Printers, 1906), 9–11, emphasis added; DKS Papers, 30.A.3B., Box 3.

55. ICC v. CGW Ry Co., 209 U.S. 121–22.

56. A. B. Stickney, *Railway Rates: A Discovery and Demonstration in Schedule Making* (St. Paul: McGill-Warner Co., 1909); A. B. Stickney, *The Defects of the Interstate Commerce Law: An Address at a Meeting of the Washington Economic Society*, Feb. 3, 1905; A. B. Stickney, *Railway Rates: An Address at a Banquet of the Railway Employees Transportation Club of St. Paul*, Feb. 2, 1907.

57. Chandler, *The Visible Hand*, 9–10; Chandler, "The Separation of Ownership and Control"; Clark, "Four Stages of Capitalism"; Richard Posner, *Economic Analysis of Law*,

2d ed. (Boston: Little, Brown & Co., 1977); Hurst, *The Legitimacy of the Business Corporation*, 39–57; Berle and Means, *The Modern Corporation and Private Property*.

58. A. B. Stickney, *A Western Trunkline Railway without a Mortgage: A Short History of the Finances of the Chicago Great Western Railway Company* (New York: Evening Post Printing House, 1900); Grant, *The Cornbelt Route*, 32–34.

59. Stickney, *Western Trunkline Railway*.

60. Grant, *The Cornbelt Route*, 45–47; *Railway World* (Sept. 13, 1902): 1041–42. See also Emily Stickney Spencer, *Alpheus Beede Stickney, His Descendents and Some of Their Ancestors*, 20, ABS Papers, 25.C.10. For a retrospective account of several times that J. P. Morgan had been enlisted to acquire control of the Great Western, see Unknown to Stickney, Dec. 19, 1907, DKS Papers, 30.A.4.2F.

61. *Chicago Great Western Railway Company Annual Report*, 1894, 10–11; *Railroad Age Gazette* 67 (Aug. 27, 1904): 348; *Commercial and Financial Chronicle* 75 (Apr. 11, 1903): 809; *Commercial and Financial Chronicle* 73 (Sept. 14, 1901): 525.

62. E. S. Meade, "The Chicago Great Western," 675.

63. "Memorandum for Mr. Root," DKS Papers, 30.A.2F., 5–6; *Proceedings at a Private Meeting of the Holders of 5 per cent. Sterling Notes, Held at the Institute of Chartered Accountants, Moorgate Place, London, E.C., on Wednesday, the 8th Day of January, 1908*, DKS Papers, 30.A.4.2F; *Commercial and Financial Chronicle* 86 (Jan. 11, 1908): 107.

64. Chicago Great Western Railway Company, Annual Letter of the Directors to the London Finance Committee, 1907, 5–17; James Thomas Craig, "The 'Big Strike' at Oelwein Shops," *Annals of Iowa* 28 (July 1946): 116–38.

65. *Commercial and Financial Chronicle* 86 (Mar. 7, 1908): 601.

66. Chicago Great Western Railway Company, *Statement of Mr. A. B. Stickney, at Private Conference of Holders of Notes due, and shortly to become due, held in London, on January 8th, 1908, at the Institute of Chartered Accountants*, DKS Papers, 30.A.4.2F.

67. Unknown to Stickney, Dec. 19, 1907, DKS Papers, 30.A.4.2F.

68. *Railway World*, Jan. 17, 1908, quoted in Grant, *The Cornbelt Route*, 74.

69. Evidence of the Great Western's continued concern with modest size regional markets through the teens and 1920s is indicated by periodic articles in its employees' magazine on small cities along the road. See, for example, C. C. Rumple, "Highlights of Great Western Cities: Fairbault, Minnesota," *The Great Western Magazine* (Oct. 1926): 9–10; "Fort Dodge, Iowa," *The Maize* 3 (Feb. 1914): 34–35; B. J. DeGroodt, "Red Wing, Minnesota," *The Maize* 4 (Feb. 1915); W. F. Muse, "Mason City, Iowa," *The Maize* 4 (Apr. 1915): 48–52; James R. Kinsole, "Winona, Minnesota," *The Maize* 4 (June 1915): 33–37; and Guy F. Boycee, "Rochester, Minnesota," *The Maize* 4 (Aug. 1915): 17-22.

70. H. Roger Grant, "Prairie Innovator," 70–82.

Chapter 6. The Predicament of Regulated Monopoly

1. For an excellent summary of pluralist assumptions about the transformation of American politics in industrialization, see Michael Paul Rogin, *The Intellectuals and McCarthy: The Radical Specter* (Cambridge: M.I.T. Press, 1969), 9–31.

2. See, for example, James Weinstein, *The Corporate Ideal in the Liberal State, 1900–1918* (Boston: Beacon Press, 1968); Martin J. Sklar, "Woodrow Wilson and the Political Economy of Modern United States Liberalism," *Studies on the Left* 1 (Fall 1960): 17–47; and Ellis

W. Hawley, "'The Study and Discovery of a 'Corporate Liberalism,'" *Business History Review* 52 (Autumn 1978): 309–20.

3. ICC *Annual Report*, 1898 (Washington, 1898), 16.

4. Quoted in Gabriel Kolko, *Railroads and Regulation, 1877–1916* (Princeton: Princeton University Press, 1965), 87.

5. ICC *Annual Report*, 1898 (Washington, 1898), 20.

6. John Moody, *The Truth about the Trusts: A Description and Analysis of the American Trust Movement* (New York: Moody Publishing Co., 1904), 429–50; Interstate Commerce Commission, *Intercorporate Relationships of Railways in the United States as of June 30, 1906* (Washington, 1908); William Z. Ripley (testimony), *U.S. Industrial Commission* 19 (1902): 304–29; William Z. Ripley, "Changes in Railroad Conditions since 1887," *The World's Work* (Oct. 1905); Louis D. Brandeis, *Other People's Money and How the Bankers Use It* (1914; reprint, New York: Harper Torchbooks, 1967).

7. ICC *Annual Report*, 1899 (Washington, 1899), 6.

8. Ibid. See also Albro Martin, *Enterprise Denied: Origins of the Decline of American Railroads, 1897–1917* (New York: Columbia University Press, 1971), 176.

9. ICC *Annual Report*, 1902 (Washington, 1902), 7.

10. Reagan v. Farmers' Loan and Trust Co., 154 U.S. 362 (1894).

11. Gerard C. Henderson, "Railway Valuation and the Courts, I," *Harvard Law Review* 33 (1920): 909. For a good discussion of Smyth v. Ames, see also Stephen A. Siegel, "Understanding the *Lochner* Era: Lessons from the Controversy over Railroad and Utility Rate Regulation, *Virginia Law Review* 70 (Mar. 1984): 187–263.

12. Smyth v. Ames, 169 U.S. 466, 546 (1898).

13. This view of Adams is best articulated by Skowronek, *Building a New American State*, 132–38. For a similar account of another "economic mugwump," Charles Francis Adams, Jr., see McCraw, *Prophets of Regulation*, 1–56.

14. Interstate Commerce Commission, *Report of the Statistics of Railways in the United States, 1888* (Washington, 1889), 5–6. (Hereafter cited as ICC *Statistics*.) In 1890 Adams wrote, "No effort has been made by the statistician's office to arrive at the cost of railway property, or the value except as represented by stocks and bonds . . . or by the capitalization of payments on capital . . . Reference was made to this question in the first report of railway statistics, and the difficulties in arriving at accurate figures pertaining to cost were suggested. Chief among these difficulties is the fact that the railway system as it exists at the present time is represented by corporations which had nothing to do with the building of these lines. There is, therefore, no record in many instances of the original cost of a line. Moreover, since the inception of the railway system in the United States, the changes in mechanical appliances and the constant fluctuation in the prices of railway supplies are so great that the cost of railway property, even though it could be taken from the books of a company, would be useless as showing the present value of the property." ICC *Statistics*, 1890, 97–98. See also ICC *Statistics*, 1891, 68.

15. ICC *Statistics*, 1888, 5–6.

16. *Report of the Industrial Commission on Transportation* 9 (Washington, 1901), 382–84. Like the ICC, state railroad commissioners also re-evaluated the feasibility of and necessity for valuation after Smyth v. Ames and rejected commercial value as useless for setting maximum rates. For the changing attitudes of the state commissioners, see National Association of Railroad Commissioners (NARC), *Proceedings of Annual Conventions* (Washing-

ton), 1905, 56–59, 67–68; 1906, 39, 82–86; 1907, 74–76; 1908, 175–215; 1909, 332–33, 418–23; 1910, 139–44.

17. ICC *Annual Report*, 1901 (Washington, 1901), 26–27.

18. On the Elkins Act, see George Mowry, *The Era of Theodore Roosevelt and the Birth of Modern America* (New York: Harper Torchbooks, 1958), 198; Kolko, *Railroads and Regulation*, 94–101; I. Leo Sharfman, *The Interstate Commerce Commission: A Study in Administrative Law and Procedure* (New York: Commonwealth Fund, 1931), 1: 35–40; Hoogenboom and Hoogenboom, *A History of the ICC*, 39–46; and W. Z. Ripley, *Railroads: Rates and Regulation* (New York: Longmans, Green, 1913), 492–94.

19. See ICC statements reproduced in *Congressional Record*, 61st Cong., 2d sess., 6892.

20. Frank Haigh Dixon, "The Interstate Commerce Act as Amended," *Quarterly Journal of Economics* 21 (Nov. 1906): 38. On the passage of the Hepburn Act more generally, see John Morton Blum, *The Republican Roosevelt* (Cambridge: Harvard University Press, 1954), 87–105; Skowronek, *Building a New American State*, 255–58; Hoogenboom and Hoogenboom, *A History of the ICC*, 46–52; Mowry, *Era of Theodore Roosevelt*, 198–206; Lewis L. Gould, *The Presidency of Theodore Roosevelt* (Lawrence: University Press of Kansas, 1991), 151–64.

21. Quoted in Kolko, *Railroads and Regulation*, 111.

22. *Congressional Record*, 59th Cong., 1st sess., v. 40, part 6, 5722.

23. Ibid., 5691.

24. Ibid., 5692, emphasis added.

25. Ibid., 5711–14.

26. See Chap. 4, 112–13.

27. *Congressional Record*, 59th Cong., 1st sess., 5695.

28. Ibid., 5706, 5708, 5714, emphasis added.

29. Hoogenboom and Hoogenboom, *A History of the ICC*, 54; Skowronek, *Building a New American State*, 258; Kolko, *Railroads and Regulation*, 155–76. Among those who joined LaFollette's demand for regulated monopoly in 1906 was the chair of the Senate Interstate Commerce Committee, Francis Newlands. "The steady trend of consolidation," he wrote, "is the outcome of economic forces which cannot be controlled or appreciably impeded by legislation. . . . Railroad monopoly has come in the course of natural evolution. We have learned that monopoly is inherent in our modern method of transportation." The industry's consolidation into six working groups, he concluded, required novel policy. Like the president, Newlands advocated national incorporation, property valuation, and maximum rate authority for the ICC. See Francis Newlands, "Common Sense on the Railroad Question," *The North American Review* 180 (1905): 576–85.

30. Kenneth W. Hechler, *Insurgency: Personalities and Politics of the Taft Era* (New York: Columbia University Press, 1940), 32–43; George E. Mowry, *Theodore Roosevelt and the Progressive Movement* (Madison: University of Wisconsin Press, 1947), 31–32, 155.

31. Mowry, *Theodore Roosevelt*, 94–95.

32. Hechler, *Insurgency*, 165–72; "Views of the Minority (To Accompany S.6737)," *Congressional Record*, 61st Cong., 2d sess., 2821–23. Looking back in 1913, LaFollette condemned Taft's initiative as "the rankest, boldest betrayal of public interest ever proposed in any legislative body." See Kolko, *Railroads and Regulation*, 184–86.

33. The amendment read, "Rates should not be advanced until found by the commission to be just and reasonable." *Congressional Record*, 61st Cong., 2d sess., 6885.

34. Hechler, *Insurgency*, 172, emphasis added.

35. *Congressional Record*, 61st Cong., 2d sess., 6882.

36. Ibid., 6885.

37. Ibid., 6888. See also the statements in the same session by Jonathan P. Dolliver (R. Iowa), ibid., 5324; and Rep. William J. Cary (R. Wis.), ibid., Appendix, 105–8.

38. Ibid., Appendix, 86–89, 99.

39. Sanders, "Farmers, Railroads, and the State," 48; Hoogenboom and Hoogenboom, *A History of the ICC*, 60; Martin, *Enterprise Denied*, 186–89.

40. *Congressional Record*, 61st Cong., 2d sess., 5745, 5748, 7575.

41. Ibid., 5858–59.

42. Ibid., 5741.

43. Ibid., 5841, 5855.

44. Ibid., Robert Turnbull, 5859.

45. Ibid., 5841.

46. Ibid., 5841. See also the statement by Rep. Clement Dickinson (D. Mo.), ibid., 5855.

47. Ibid., speech by Rep. Martin Madden (R. Ill.), 5844.

48. Ibid., 5849.

49. Ibid., Jonathan Dolliver (R. Iowa), 5324.

50. Ibid., speech by Francis Newlands (D. Nev.), 2824–27; Hechler, *Insurgency*, 171–72. See also the discussion of antitrust led by Senator Borah, *Congressional Record*, 61st Cong., 2d sess., 5261–71; and the speech by Dolliver, ibid., 5323–30. For scholars who have explained the failure of a pooling provision in this way, see Skowronek, *Building a New American State*, 264; and Sanders, "Farmers, Railroads, and the State," 45.

51. Frank Haigh Dixon, "The Mann-Elkins Act, Amending the Act to Regulate Commerce," *Quarterly Journal of Economics* 24 (Aug. 1910): 601–5, 612–13, 631–32.

52. Dixon, "The Mann-Elkins Act"; Hechler, *Insurgency*, 173–77; *Congressional Record*, 61st Cong., 2d sess., 7568–77.

53. Dixon, "The Mann-Elkins Act," 619.

54. Ripley, *Railroads*, 581.

55. Sharfman, *The Interstate Commerce Commission*, 1: 124–27; Sanders, "Farmers, Railroads, and the State," 49–50; Kolko, *Railroads and Regulation*, 198–202; Hoogenboom and Hoogenboom, *A History of the ICC*, 66–70.

56. C. A. Prouty to Hon. C. L. Bartlett, reprinted in *Congressional Record*, 61st Cong., 2d sess., 5214, emphasis added.

57. Kolko, *Railroads and Regulation*, 192.

58. See Skowronek, *Building a New American State*, 269; Hoogenboom and Hoogenboom, *A History of the ICC*, 66; Martin, *Enterprise Denied*, 223–25; and Sanders, "Farmers, Railroads, and the State," 50.

59. The phrase "interest group liberalism" derives from Theodore Lowi, *The End of Liberalism: The Second Republic of the United States* (New York: W. W. Norton, 1979). The idea of "countervailing power" is explored by John Kenneth Galbraith, *American Capitalism: The Concept of Countervailing Power* (Boston: Houghton Mifflin, 1952).

60. On the exercise of power by subordinates within hierarchical arrangements by holding rigidly to rules that mark the limits of their authority, more generally, see Pierre Bourdieu, *Outline of a Theory of Practice*, trans. Richard Nice (Cambridge: Cambridge University Press, 1977), 159; E. P. Thompson, *Whigs and Hunters: The Origins of the Black Act*

(New York: Pantheon, 1975), 258–65; and Joel F. Handler, *The Conditions of Discretion: Autonomy, Community, Bureaucracy* (New York: Russell Sage, 1986), 130–43.

61. 35 ICC 500–505.

62. 31 ICC 359–60.

63. This quotation is Albro Martin's summary of McCrea's testimony before the ICC. See Martin, *Enterprise Denied,* 208.

64. 20 ICC 280, 284.

65. Interstate Commerce Commission, *Advance in Rates by Carriers, Reports of the Commission* 10 (Washington, 1912): 5403, 5472.

66. Ibid., 5403.

67. 35 ICC 507; Martin, *Enterprise Denied,* 308–9.

68. *Hearings before the ICC in the "Five Per Cent Case,"* Senate Document 466, 63d Cong., 2d sess., 699, 702, 705, 709, 711–13, quoted and summarized in Martin, *Enterprise Denied,* 277.

69. 35 ICC 505.

70. 20 ICC 256, 263, 275.

71. 20 ICC 305.

72. 31 ICC 371.

73. Summarized in Martin, *Enterprise Denied,* 275–76.

74. 20 ICC 268. Note Martin's distortion of the commission's logic here. The ICC, he correctly points out, says that "each generation may well be required to bear the burden, and the stockholder should not obtain both an adequate dividend upon his stock and an addition to the value of his property." But the commission does not conclude from this, as Martin says, that "rates need not be high enough to ensure a surplus." The ICC concedes there are a number of legitimate reasons to carry a surplus. But more important, it goes on to qualify the sentence quoted by Martin, adding that investment does justify a greater return for railroads. Hence, the ICC sees its mission as one of locating the criteria to resolve a distributive problem. In the passage referred to, the commission is merely saying that an unqualified rule allowing the railroads to finance from surplus does not resolve the problem. See Martin, *Enterprise Denied,* 229 and 229n59, where he refers to the ICC's reasoning as a "childlike ignorance of the dynamics of investment."

75. Summarized in Martin, *Enterprise Denied,* 208–9.

76. 20 ICC 267, 334.

77. 31 ICC 358–59.

78. 20 ICC 334.

79. Gerard Henderson, "Railway Valuation and the Courts, III," *Harvard Law Review* 33 (1920): 1031–32.

80. Ibid., 1035.

81. Ibid., 1051.

82. The classic statement of pluralist bargaining as "partisan mutual adjustment" is Charles Lindblom, *The Intelligence of Democracy* (New York: Free Press, 1965). See also Rogin, *The Intellectuals and McCarthy.*

83. Among the new institutionalists and organizational historians, see David Vogel, "Why Businessmen Distrust Their State: The Political Consciousness of American Corporate Executives," *British Journal of Political Science* (Jan. 1978): 45–78; Thomas K. McCraw, "Business and Government: Origins of the Adversary Relationship," *California Management Review* 26 (Winter 1984); and Alfred D. Chandler, "Government versus Business: An

American Phenomenon," in John T. Dunlop, ed., *Business and Public Policy* (Boston: Harvard Business School Press, 1980), 1-11.

84. This argument is best made by Weinstein, *The Corporate Ideal in the Liberal State.* See also Sklar, "Woodrow Wilson and the Political Economy of Modern United States Liberalism"; and Hawley, "The Study and Discovery of a 'Corporate Liberalism.'" Two recent versions of this "corporate liberal" thesis concerned much more with the (re)construction of cultural authority, rather than the instrumental exercise of business power over the state or the functionalist imperatives of accumulation and legitimation, are Martin J. Sklar, *The Corporate Reconstruction of American Capitalism, 1890-1916: The Market, the Law, and Politics* (Cambridge: Cambridge University Press, 1988); and James Livingston, *Origins of the Federal Reserve: Money, Class, and Corporate Capitalism, 1890-1913* (Ithaca, N.Y.: Cornell University Press, 1986). For a more detailed discussion of the last two works, see Gerald Berk, "Corporate Liberalism Reconsidered: A Review Essay," *Journal of Policy History* 3 (Winter 1991): 70-84.

Chapter 7. Beyond Corporate Liberalism

1. This picture of pluralist scholarship is intended as an ideal typical account of a research program quite varied in practice. Among political scientists, see Robert Dahl, *Who Governs? Democracy and Power in an American City* (New Haven: Yale University Press, 1961); Nelson Polsby, "How to Study Community Power: The Pluralist Alternative," *Journal of Politics* 22 (Aug. 1960); Lindblom, *The Intelligence of Democracy*; Seymour Martin Lipset, *Political Man* (Garden City, N.Y.: Doubleday, 1960); and Daniel Bell, *The End of Ideology* (Glencoe, Ill.: Free Press, 1960). Among historians, see especially Richard Hofstadter, *The American Political Tradition and the Men Who Made It* (New York: Alfred A. Knopf, 1948); and Richard Hofstadter, *The Age of Reform: From Bryan to Roosevelt* (New York: Vintage Books, 1955). For an excellent account and critique of midcentury pluralism's assumptions about industrialization and mass politics, see Rogin, *The Intellectuals and McCarthy*, 9-31.

2. Walter Dean Burnham, *The Current Crisis in American Politics* (New York: Oxford University Press, 1982); Samuel P. Huntington, "The Democratic Distemper," in Michel Crozier, Samuel P. Huntington, and Joji Watanuki, eds., *The Crisis of Democracy: Report on the Governability of Democracies to the Trilateral Commission* (New York: New York University Press, 1975); Mancur Olson, *The Rise and Decline of Nations: Economic Growth, Stagflation, and Social Rigidities* (New Haven: Yale University Press, 1982); Lester Thurow, *The Zero-Sum Society: Distribution and the Possibilities for Economic Change* (New York: Penguin Books, 1981).

3. Compare Daniel Bell, *The End of Ideology* to Daniel Bell, *The Cultural Contradictions of Capitalism* (New York: Basic Books, 1976).

4. Charles Lindblom, "The Market as Prison," in Thomas Ferguson and Joel Rogers, eds., *The Political Economy* (Armonk, N.Y.: M. E. Sharpe, 1984), 3-11; Joshua Cohen and Joel Rogers, *On Democracy* (New York: Penguin Books, 1984), 47-87; Adam Przeworski, *Capitalism and Social Democracy* (Cambridge: Cambridge University Press, 1985), 133-69; Arthur M. Okun, *Equality and Efficiency: The Big Trade-Off* (Washington: Brookings Institution, 1975); George Gilder, *Wealth and Poverty* (New York: Basic Books, 1981).

5. Alan Fox, *Beyond Contract: Work, Power, and Trust Relations* (London: Faber & Faber, 1974).

6. Thomas J. Peters, *Thriving on Chaos: Handbook for a Management Revolution* (New York: Alfred A. Knopf, 1987); Rosabeth Moss Kanter, *When Giants Dance: Mastering the Challenges of Strategy, Management, and Careers in the 1990s* (New York: Simon & Schuster, 1989); Arnold O. Putnam, "A Redesign for Engineering, " *Harvard Business Review* 63 (May–June 1985): 139–44; Hirotaka Takeuchi and Ikujiro Nonaka, "The New Product Development Game," *Harvard Business Review* 64 (Jan.–Feb. 1986): 137–46.

7. On the surprising convergence of left and right on deregulation, see Martha Derthick and Paul J. Quirk, *The Politics of Deregulation* (Washington: Brookings Institution, 1985).

8. On the macroeconomic results of wealth redistribution in the 1980s, see Kevin Phillips, *The Politics of Rich and Poor: Wealth and the American Electorate in the Reagan Aftermath* (New York: Random House, 1990); Steven Schlossstein, *The End of the American Century* (New York: Congdon, 1989).

9. See, for example, David Stockman, *The Triumph of Politics: Why the Reagan Revolution Failed* (New York: Harper & Row, 1986); Benjamin Ginsburg and Martin Shefter, *Politics by Other Means: The Declining Importance of Elections in America* (New York: Basic Books, 1990), 171–75; Susan J. Tolchin and Martin Tolchin, *Dismantling America: The Rush to Deregulate* (New York: Oxford University Press, 1983); and Marc P. Petracca, "The Rediscovery of Interest Group Politics," in Marc P. Petracca, ed., *The Politics of Interests: Interest Groups Transformed* (Boulder: Westview Press, 1992), 13–18.

10. On the implications of this point for the difficulties in American economic adjustment in the 1980s, see Robert B. Reich, *The Next American Frontier* (New York: Penguin, 1983), 20–21, 255–82.

11. Dahl, "On Removing Certain Impediments to Democracy in the United States," 320.

BIBLIOGRAPHY

Social Theory and Political Economy

Abernathy, William. *The Productivity Dilemma: Roadblock to Innovation in the Automobile Industry.* Baltimore: Johns Hopkins University Press, 1978.

Ackerman, Bruce. *We the People 1: Foundations.* Cambridge: Harvard University Press, 1991.

Aglietta, Michel. *A Theory of Capitalist Regulation.* London: New Left Books, 1979.

Amenta, Edwin, and Theda Skocpol. "Taking Exception: Explaining the Distinctiveness of American Public Policies in the Last Century." In *The Comparative History of Public Policy,* edited by Francis G. Castles. New York: Oxford University Press, 1989: 292–333.

Arnold, Thurman. *The Folklore of Capitalism.* New Haven: Yale University Press, 1937.

Bell, Daniel. *The End of Ideology.* Glencoe: Free Press, 1960.

———. *The Cultural Contradictions of Capitalism.* New York: Basic Books, 1976.

Berger, Suzanne, and Michael J. Piore. *Dualism and Discontinuity in Industrial Societies.* Cambridge: Cambridge University Press, 1981.

Berle, Adolf, and Gardiner Means. *The Modern Corporation and Private Property.* New York: Harcourt, Brace & World, 1967.

Berry, Brian J. L., and W. C. Garrison. "Functional Bases of the Central Place Hierarchy." *Economic Geography* 34 (1958): 98–107.

Best, Michael. *The New Competition: Institutions of Industrial Restructuring.* Cambridge: Harvard University Press, 1990.

Block, Fred. "The Ruling Class Does Not Rule: Notes on the Marxist Theory of the State." *Socialist Revolution* 33 (May–June 1977).

Bourdieu, Pierre. *Outline of a Theory of Practice.* Translated by Richard Nice. Cambridge: Cambridge University Press, 1977.

Brenner, Robert. "The Origins of Capitalism: A Critique of Neo-Smithian Economics." *New Left Review* 104 (1977).

———. "Economic Backwardness in Eastern Europe in Light of Developments in the West." In *The Origins of Backwardness in Eastern Europe,* edited by Daniel Chirot. Berkeley: University of California Press, 1989: 15–52.

Burnham, James. *The Managerial Revolution: What Is Happening in the World*. New York: John Day, 1941.

Ceaser, James W. "In Defense of Republican Constitutionalism: A Reply to Dahl." In *The Moral Foundations of the American Republic*, edited by Robert H. Horowitz. 3d ed. Charlottesville: University Press of Virginia, 1986: 253–81.

Chandler, Alfred D., and Herman Daems, eds. *Managerial Hierarchies: Comparative Perspectives on the Rise of the Modern Industrial Enterprise*. Cambridge: Harvard University Press, 1980.

Clark, Robert Charles. "Four Stages of Capitalism: Reflections on Investment Management Treatises." *Harvard Law Review* 94 (1981): 561–82.

Cohen, Joshua, and Joel Rogers. *On Democracy*. New York: Penguin Books, 1984.

Crozier, Michel. *The Bureaucratic Phenomenon*. Chicago: University of Chicago Press, 1964.

Dahl, Robert. *Dilemmas of Pluralist Democracy: Autonomy versus Control*. New Haven: Yale University Press, 1982.

———. "On Removing Certain Impediments to Democracy in the United States." In *The Moral Foundations of the American Republic*, edited by Robert H. Horowitz. 3d ed. Charlottesville: University Press of Virginia, 1986: 230–52.

Dore, Ronald. *Taking Japan Seriously: A Confucian Perspective on Leading Economic Issues*. Stanford: Stanford University Press, 1987.

Eisenstadt, S. N. "Studies of Modernization and Sociological Theory." *History and Theory* 13 (1974): 225–53.

Elbaum, Bernard, and William Lazonick, eds. *The Decline of the British Economy*. Oxford: Oxford University Press, 1986.

Field, Alexander James. "The Problem with Neoclassical Institutional Economics: A Critique with Special Reference to the North/Thomas Model of Pre-1500 Europe." *Explorations in Economic History* 18 (1981): 174–98.

Fligstein, Neil. *The Transformation of Corporate Control*. Cambridge: Harvard University Press, 1990.

Fox, Alan. *Beyond Contract: Work, Power, and Trust Relations*. London: Faber & Faber, 1974.

Galbraith, John Kenneth. *The New Industrial State*. Boston: Houghton Mifflin, 1967.

Gaventa, John. *Power and Powerlessness: Quiescence and Rebellion in an Appalachian Valley*. Urbana: University of Illinois Press, 1980.

Geertz, Clifford. *The Interpretations of Cultures*. New York: Basic Books, 1973.

———. *Local Knowledge*. New York: Basic Books, 1983.

Goldhar, J., and M. Jelinek. "Plan for Economies of Scope." *Harvard Business Review* (Nov.–Dec. 1983): 141–48.

Gordon, Robert W. "Critical Legal Histories." *Stanford Law Review* 36 (Jan. 1984): 57–125.

Gourevich, Peter. "The Second Image Reversed: International Trade and Domestic Coalitions." *International Organization* 32 (Autumn 1978): 881–912.

Gramsci, Antonio. *Selections from the Prison Notebooks*. Translated by Quintin Hoare and Geoffrey Nowell Smith. New York: International Publishers, 1980.

Hall, Peter. *Governing the Economy: The Politics of State Intervention in Britain and France*. New York: Oxford University Press, 1986.

Hirst, Paul, and Jonathan Zeitlin. "Flexible Specialization versus Post-Fordism: Theory, Evidence, and Policy Implications." *Economy and Society* 20 (Feb. 1991): 1–56.

Kanter, Rosabeth Moss. *When Giants Dance: Mastering the Challenges of Strategy, Management, and Careers in the 1990s*. New York: Simon & Schuster, 1989.

Keller, Morton. "Public Policy and Large Enterprise: Comparative and Historical Perspectives." In *Law and the Formation of the Big Enterprises in the Nineteenth and Early Twentieth Centuries*, edited by Norbert Horn and Jurgen Kocka. Göttingen: Vandenhoek & Ruprecht, 1979: 519–23.

Kennedy, Duncan. "Cost Reduction Theory as Legitimation." *Yale Law Journal* 90 (Apr. 1981): 1275–83.

———. "The Stages of the Decline of the Public/Private Distinction." *University of Pennsylvania Law Review* 130 (June 1982): 1349–57.

Kennedy, Duncan, and Frank I. Michelman. "Are Property and Contract Efficient?" *Hofstra Law Review* 88 (1980): 711–70.

Kindleberger, Charles. *Economic Response*. Cambridge: Harvard University Press, 1978.

Kurth, James R. "The Political Consequences of the Product Cycle: Industrial History and Political Outcomes." *International Organization* 33 (Winter 1979): 1–35.

Lindblom, Charles. *The Intelligence of Democracy*. New York: Free Press, 1965.

———. *Politics and Markets: The World's Political-Economic Systems*. New York: Basic Books, 1977.

———. "The Market as Prison." In *The Political Economy*, edited by Thomas Ferguson and Joel Rogers. Armonk: M. E. Sharpe, 1984: 3–11.

Lipset, Seymour Martin. *Political Man*. Enl. ed. Baltimore: Johns Hopkins University Press, 1981.

Lorenz, Edward. "Neither Friends nor Strangers: Informal Networks of Subcontracting in French Industry." In *Trust: Making and Breaking Cooperative Relations*, edited by Diego Gambetta. New York: Basil Blackwell, 1988: 194–210.

Lowi, Theodore. *The End of Liberalism: The Second Republic of the United States*. New York: W. W. Norton, 1979.

Lukes, Stephen. *Power: A Radical View*. London: Macmillan, 1989.

Lynch, Frederick R. "Social Theory and the Progressive Era." *Theory and Society* 2 (Summer 1977): 159–210.

McConnell, Grant. *Private Power and American Democracy*. New York: Alfred A. Knopf, 1966.

MacIntyre, Alasdair. "The Relationship of Philosophy to Its Past." In *Philosophy in History: Essays on the Historiography of Philosophy*, edited by Richard Rorty, J. B. Schneedwind, and Quentin Skinner. Cambridge: Cambridge University Press, 1984.

Marris, Robin. *The Economic Theory of "Managerial" Capitalism*. New York: Free Press, 1964.

Milliband, Ralph. *The State in Capitalist Society*. New York: Basic Books, 1969.

Okun, Arthur M. *Equality and Efficiency: The Big Trade-Off*. Washington: Brookings Institution, 1975.

Olson, Mancur. *The Rise and Decline of Nations: Economic Growth, Stagflation, and Social Rigidities*. New Haven: Yale University Press, 1982.

Parsons, Talcott. *The Social System*. Glencoe, Ill.: Free Press, 1951.

———. *On Institutions and Social Evolution*. Edited by Leon H. Mayhew. Chicago: University of Chicago Press, 1982.

Piore, Michael J., and Charles F. Sabel. *The Second Industrial Divide: Possibilities for Prosperity*. New York: Basic Books, 1985.

Pizzorno, Alessandro. "On the Rationality of Democratic Choice." *Telos* 63 (Spring 1986): 55–59.

Polanyi, Karl. *The Great Transformation*. Boston: Beacon Press, 1957.

Polsby, Nelson. "How to Study Community Power: The Pluralist Alternative." *Journal of Politics* 22 (Aug. 1960): 474–84.

Posner, Richard A. "Theories of Economic Regulation." *Bell Journal of Economics and Management Science* 5 (Autumn 1974): 335–58.

————. *Economic Analysis of Law*. 2d ed. Boston: Little, Brown & Co., 1977.

Poulantzas, Nicos. *Political Power and Social Class*. London: New Left Books, 1975.

Sabel, Charles F. *Work and Politics: The Division of Labor in Industry*. Cambridge: Cambridge University Press, 1982.

————. "Flexible Specialization and the Re-emergence of Regional Economies." In *Reversing Industrial Decline? Industrial Structure and Policy in Britain and Her Competitors*, edited by Paul Hirst and Jonathan Zeitlin. Oxford: Berg Publishers, 1989: 26–31.

Sabel, Charles F., and Jonathan Zeitlin. "Historical Alternatives to Mass Production: Politics, Markets, and Technology in Nineteenth-Century Industrialization." *Past and Present* 108 (Aug. 1985): 133–76.

Schattschneider, E. E. *The Semisovereign People: A Realist's View of Democracy*. New York: Holt, Rinehart & Winston, 1960.

Schumpeter, Joseph. *Capitalism, Socialism, and Democracy*. 1947. Reprint. New York: Harper & Row, 1976.

Scott, James. *The Moral Economy of the Peasant: Rebellion and Subsistence in Southeast Asia*. New Haven: Yale University Press, 1976.

Skocpol, Theda. "Bringing the State Back In: Strategies of Analysis in Current Research." In *Bringing the State Back In*, edited by Peter B. Evans, Dietrich Rueschemeyer, and Theda Skocpol. Cambridge: Cambridge University Press, 1985.

Smith, Rogers M. "Political Jurisprudence, the 'New Institutionalism,' and the Future of Public Law." *American Political Science Review* 82 (Mar. 1988): 89–108.

Stinchecombe, Arthur L. "Bureaucratic and Craft Administration of Production: A Comparative Study." *Administrative Science Quarterly* 4 (Sept. 1959): 168–87.

————. *Theoretical Methods in Social History*. New York: Academic Press, 1978.

Thompson, E. P. "The Moral Economy of the English Crowd in the Eighteenth Century." *Past and Present* 50 (Feb. 1971): 76–136.

————. *Whigs and Hunters: The Origins of the Black Act*. New York: Pantheon, 1975.

Truman, David. *The Governmental Process*. New York: Alfred A. Knopf, 1951.

Unger, Roberto M. *Knowledge and Politics*. New York: Free Press, 1975.

————. *Law in Modern Society*. New York: Free Press, 1976.

————. *Politics, a Work in Constructive Social Theory*. 3 vols. Cambridge: Cambridge University Press, 1987.

Weber, Max. *From Max Weber: Essays in Sociology*. Edited by H. H. Gerth and C. Wright Mills. New York: Oxford University Press, 1946.

————. *The Methodology of the Social Sciences*. Translated and edited by Edward A. Shils and Henry A. Finch. New York: Free Press, 1949.

————. *Economy and Society*. 2 vols. Edited by Guenther Roth and Claus Wittich. Berkeley: University of California Press, 1970.

Williamson, Oliver. *Markets and Hierarchies*. New York: Free Press, 1975.

————. "The Modern Corporation: Origins, Evolution, Attributes." *Journal of Economic Literature* 19 (Dec. 1981): 1537–68.

———. *The Economic Institutions of Capitalism: Firms, Markets, Relational Contracting.* New York: Free Press, 1985.

Wilson, Graham. "Why Is There No Corporatism in the United States?" In *Patterns of Corporatist Policy-Making*, edited by Gerhard Lembruch and Philippe Schmitter. Beverly Hills: Sage, 1982.

Wilson, James Q. "The Politics of Regulation." In *The Politics of Regulation*, edited by James Q. Wilson. New York: Basic Books, 1980.

Wright, Erik Olin. *Class, Crisis, and the State.* London: New Left Review Books, 1978.

American Political and Economic Development

Bailyn, Bernard. *The Ideological Origins of the American Revolution.* Cambridge: Harvard University Press, 1967.

Bensel, Richard. *Sectionalism and American Political Development.* Madison: University of Wisconsin Press, 1984.

Berk, Gerald. "Corporate Liberalism Reconsidered: A Review Essay." *Journal of Policy History* 3 (Winter 1991): 70–84.

Blum, John Morton. *The Republican Roosevelt.* Cambridge: Harvard University Press, 1954.

Burnham, Walter Dean. *Critical Elections and the Mainsprings of American Politics.* New York: W. W. Norton, 1970.

———. *The Current Crisis in American Politics.* New York: Oxford University Press, 1982.

Chandler, Alfred D., Jr. *The Visible Hand: The Managerial Revolution in American Business.* Cambridge: Harvard University Press, 1978.

———. "Government versus Business: An American Phenomenon." In *Business and Public Policy*, edited by John T. Dunlop. Boston: Harvard Business School Press, 1980.

———. *Scale and Scope: The Dynamics of Industrial Capitalism.* Cambridge: Harvard University Press, 1989.

Chandler, Alfred D., Jr., and Richard S. Tedlow. *The Coming of Managerial Capitalism: A Casebook on the History of American Economic Institutions.* Homewood, Ill.: Richard D. Irwin, 1985.

Cochran, Thomas C. "Did the Civil War Retard Industrialization?" In *The Economic Impact of the Civil War*, edited by Ralph Andreano. Cambridge, Mass.: Schenkman, 1967: 167–79.

———. *Two Hundred Years of American Business.* New York: Dell, 1977.

Davis, Mike. *Prisoners of the American Dream: Politics and Economy in the History of the U.S. Working Class.* London: Verso Books, 1986.

Dawley, Alan. *Class and Community: The Industrial Revolution in Lynn.* Cambridge: Harvard University Press, 1976.

Derthick, Martha, and Paul Quirk. *The Politics of Deregulation.* Washington: Brookings Institution, 1985.

Dorfman, Joseph. *The Economic Mind in American Civilization.* 5 vols. New York: Viking, 1949.

DuBoff, Richard B., and Edward S. Herman. "Alfred Chandler's New Business History: A Review." *Politics and Society* 10 (1980): 100–102.

Eichner, Alfred S. *The Emergence of Oligopoly: Sugar Refining as a Case Study.* Baltimore: Johns Hopkins Press, 1969.

Eichner, Alfred S., and Davis R. B. Ross. "Competition." In *Encyclopedia of American Economic History*, edited by Glenn Porter. New York: Charles Scribner, 1980.

Engerman, Stanley L. "The Economic Impact of the Civil War." *Explorations in Economic History*, 2d ser., 3 (1966): 176–99.

Evans, Sara M., and Harry C. Boyte. *Free Spaces: The Sources of Democratic Change in America*. New York: Harper & Row, 1986.

Ferguson, Thomas. "From Normalcy to New Deal: Industrial Structure, Party Competition and American Public Policy in the Great Depression." *International Organization* 38 (Winter 1984): 41–94.

Fine, Nathan. *Labor and Farmer Parties in the United States, 1828–1928*. New York: Russell & Russell, 1961.

Fink, Leon. *Workingmen's Democracy: The Knights of Labor and American Politics*. Urbana: University of Illinois Press, 1983.

Foner, Eric. *Free Soil, Free Labor, Free Men: The Ideology of the Republican Party before the Civil War*. London: Oxford University Press, 1970.

Friedman, Lawrence M. *A History of American Law*. New York: Simon & Schuster, 1973.

Friedman, Lawrence M., and Jack Landinsky. "Social Change and the Law of Industrial Accidents." *Columbia Law Review* 67 (1967): 51–82.

Frug, Gerald. "The City as a Legal Concept." *Harvard Law Review* 93 (Apr. 1980).

Galambos, Louis. "The Emerging Organizational Synthesis in American History." *Business History Review* 44 (1983): 279–90.

———. "Technology, Political Economy, and Professionalization: Central Themes of the Organizational Synthesis." *Business History Review* 57 (Winter 1983): 471–93.

Galbraith, John Kenneth. *American Capitalism: The Concept of Countervailing Power*. Boston: Houghton Mifflin Company, 1952.

———. *The New Industrial State*. Boston: Houghton Mifflin, 1967.

Garvey, George E., and Gerald J. Garvey. *Economic Law and Economic Growth: Antitrust, Regulation, and the American Growth System*. New York: Praeger, 1990.

Ginsburg, Benjamin, and Martin Shefter. *Politics by Other Means: The Declining Importance of Elections in America*. New York: Basic Books, 1990.

Goodwyn, Lawrence. *Democratic Promise: The Populist Moment in America*. New York: Oxford University Press, 1976.

Gordon, David. "Capitalist Development and the History of American Cities." In *Marxism and the Metropolis*, edited by William Tabb and Larry Sawers. New York: Oxford University Press, 1978.

Gordon, Robert W. "Legal Thought and Legal Practice in the Age of Enterprise, 1870–1920." In *Professions and Professional Ideologies in America*, edited by G. L. Geison. Chapel Hill: University of North Carolina Press, 1984, 70–139.

Gould, Lewis L. *The Presidency of Theodore Roosevelt*. Lawrence: University Press of Kansas, 1991.

Harris, Richard A., and Sidney Milkis. *The Politics of Regulatory Change: A Tale of Two Agencies*. New York: Oxford University Press, 1989.

Hartz, Louis. *The Liberal Tradition in America*. New York: Harcourt, Brace & World, 1955.

Hattam, Victoria. "Economic Visions and Political Strategies: American Labor and the State, 1865–1905." *Studies in American Political Development* 4 (1990): 82–129.

Hawley, Ellis W. "The Study and Discovery of a 'Corporate Liberalism.'" *Business History Review* 52 (Autumn 1978): 309–20.

Haynes, Fred Emory. *James Baird Weaver*. Iowa City: State Historical Society of Iowa, 1916.

———. *Third Party Movements since the Civil War*. Iowa City: State Historical Society of Iowa, 1916.

Hays, Samuel P. *The Response to Industrialism, 1885–1914*. Chicago: University of Chicago Press, 1957.

———. "Political Parties and the Community-Society Continuum." In *The American Party Systems: Stages of Political Development*, edited by William N. Chambers and Walter Dean Burnham. London: Oxford University Press, 1979: 152–81.

Hofstadter, Richard. *The Age of Reform: From Bryan to FDR*. New York: Vintage Books, 1955.

Horwitz, Morton J. *The Transformation of American Law, 1780–1860*. Cambridge: Harvard University Press, 1977.

———. "The History of the Public/Private Distinction." *University of Pennsylvania Law Review* 130 (June 1982).

———. "Santa Clara Revisited: The Development of Corporate Theory." *West Virginia Law Review* 88 (1985): 173–224.

Huntington, Samuel P. "Political Modernization: America vs. Europe," Chapter 2 of *Political Order in Changing Societies*. New Haven: Yale University Press, 1968.

———. "The Democratic Distemper." In *The Crisis of Democracy: Report on the Governability of Democracies to the Trilateral Commission*, edited by Michel Crozier, Samuel P. Huntington, and Joji Watanuki. New York: New York University Press, 1975.

———. *American Politics: The Promise of Disharmony*. Cambridge: Harvard University Press, 1981.

Hurst, James Willard. *The Legitimacy of the Business Corporation in the Law of the United States, 1780–1970*. Charlottesville: University Press of Virginia, 1970.

Josephson, Matthew. *The Politicos*. 1938. Reprint. New York: Harcourt, Brace & World, 1966.

Keller, Morton. *Affairs of State: Public Life in Late Nineteenth-Century America*. Cambridge: Harvard University Press, 1977.

Kolko, Gabriel. *The Triumph of Conservatism: A Re-Interpretation of American History, 1900–1916*. Chicago: Quadrangle Books, 1963.

Lamoreaux, Naomi. *The Great Merger Movement in American Business, 1895–1904*. Cambridge: Cambridge University Press, 1985.

Lebergott, Stanley. *The Americans: An Economic Record*. New York: W. W. Norton, 1984.

Lippmann, Walter. *Drift and Mastery: An Attempt to Diagnose the Current Unrest*. 1914. Reprint. Englewood Cliffs, N.J.: Prentice-Hall, 1961.

McCraw, Thomas K. "Regulation in America: A Review Article." *Business History Review* 49 (Summer 1975): 159–83.

———. "Business and Government: The Origins of the Adversary Relationship." *California Management Review* 26 (Winter 1984): 33–52

———. *Prophets of Regulation: Charles Francis Adams, Louis D. Brandeis, James M. Landis, Alfred E. Kahn*. Cambridge: Belknap Press, 1984.

Merrill, Horace Samuel. *Bourbon Democracy of the Middle West, 1865–1896*. Baton Rouge: Louisiana State University Press, 1953.

North, Douglass C. *Economic Growth of the United States, 1790–1860*. Englewood Cliffs, N.J.: Prentice-Hall, 1961.

Oestreicher, Richard. "Terrence Powderly, the Knights of Labor, and Artisanal Republicanism." In *Labor Leaders in America*, edited by Melvyn Dubofsky and Warren Van Tine. Urbana: University of Illinois Press, 1987.

Paul, Arnold M. *Conservative Crisis and the Rule of Law: Attitudes of the Bar and Bench, 1887–1895*. Gloucester, Mass.: Peter Smith, 1976.

Petracca, Marc P. "The Rediscovery of Interest Group Politics." In *The Politics of Interests: Interest Groups Transformed*, edited by Marc P. Petracca. Boulder: Westview Press, 1992.

Pocock, J. G. A. *Politics, Language and Time*. New York: Atheneum, 1971.

Pollack, Norman. *The Populist Response to Industrial America*. Cambridge: Harvard University Press, 1962.

Reich, Robert B. *The Next American Frontier*. New York: Times Books, 1983.

Rogin, Michael Paul. *The Intellectuals and McCarthy: The Radical Specter*. Cambridge: M.I.T. Press, 1967.

Salvatore, Nick. *Eugene V. Debs: Citizen and Socialist*. Urbana: University of Illinois Press, 1982.

Sanders, Elizabeth. "Industrial Concentration, Sectional Competition, and Antitrust Politics in America, 1880–1890." *Studies in American Political Development* 1 (1986): 142–214.

Scheiber, Harry S. "Economic Change in the Civil War: An Analysis of Recent Studies." *Civil War History* (Dec. 1965), 396–411.

Scranton, Philip. *Proprietary Capitalism: The Textile Manufacture at Philadelphia, 1800–1885*. Cambridge: Cambridge University Press, 1983.

Shallope, Robert. "Republicanism and Early American Historiography." *William and Mary Quarterly* 39 (Apr. 1982): 334–56.

Shefter, Martin. "Trade Unions and Political Machines: The Organization and Disorganization of the American Working Class in the Late Nineteenth Century." In *Working Class Formation: Nineteenth-Century Patterns in Western Europe and the United States*, edited by Ira Katznelson and Aristedes Zolberg. Princeton: Princeton University Press, 1986.

Sklar, Martin J. "Woodrow Wilson and the Political Economy of Modern United States Liberalism." *Studies on the Left* 1 (Fall 1960): 17–47.

———. *The Corporate Reconstruction of American Capitalism, 1890–1916: The Market, the Law, and Politics*. Cambridge: Cambridge University Press, 1988.

Skocpol, Theda, and Kenneth Finegold. "State, Party, and Industry: From Business Recovery to the Wagner Act in America's New Deal." In *Statemaking and Social Movements: Essays in History and Theory*, edited by Charles C. Bright and Susan F. Harding. Ann Arbor: University of Michigan Press, 1984.

Skocpol, Theda, and John Ikenberry. "The Political Formation of the American Welfare State in Historical and Comparative Perspective." *Comparative Social Research* 6 (1983): 25–27.

Skowronek, Stephen. *Building a New American State: The Expansion of National Administrative Capacities, 1877–1920*. Cambridge: Cambridge University Press, 1982.

Stewart, Richard B. "The Reformation of American Adminstrative Law." *Harvard Law Review* 88 (June 1975): 1667–1813.

Tolchin, Susan J., and Martin Tolchin. *Dismantling America: The Rush to Deregulate*. New York: Oxford University Press, 1983.

Vogel, David. "Why Businessmen Distrust Their State: The Political Consciousness of American Corporate Executives." *British Journal of Political Science* 8 (Jan. 1978): 45–78.

Weinstein, James. *The Corporate Ideal in the Liberal State, 1900–1918.* Boston: Beacon Press, 1968.

Weir, Margaret, Ann Shola Orloff, and Theda Skocpol. *The Politics of Social Policy in the United States.* Princeton: Princeton University Press, 1988.

Wiebe, Robert. *Businessmen and Reform: A Study of the Progressive Movement.* Chicago: Quadrangle Books, 1962.

———. *The Search for Order, 1877–1920.* New York: Hill & Wang, 1967.

Womack, James P. *The Machine That Changed the World.* New York: Rawson Associates, 1990.

Money and Banking

Anderson, George L. "Western Attitudes toward the National Banks, 1873–1874." *Mississippi Valley Historical Review* 23 (Sept. 1936): 205–16.

Berkey, William A. *The Money Question: The Wealth and Resources of the United States, and Why the People Do Not Enjoy General Prosperity.* Grand Rapids, Mich., 1878.

Campbell, Alexander. *The True American System of Finance: The Rights of Labor and Capital; and the Common Sense Way of Doing Justice to the Soldiers and Their Families* (Chicago: Evening Journal and Job Print, 1864).

Carleton, William G. "The Money Question in Indiana Politics." *Indiana Magazine of History* 42 (June 1946).

———. "Why Was the Democratic Party in Indiana a Radical Party, 1865–1890?" *Indiana Magazine of History* 42 (Sept. 1946): 207–28.

Carosso, Vincent P. *Investment Banking in America: A History.* Cambridge: Harvard University Press, 1970.

———. *The Morgans, Private International Bankers, 1854–1913.* Cambridge: Harvard University Press, 1984.

Chernow, Ron. *The House of Morgan: An American Banking Dynasty and the Rise of Modern Finance.* New York: Atlantic Monthly Press, 1990.

Davis, Andrew McFarland. *The Origin of the National Banking System.* National Monetary Commission, Senate, 61st Cong., 2d sess., Document #582. Washington: Government Printing Office, 1910.

Davis, Lance. "The Capital Markets and Industrial Concentration: The U.S. and U.K., a Comparative Study." *Economic History Review* 19 (1966): 255–72.

Destler, Chester McArthur. *American Radicalism, 1865–1901.* 1946. Reprint. Chicago: Quadrangle Books, 1966.

Grossman, Jonathan. *William Sylvis, Pioneer of American Labor.* New York: Octagon, 1945.

James, John. *Money and Capital Markets in Postbellum America.* Princeton: Princeton University Press, 1978.

Kellogg, Edward. *A New Monetary System: The Only Means of Securing the Respective Rights of Labor and Property, and of Protecting the Public from Financial Revulsions.* New York: Rudd & Carleton, 1861.

Larson, Henrietta M. *Jay Cooke, Private Banker.* Cambridge: Harvard University Press, 1936.

Libby, Orin G. "A Study of the Greenback Movement, 1876–1884." *Transactions of the Wisconsin Academy of Sciences, Arts, and Letters* 12 (1898): 530–43.

Livingston, James. *Origins of the Federal Reserve System: Money, Class, and Corporate Capitalism, 1890–1913.* Ithaca, N.Y.: Cornell University Press, 1986.

McGrane, R. C. "Ohio and the Greenback Movement." *Mississippi Valley Historical Review* 11 (Mar. 1925): 526–42.

McPherson, Edward. *A Handbook of Politics for 1870 (to 1894).* Annual. New York: Negro Universities Press, 1969.

Myers, Margaret G. *The New York Money Market.* New York: Columbia University Press, 1931.

———. *A Financial History of the United States.* New York: Columbia University Press, 1970.

Navin, Thomas R., and Marian V. Sears. "The Rise of a Market for Industrial Securities, 1887–1902." *Business History Review* 29 (June 1955): 105–38.

Noyes, Alexander Dana. *Forty Years of Finance: A Short Financial History of the Government and People of the United States since the Civil War, 1865–1907.* New York: G. P. Putnam's Sons, 1909.

Nugent, Walter T. K. *Money and American Society, 1865–1880.* New York: Free Press, 1968.

Redlich, Fritz. *The Molding of American Banking: Men and Ideas.* 1947. Reprint. New York: Johnson Reprint Company, 1968.

Ricker, Ralph R. *The Greenback Labor Movement in Pennsylvania.* Bellefont: Pennsylvania Heritage, 1966.

Shannon, Fred A. *The Farmer's Last Frontier: Agriculture, 1860–1897.* New York: Farrar & Rinehart, 1945.

Sharkey, Robert P. *Money, Class, and Party: An Economic Study of Civil War and Reconstruction.* The Johns Hopkins University Studies in Historical and Political Science. Series 77, 1959. Baltimore: Johns Hopkins Press, 1959.

———. "Commercial Banking." In *Economic Change in the Civil War Era,* edited by David T. Gilchrist and W. David Lewis. Greenville, Del: Eleutherian Mills-Hagley Foundation, 1965.

Sobel, Robert. *The Big Board: A History of the New York Stock Market.* New York: Free Press, 1965.

Sprague, O. M. W. "History of Crises under the National Banking System." In *The National Banking System.* Publications of the U.S. National Monetary Commission. Washington, 1911.

Studenski, Paul, and Herman E. Krooss. *A Financial History of the United States.* New York: McGraw-Hill, 1963.

Supple, Barry. "A Business Elite: German-Jewish Financiers in Nineteenth-Century New York." *Business History Review* 31 (Summer 1957): 143–51.

Sylla, Richard Eugene. *The American Capital Market, 1846–1914.* New York: Arno Press, 1975.

Trescott, Paul. *Financing American Enterprise: The Story of Commercial Banking.* New York: Harper & Row, 1963.

Unger, Irwin. "Businessmen and Species Resumption." *Political Science Quarterly* 74 (Mar. 1959): 46–70.

———. *The Greenback Era: A Social and Political History of American Finance, 1865–1879.* Princeton: Princeton University Press, 1964.

Usher, Ellis B. *The Greenback Movement of 1875–1884 and Wisconsin's Part in It.* Milwaukee, 1911.

Willis, H. Parker, and Julius I. Bogen. *Investment Banking.* New York: Harper & Brothers, 1929.

The Railroad Corporation

Ackerman, William K. *Historical Sketch of the Illinois Central Railroad.* Chicago: Fergus Printing, 1890.

Adams, Charles Francis. *Railroads: Their Origin and Problems.* New York: G. P. Putnam's Sons, 1887.

Adams, Charles Francis, and Henry Adams. *Chapters of Erie.* 1886. Reprint. Ithaca, N.Y.: Cornell University Press, 1968.

Association of the Bar of the City of New York. *Some Legal Phases of Corporate Financing, Reorganization and Regulation.* New York: Macmillan, 1917.

Beach, Charles Fisk, Jr. *Commentaries on the Law of Receivers.* New York: L. K. Strouse, 1894.

Berle, A. A. "Receivership." *Encyclopedia of the Social Sciences* (1936): 50.

Bonbright, James C. *Railroad Capitalization: A Study of the Principles of Regulation of Railroad Securities.* Studies in History, Economics, and Public Law. Columbia University, 95. New York: Columbia University Press, 1920.

Brandeis, Louis D. *Other People's Money and How Bankers Use It.* 1914. Reprint. New York: Harper Torchbooks, 1967.

Brownson, Howard Gray. *History of the Illinois Central Railroad to 1870.* Urbana: University of Illinois Press, 1950.

Campbell, Edward G. *The Reorganization of the American Railroad System, 1893–1900.* New York: Columbia University Press, 1938.

Chamberlain, D. H. "New Fashioned Receiverships." *Harvard Law Review* 10 (Oct. 1896): 139–49.

Chandler, Alfred D., Jr. *Henry Varnum Poor: Business Editor, Analyst, and Reformer.* Cambridge: Harvard University Press, 1956.

———. *The Railroads: The Nation's First Big Business.* New York: Harcourt, Brace & World, 1965.

———. "The Revolution in Transportation and Communication." Part I of *The Visible Hand.* Cambridge: Belknap Press, 1977.

———. "The Separation of Ownership and Control." Harvard Business School Case No. 1–380–215, 1980.

———. "Jay Gould and the Coming of Railroad Consolidation." In *The Coming of Managerial Capitalism,* edited by Alfred D. Chandler and Richard S. Tedlow. Homewood, Ill.: Richard D. Irwin, 1985.

Cleveland, Frederick A., and Fred Wilbur Powell. *Railroad Promotion and Capitalization in the United States.* New York: Longmans, Green, 1909.

Cochran, Thomas C. *Railroad Leaders, 1845–1890: The Business Mind in Action.* Cambridge: Harvard University Press, 1953.

Corliss, Carleton J. *Main Line of Mid-America: The Story of the Illinois Central.* New York: Creative Age Press, 1950.

Craig, James Thomas. "Oelwein Secures the Machine Shops of the Chicago Great Western Railway Company, 1894." *Annals of Iowa* 24 (Jan. 1943): 211–15.

————. "Great Western Builds Oelwein Shops: Construction of the Chicago Great Western Railway Machine Shops in 1894–1899." *Annals of Iowa* 26 (July 1944): 90–128.

————. "The "Big Strike" at Oelwein Shops." *Annals of Iowa* 78 (July 1946): 116–38.

Crowell, J. F. "Railway Receiverships in the United States." *Yale Review* (1898): 326.

Daggett, Stuart. *Railroad Reorganization.* Cambridge: Harvard University Press, 1908.

Dewing, Arthur Stone. *Corporate Promotions and Reorganizations.* Cambridge: Harvard University Press, 1914.

————. "The Theory of Railroad Reorganization." *American Economic Review* 8 (Dec. 1918): 774–95.

————. "The Procedure of Contemporary Railroad Reorganization." *American Economic Review* 9 (March 1919): 1–33.

————. "The Purposes Achieved by Railroad Reorganization." *American Economic Review* 9 (June 1919): 227–310.

————. *The Financial Policy of Corporations.* 2 vols. New York: Ronald Press, 1941.

Donovan, Frank P., Jr. "The Amazing Great Western." *Railroad Magazine* 61 (Sept. 1953): 29–31.

————. "The Great Western in Iowa." *The Palimpsest* 34 (June 1953): 266–83.

Donovan, Frank P., Jr., and W. B. Davids. "A. B. Stickney." *Railway Progress* (Dec. 1952): 15–19.

Fogel, Robert W. *Railroads and American Economic Growth.* Baltimore: Johns Hopkins Press, 1964.

————. *The Union Pacific Railroad, A Case in Premature Enterprise.* Baltimore: Johns Hopkins Press, 1964.

Goodrich, Carter. *Government Promotion of Canals and Railroads, 1800–1890.* New York: Columbia University Press, 1960.

Grant, H. Rodger. "Courting the Great Western Railway: An Episode of Town Rivalry." *Missouri Historical Review* 76 (July 1982): 405–20.

————. "Iowa's New Communities: Townsite Promotion along the Chicago Great Western Railway's Omaha Extension." *Upper Midwest History* 2 (1982): 53–63.

————. "A. B. Stickney and James J. Hill: The Railroad Relationship." *Railroad History* 146 (Spring 1982).

————. "Prairie Innovator: The Chicago Great Western Railway." *Railroad History* (Autumn 1983): 74–77.

————. *The Cornbelt Route: A History of the Chicago Great Western Railroad Company.* DeKalb: Northern Illinois University Press, 1984.

Greenberg, Dolores Breitman. *Financiers and Railroads, 1869–1889: A Case Study of Morton, Bliss and Company.* Newark: University of Delaware Press, 1980.

Grodinsky, Julius. *The Iowa Pool: A Study in Railroad Competition, 1870–1884.* Chicago: University of Chicago Press, 1950.

————. *Jay Gould, His Business Career.* Philadelphia: University of Pennsylvania Press, 1957.

————. *Transcontinental Railway Strategy, 1869–1893: A Study of Businessmen.* Philadelphia: University of Pennsylvania Press, 1957.

Hungerford, Edward. *The Story of the Baltimore and Ohio Railroad, 1827–1927.* New York: G. P. Putnam's Sons, 1928.

————. *Men and Iron: History of the New York Central.* New York: Thomas Y. Crowell, 1938.

Kirkland, Edward C. *Men, Cities and Transportation*. Cambridge: Harvard University Press, 1948.

Klein, Maury. "Strategy of Southern Railroads." *American Historical Review* 73 (Apr. 1968): 1052–68.

———. *The Great Richmond Terminal*. Charlottesville: University Press of Virginia, 1970.

———. *The Life and Legend of Jay Gould*. Baltimore: Johns Hopkins University Press, 1986.

Lambie, Joseph T. *From Mine to Market: The History of Coal Transportation on the Norfolk and Western Railway*. New York: New York University Press, 1954.

Larson, John Lauritz. *Bonds of Enterprise: John Murray Forbes and Western Development in America's Railway Age*. Cambridge: Harvard University Press, 1984.

Lasdon, Oscar. "The Evolution of Railroad Reorganization." *The Banking Law Journal* 88 (Jan. 1971): 3–9.

Marsh, Harold, Jr. "Are Directors Trustees: Conflict of Interest and Corporate Morality." *The Business Lawyer* 22 (Nov. 1966): 35–39.

Martin, Albro. "Railroads and the Equity Receivership: An Essay on Institutional Change." *Journal of Economic History* 34 (Sept. 1974): 685–710.

Meade, Edward Sherwood. "The Reorganization of Railroads." *Annals of the American Academy of Political and Social Science* 17 (Mar. 1901): 205–42.

———. "The Chicago Great Western." *Railway World* (Aug. 25, 1905): 675.

Mitchell, Thomas Warner. "The Collateral Trust Mortgage in Railway Finance." *Quarterly Journal of Economics* 20 (1906): 443–67.

Moody, John. *The Truth about the Trusts: A Description and Analysis of the American Trust Movement*. New York: Moody Publishing Co., 1904.

Morris, Ray. *Railroad Administration*. New York: D. Appleton, 1910.

Overton, Richard C. *Perkins–Budd: Railway Statesmen of the Burlington*. Westport, Conn.: Greenwood, 1982.

Poor, Henry Varnum. *Railroad Manual of the United States, 1870–1910*.

Riegel, Robert Edgar. *The Story of the Western Railroads*. New York: Macmillan, 1926.

Ripley, William Z. *Railroads: Finance and Organization*. New York: Longmans, Green, 1915.

———. "Railroad Overcapitalization." *Quarterly Journal of Economics* (Aug. 1914), 601–29.

Sakolski, A. M. *American Railroad Economics*. New York: Macmillan, 1913.

Stover, John. *The Railroads of the South, 1865–1900*. Chapel Hill: University of North Carolina Press, 1955.

Swain, Henry H. "Economic Aspects of Railroad Receiverships." *Economic Studies of the American Economic Association* 3 (1889): 50–161.

Taylor, George Rodgers, and Irene D. Neu. *The American Railroad Network, 1861–1890*. Cambridge: Harvard University Press, 1956.

Trottman, Nelson. *History of the Union Pacific: A Financial and Economic Survey*. New York: Ronald Press, 1923.

Wollman, Henry. "The Bane of Friendly Receiverships." *North American Review* 158 (1894): 251.

Railroad Regulation

Adams, Charles Francis, Jr. "The Granger Movement." *North American Review* 120 (Apr. 1875): 394–424.

Adams, Henry C. "A Decade of Federal Railway Regulation." *Atlantic Monthly* 81 (Apr. 1898): 433–43.

Barns, William D. "Oliver Hudson Kelley and the Genesis of the Grange: A Reappraisal." *Agricultural History* 41 (July 1967): 229–42.

Benson, Lee. *Merchants, Farmers, and Railroads: Railroad Regulation and New York Politics, 1850–1887.* Cambridge: Harvard University Press, 1955.

Berk, Gerald. "Constituting Corporations and Markets: Railroads in Gilded Age Politics." *Studies in American Political Development* 4 (1990): 130–68.

Bernstein, Marver. *Regulating Business by Independent Commission.* Princeton: Princeton University Press, 1955.

Brewer, Hon. D. J. *Protection to Property from Public Attack.* New Haven: Hoggson & Robinson, 1891.

Buck, Solon Justice. *The Granger Movement: A Study of Agricultural Organization and Its Political, Economic, and Social Manifestations, 1870–1880.* Lincoln: University of Nebraska Press, 1965.

Cooley, Thomas McIntyre. "State Regulation of Corporate Profits." *North American Review* 137 (Sept. 1883): 205–17.

———. "Popular and Legal Views of Traffic Pooling." *Railway Review* 24 (Apr. 26, 1884): 212–14.

Cushman, Robert. *The Independent Regulatory Commissions.* New York: Oxford University Press, 1941.

Destler, Chester MacArthur. *Henry Demerest Lloyd and the Empire of Reform.* Philadelphia: University of Pennsylvania Press, 1963.

———. *Roger Sherman and the Independent Oil Men.* Ithaca, N.Y.: Cornell University Press, 1967.

Detrick, Charles R. "The Effects of the Granger Acts." *Journal of Political Economy* 11 (Mar. 1903): 237–56.

Dewey, Ralph L. *The Long and Short Haul Principle of Rate Regulation.* Columbus: Ohio State University Press, 1935.

Dixon, Frank Haigh. "The Interstate Commerce Act as Amended." *Quarterly Journal of Economics* 21 (Nov. 1906): 22–51.

———. "The Mann-Elkins Act, Amending the Act to Regulate Commerce." *Quarterly Journal of Economics* 24 (Aug. 1910): 593–633.

Fletcher, Henry J. "The Doom of the Small Town." *The Forum* 19 (Apr. 1895): 214–23.

Friedlander, Ann F. *The Dilemma of Freight Transport Regulation.* Washington: Brookings Institution, 1969.

Gilligan, Thomas W., William J. Marshall, and Barry R. Weingast. "Regulation and the Theory of Legislative Choice: The Interstate Commerce Act of 1887." *Journal of Law and Economics* 33 (Apr. 1989): 35–62.

———. "The Economic Incidence of the Interstate Commerce Act of 1887: A Theoretical and Empirical Analysis of the Shorthaul Pricing Constraint." Hoover Institution, Domestic Studies Program, Working Paper No. P-90–6, Apr. 1990.

Hadley, Arthur Twining. *Railroad Transportation: Its History and Its Laws.* New York: G. P. Putnam's Sons, 1885.

———. "Legal Theories of Price Regulation." *Yale Review* 56 (1892).

Hammond, M. B. *Railway Rate Theories of the Interstate Commerce Commission.* Cambridge: Harvard University Press, 1911.

Haney, Lewis H. *A Congressional History of Railroads in the United States.* Bulletin of the University of Wisconsin, No. 342. Madison, 1910.

Hechler, Kenneth W. *Insurgency: Personalities and Politics of the Taft Era.* New York: Columbia University Press, 1940.

Henderson, Gerard. "Railway Valuation and the Courts." *Harvard Law Review* 33 (190): 902–28, 1031–57.

Hines, Walker. *War History of American Railroads.* New Haven: Yale University Press, 1928.

Hoogenboom, Ari, and Olive Hoogenboom. *A History of the ICC: From Panacea to Palliative.* New York: W. W. Norton, 1976.

Huntington, Samuel P. "The Marasmus of the ICC: The Commission, the Railroads, and the Public Interest." *Yale Law Journal* 51 (Apr. 1952): 467–509.

Jones, Alan. "Thomas M. Cooley and 'Laissez-Faire Constitutionalism': A Reconsideration." *Journal of American History* 53 (March 1967): 751–71.

Joubert, William H. *Southern Freight Rates in Transition.* Gainesville: University of Florida Press, 1949.

Kerr, K. Austin. *American Railroad Politics, 1914–1920.* Pittsburgh: University of Pittsburgh Press, 1968.

Kolko, Gabriel. *Railroads and Regulation, 1877–1916.* Princeton: Princeton University Press, 1965.

LaFollette, Robert. *Railway Regulation, State and Interstate.* Chicago: Slayton Lyceum Bureau, 1905.

Latham, Earl. *The Group Basis of Politics: A Study in Basing-Point Legislation.* Ithaca, N.Y.: Cornell University Press, 1952.

Lloyd, Henry Demerest. "Story of a Great Monopoly." *Atlantic* (Mar. 1881): 317–34.

———. *Wealth against Commonwealth.* New York: Harper & Brothers, 1894.

MacAvoy, Paul W. *The Economic Effects of Regulation: The Trunk Line Cartels and the Interstate Commerce Commission before 1900.* Cambridge: M.I.T. Press, 1965.

McCraw, Thomas K. "Adams and the Sunshine Commission." Chapter 1 of *Prophets of Regulation.* Cambridge: Belknap Press, 1984.

McCurdy, Charles W. "Justice Field and the Jurisprudence of Business-Government Relations: Some Parameters of Laissez-Faire Constitutionalism, 1863–1897." *Journal of American History* 61 (Mar. 1975): 970–1005.

Martin, Albro. *Enterprise Denied: Origins of the Decline of American Railroads, 1897–1917.* New York: Columbia University Press, 1971.

———. "The Troubled Subject of Railroad Regulation in the Gilded Age–A Reassessment." *Journal of American History* 61 (Sept. 1974): 339–71.

Meyer, Hugo Richard. *Government Regulation of Railway Rates.* New York: Macmillan, 1905.

Miller, George H. *Railroads and the Granger Laws.* Madison: University of Wisconsin Press, 1965.

Miller, Sidney L. *Inland Transportation: Principles and Policies.* New York: McGraw-Hill, 1933.

Mowry, George. *Theodore Roosevelt and the Progressive Movement.* Madison: University of Wisconsin Press, 1947.

———. *The Era of Theodore Roosevelt and the Birth of Modern America.* New York: Harper Torchbooks, 1958.

Nash, Gerald D. "The Reformer Reformed: John H. Reagan and Railroad Regulation." *Business History Review* 29 (June 1955): 189–96.

———. "Origins of the Interstate Commerce Act of 1887." *Pennsylvania History* 24 (July 1957): 181–90.

Newlands, Francis. "Common Sense of the Railroad Question." *The North American Review* 180 (1905): 576–85.

Purcell, Edward A., Jr. "Ideas and Interests: Businessmen and the Interstate Commerce Act." *Journal of American History* 54 (Dec. 1967): 561–78.

Ripley, William Z. *Railroads: Rates and Regulation.* New York: Longmans, Green, 1912.

Sanders, Elizabeth. "Farmers, Railroads, and the State: A Political Economy Perspective." Paper Delivered at the Annual Meeting of the American Political Science Association, Aug. 1990.

Seigel, Stephen A. "Understanding the *Lochner* Era: Lessons from Railroad and Utility Regulation." *Virginia Law Review* 70 (Mar. 1984): 187–263.

Sharfman, I. L. *The Interstate Commerce Commission: A Study in Administrative Law and Procedure.* New York: Commonwealth Fund, 1931.

Spann, Robert M., and Edward W. Erikson. "The Economics of Railroading: The Beginning of Cartelization and Regulation." *Bell Journal of Economics and Management Science* 1 (Autumn 1970): 227–44.

Stickney, A. B. *The Railroad Problem.* St. Paul: D. D. Merrill, 1891.

Tarbell, Ida. *The History of the Standard Oil Company.* New York: Macmillan, 1904.

Throne, Mildred. "Repeal of the Iowa Granger Law." *Iowa Journal of History* 51 (Apr. 1953): 99.

Vietor, Richard H. K. "Businessmen and the Political Economy: The Railroad Rate Controversy of 1905." *Journal of American History* 64 (June 1977): 47–66.

Zerbe, Richard O. "The Costs and Benefits of Early Regulation of the Railroads." *Bell Journal of Economics and Management Science* 11 (Spring 1980): 343–50.

Government Documents

Bureau of Corporations. *Report of the Commissioner of Corporations on the Petroleum Industry.* Washington, 1907–1909.

Comptroller of the Currency. *Annual Report,* 1873.

U.S. Congress. House. Interstate Commerce. *Debate in 48th Cong., 2d Sess. on the Bill (H.R. 5461) to Establish a Board of Commissioners of Interstate Commerce, and to Regulate Such Commerce, etc.* Washington, 1884.

———. *Debate in 49th Cong. on Bill to Establish a Board of Commissioners, etc.* Compiled by V. H. Painter. Washington, 1887.

———. Committee on Interstate and Foreign Commerce. *Hearings.* 58th Cong., 3d sess., 1904–1905. H. Doc. 422. Washington, 1905.

———. *Hearings on Physical Valuation of Railroad Properties.* 61st Cong., 2d sess., Washington, 1911.

———. *Regulation of the Issuance of Stocks and Bonds by Common Carriers.* 63d Cong., 2d sess., 1914. Washington, 1914.

U.S. Congress. Senate. Committee on Interstate and Foreign Commerce. *Regulation of Railway Rates.* 59th Cong., 1st sess., 1904–1905. S. Doc. 243. Washington, 1905.

————. Committee on Interstate Commerce. *Hearings on Physical Valuation of Property of Common Carriers*. 62d Cong., 3d sess. Washington, 1913.

————. *Hearings before the ICC in the "Five Per Cent Case."* Senate Document 466, 63d Cong., 2d sess, 1914.

Industrial Commission. *Report of the Industrial Commission on Transportation*, No. 9. Washington, 1901.

Interstate Commerce Commission. *Annual Report*, 1887–1907. Washington, 1887–1907.

————. *Report of the Statistics of Railways in the United States, 1889–1907*. Washington, 1889–1907.

————. *Report on Intercorporate Relationships of Railways of the United States as of June 30, 1906*. Washington, 1906.

————. "In Re Investigation of Advances in Rates By Carriers in Official Classification Territory." No. 3400. Washington, 1911.

————. "In Re Investigation of Advances in Rates by Carriers in Western Trunk Line, Trans-Missouri, and Illinois Freight Committee Territories." No. 3500. Washington, 1911.

————. *Advance in Rates by Carriers, Reports of the Commission*. 10 vols. Washington, 1912.

LaFollette, Robert M. *Regulation of Railway Rates and Services. Relation of Government to Commerce and Transportation. Speeches of Hon. Robert M. LaFollette of Wisconsin in the Senate of the United States*. Washington, 1906.

National Association of Railroad Commissioners. *Proceedings of Annual Conventions*, 1900–1910. Washington, 1900–1910.

New York. State Assembly. *Report of the Special Committee on Railroads. Appointed under a Resolution of the Assembly, Feb. 28, 1878 to Investigate the Alleged Abuses in the Management of Railroads*. Albany: Weed, Parsons & Co., 1880.

Securities and Exchange Commission. *Report on the Study and Investigation of the Work, Activities, Personnel and Functions of Protective and Reorganization Committees: Pursuant to Section 211 of the Securties and Exchange Act of 1934*. Washington, 1937.

INDEX

Ackerman, Bruce, 4, 10

Adams, Charles Francis, Jr., 28, 83–85, 95–96, 157; criticized by regionalists, 97–98

Adams, Henry Carter, 97; changing views on regulation, 157–58

Adamson, William, 164

Advance rate cases, 168–77

Adversarial regulation: and advance rate cases, 168–77; and corporate liberal theory, 82–83, 102–3, 156; and equity-efficiency trade-off, 82–83, 184–87. *See also* Field, Stephen J.; Liberal positivism

Affectation doctrine: and railroad regulation, 81–83

Agriculture: diversification of, 131

Alabama Midland Railway, 107–8. See also *Interstate Commerce Commission* v. *Alabama Midland Railway*

Alton Railroad, 130

American Economic Association, 155

American Tobacco Company, 111

Anglo-American Provision Company, 135

Antitrust: and railroad regulation, 110, 165

Arlington Heights Fruit Exchange v. *Southern Pacific*, 111–13, 184

Armour & Company, 111

Atchison, Topeka and Santa Fe Railroad, 61–62, 65; compared to Chicago Great Western, 117, 130

Baker, George, 30

Baltimore and Ohio Railroad, 61–65, 142, 172, 174

Banks. *See* Commercial banking; Investment banking; National banking system

Bartlett, Charles, 164, 167

Beach, Charles, 57

Beck, James Burnie, 94

Belmont, August, 65

Bensen, Lee, 114

Beveridge, Albert, 161

Bonds: and Chicago Great Western, 146–47; and greenback monetary reform, 43; income, 69; and overseas investment in railroads, 34–35, 50, 70; railroad mortgage, 49–51; reduction of principal on, in receivership, 54–55, 64–71. *See also* Finance, corporate; Finance, public

Borah, William, 161

Borland, William, 163

Bradley, Joseph P., 81

Brandeis, Louis D., 2

Brewer, David, 53, 102, 104, 156

Bristow, Joseph, 161

Buck, Solon, 79

Bureaucracy: limited efficiency of, 124–29; U.S. compared to European, 9. *See also* Corporation, modern

Burnham, Walter Dean, 11

Business cycle: and corporate finance, 62–71; and money and banking reform, 36–45. *See also* Panic of 1873

Cairo and Vincennes Railroad, 63

Call-loan market, 33–34. *See also* New York money market

Library of Congress Cataloging-in-Publication Data

Berk, Gerald.
   Alternative tracks : the constitution of American industrial order, 1865–1917 / Gerald Berk.
      p.   cm. — (The Johns Hopkins series in constitutional thought)
   Includes bibliographical references (pp. 205–221) and index.
   ISBN 0-8018-4656-0 (hc. : acid-free paper)
   1. Railroads and state—United States—History.   2. Railroads—Political aspects—United States—
History.   3. Railroad legislation—United States—History.   4. Corporations—Political aspects—
United States—History.   5. Corporation law—United States—History.   6. Industry and state—
United States—History.   I. Title.   II. Series.
HE2757.B47   1994
385'.0973—dc20   93-1753

Printed in the United States
3900